WITHDRAWN
NDSU

D1565759

HAWTHORNE'S
AMERICAN TRAVEL SKETCHES

HAWTHORNE'S
AMERICAN TRAVEL SKETCHES

Alfred Weber, Beth L. Lueck, and Dennis Berthold

UNIVERSITY PRESS OF NEW ENGLAND
Hanover and London

University Press of New England

Brandeis University
Brown University
Clark University
University of Connecticut
Dartmouth College
University of New Hampshire
University of Rhode Island
Tufts University
University of Vermont

© 1989 by University Press of New England

All rights reserved. Except for brief quotation in critical articles or reviews, this book, or parts thereof, must not be reproduced in any form without permission in writing from the publisher. For further information contact University Press of New England, Hanover, NH 03755.

Printed in the United States of America
∞

Library of Congress Cataloging in Publication Data
Hawthorne, Nathaniel, 1804–1864.
[American travel sketches]
Hawthorne's American travel sketches / [edited by] Alfred Weber,
Beth L. Lueck, Dennis Berthold.
p. cm.
Bibliography: p.
Includes index.
ISBN 0–87451–498–3
1. Hawthorne, Nathaniel, 1804–1864—Journeys—New England.
2. Hawthorne, Nathaniel, 1804–1864—Journeys—New York (State).
3. Novelists, American—19th century—Journeys. 4. New England—
Description and travel—1775–1865. 5. New York (State)—
Description and travel. I. Weber, Alfred. II. Lueck, Beth L.
III. Berthold, Dennis. IV. Title. V. Title: American
travel sketches.
PS1865.A2W43 1989
818.'303—dc20 89–40235
CIP

5 4 3 2 1

CONTENTS

List of Illustrations vii

Preface ix

**Hawthorne's Tour of 1832 through New England
and Upstate New York** (Alfred Weber) 1

**An Edition of Hawthorne's American Travel Sketches
with Textual Introductions** (Alfred Weber) 25

   SKETCHES FROM MEMORY. BY A PEDESTRIAN. NO. I 26

      THE NOTCH. 27

      OUR EVENING PARTY AMONG THE MOUNTAINS. 30

   SKETCHES FROM MEMORY. BY A PEDESTRIAN. NO. II 34

      THE CANAL-BOAT. 35

      THE INLAND PORT. 43

      ROCHESTER. 45

      AN AFTERNOON SCENE. 47

      A NIGHT SCENE. 48

   AN ONTARIO STEAM-BOAT. 49

   MY VISIT TO NIAGARA. 55

   FRAGMENTS FROM THE JOURNAL OF A SOLITARY
   MAN. [TWO EXTRACTS] 62

      [1] "ON REACHING THE FERRY-HOUSE . . ." 62

      [2] "A SOUND OF MERRIMENT . . ." 63

   OLD TICONDEROGA. A PICTURE OF THE PAST. 64

**The Northern Tour in Contemporary
Paintings and Engravings** 71

**A Literary and Pictorial Iconography of
Hawthorne's Tour** (Dennis Berthold) 99

**History and Nationalism in "Old Ticonderoga"
and Other Travel Sketches** (Dennis Berthold) 131

**Hawthorne's Ironic Traveler and the
Picturesque Tour** (Beth L. Lueck)   153

Notes   181
Bibliography   199
  I: Works Cited   199
  II: Tourist Guides and Gazetteers Cited and Consulted   205
Index   209

ILLUSTRATIONS

Map of the Places of Interest in Hawthorne's
Travel Sketches   xvi

1. Title page, Theodore Dwight's *The Northern Traveller*, 1830   73

2. Thomas Cole, *View of the White Mountains*   74

3. Anonymous, *One of the White Hills, Stripped of Forest and Soil by the Storm of 1826*   75

4. William Henry Bartlett, *The Willey House*   76

5. William Henry Bartlett, *The Notch-House, White Mountains*   77

6. William Henry Bartlett, *Mount Jefferson (from Mount Washington)*   78

7. William Henry Bartlett, *Mount Washington and the White Hills*   79

8. Henry Inman, *Travelling on the Erie Canal*   80

9. William Henry Bartlett, *Village of Little Falls*   81

10. John William Hill, *Erie Canal, 1831*   82

11. John William Hill, *[View of the Erie Canal]*   83

12. William Henry Bartlett, *Utica*   84

13. John William Hill, *[Scene of Night-Time Traffic on the Erie Canal]*   85

14. John W. Barber and Henry Howe, *Western view in the central part of Syracuse*   86

15. John W. Barber and Henry Howe, *View of Ogdensburg*   87

16. John W. Barber and Henry Howe, *Central Part of Buffalo Street, Rochester, N.Y.*   88

17. J. H. Bufford, *The Upper Falls of the Genesee at Rochester, N.Y.*   89

18. Anonymous, *Falls of the Genesee, N.Y.*   90

19. William James Bennett, *View of the British Fall Taken From Goat Island*   91

20. George Catlin, *View of Niagara: No. 6, Table Rock from Below*   92

21. John F. Vanderlyn, *Niagara Falls from Table Rock*   93
22. William Henry Bartlett, *Ferry Landing on
    the American Side*   94
23. Henry Reinagle, *View of the Ruins of Ticonderoga Forts
    on Lake Champlain*   95
24. Anonymous, *Ticonderoga from Mount Independence*   96
25. Thomas Cole, *Ruins of Fort Ticonderoga, New York*   97
26. William Henry Bartlett, *View of the Ruins of
    Fort Ticonderoga*   98

PREFACE

This book originated at the 1986 conference of the Nathaniel Hawthorne Society at Bowdoin College, where the three coauthors appeared together at a session on Hawthorne and the landscapes of New England. Discovering a mutual interest in Hawthorne's travels and the sketches resulting from his 1832 tour of New England and New York, we decided to collaborate on an edition of the travel sketches combined with a series of independent but related essays. As our work progressed, we became increasingly convinced of the biographical, historical, and literary importance of the sketches; thus, we examine them thoroughly from each of these critical perspectives.

The travel sketches have been neglected by critics in favor of Hawthorne's imaginative writing, the tales and the novels. Except as source material for discussions of his fiction, they have been considered mere journalistic exercises, too unimportant to be analyzed for their own merits. In fact, when studied as a related group of texts, as they are for the first time here, they have much to offer scholars concerning the author's years in the "haunted chamber": not only do they offer examples of Hawthorne's excursions into the world, traveling and meeting people at a time when he was generally thought to have been isolated in a study, but they also offer insights into his ideas, aesthetics, and literary development during the earliest phase of his career, the late 1820s and early 1830s.

In order to understand Hawthorne's use of his travels in September of 1832, first the actual journey had to be painstakingly reconstructed, through both research and actual travel along the routes Hawthorne might have followed. Next, the relationship of the travel sketches to the framed story cycle called "The Story Teller" had to be settled: the sketches are, after all, fragments of a larger work which an editor, Park Benjamin, independently selected and altered for magazine publication. While the sketches blend autobiography and fiction, their first-person narrator is not necessarily Hawthorne himself, only his *persona*. Thus, we distinguish between the traveling storyteller, who is the narrator and protagonist of the work of fiction, and the author, Nathaniel Hawthorne, who traveled as a tourist in 1832 through New England and upstate New York. The introductory essay by Alfred Weber explores these and related problems and forms the groundwork for the critical analyses that follow.

The travel sketches are reprinted because they have never before appeared as a group. Although we omit the tales that Hawthorne originally intended to accompany them, their cohesiveness becomes evident in this edition. "An Ontario Steam-Boat" is included since its thematic concerns, style, and subject all argue strongly for its authorship by Hawthorne and connect it firmly to his 1832 tour. The texts are those of the first appearance in periodicals because these are closer to Hawthorne's original manuscript than the Centenary Edition, which uses later book publication as copy-text, and they are arranged geographically, according to Hawthorne's probable itinerary. These practices provide texts closer to the author's original intention, eliminate later alterations which could have been made by either editors or the author, and establish more accurately and completely the historical context of Hawthorne's actual journey in 1832. Alfred Weber collected and collated the sketches and provides full bibliographic commentary in his textual introductions.

The tour was young Hawthorne's conscious attempt to gather materials for a national literature that celebrated the history, natural beauty, and future progress of the United States. This is evident in the sketches' descriptions of America's scenery and monuments and in their more critical comments upon the rapid commercial growth along the lakes and waterways of the northeast. It is also evident in another unrecognized source for Hawthorne's travel writing, contemporary illustrations of the scenery along his tour route. The engravings and paintings reprinted here from tourist guides and other sources testify to Hawthorne's affinities with early artists and topographers who also sketched the evolving American landscape. He shared with these illustrators a common iconography, sometimes anticipating, sometimes borrowing, and sometimes criticizing the visual conventions of the day. The inaccessibility of these illustrations, some of which have never been reprinted, has led us to include as many as feasible, in order to provide scholars with source materials for future study while also showing readers how the scenes Hawthorne describes might have appeared at the time of his tour. Dennis Berthold's essays focus on these interrelated problems of history, literary nationalism, and landscape iconography.

Finally, the tour places Hawthorne and his art in the context of the times, particularly the increasing popularity of picturesque touring in New England and New York in the 1820s and 1830s. This new way of viewing landscape revealed the influence of the aesthetics of William Gilpin on American culture, an influence evident in Hawthorne's sketches and other travel writings. Furthermore, historical research reveals Hawthorne's indebtedness to the new genre of tourist guides, works which combined facts, descriptions, and anecdotes as they led travelers to the scenic and historic attractions of the northeastern United States. These guidebooks represent an unrecognized source for Hawthorne's travel writing and help identify the conventions and norms that inform his approach to tourism. This influence forms the basis of Beth L. Lueck's essay, which demonstrates that Hawthorne both exploited his sources and commented upon them through persona, irony, and parody.

This book is written not only for Hawthorne specialists and those interested in nineteenth-century American literature and American Studies, but also for a wider audience, particularly scholars interested in cultural history, travel writing, or the relationships between literature, scenery, and visual art. We hope that it will also have reference value for its map, illustrations, and bibliographies, particularly the list of tourist guides used by such travelers as Hawthorne during the period.

We owe many debts for the successful completion of this book, and wish to acknowledge them here.

Alfred Weber is grateful for the support he received from the Deutsche Forschungsgemeinschaft, Bonn, and the Council for the International Exchange of Scholars, Washington, D. C. He also expresses his thanks to the following libraries and historical societies: American Antiquarian Society, Worcester; Erie Canal Museum, Syracuse; Essex Institute, Salem, Massachusetts; Library of Cornell University, Ithaca; Massachusetts Historical Society, Boston; New-York Historical Society, New York City; New York Public Library; Ticonderoga Historical Society, Ticonderoga; Widener Library, Harvard.

Beth L. Lueck thanks the University of Wisconsin—Milwaukee for its Committee on Institutional Cooperation's Summer Research Opportunity Program grant for the summer of 1987, both for its research support and for the assistance of Vivian M. Norwood with this project. In addition, she thanks Howard Deller, Literature Analyst, of the Golda Meir Library at the University of Wisconsin—Milwaukee for his expert assistance with the travel guides and maps in the American Geographical Society Collection. The university's Cartographic Services Laboratory also deserves recognition for the map of New England and New York that appears on page xvi of this book. She also thanks her colleague Ralph Aderman for his generous help and encouragement. Finally, she wishes to thank her husband, Roger E. Carp, for his endless patience and support while she was working on this book.

Dennis Berthold thanks the National Endowment for the Humanities for a Senior Research Fellowship on which the original research for the Ticonderoga essay was conducted as part of a larger project. He also received support from the administration at Texas A&M University, including Hamlin Hill, Head, Department of English; Daniel Fallon, Dean, College of Liberal Arts; and the University Mini-Grant Committee. Invaluable personal collaboration in Tübingen with Alfred Weber was made possible by a teaching exchange between Texas A&M and the University of Zagreb, Yugoslavia, directed by Hamlin Hill under the auspices of the United States Information Agency. During the final stages of manuscript preparation, he received much-needed support, domestic as well as academic, from his wife, Pamela R. Matthews.

Finally, we are all grateful for the two events that brought us together. The 1986 Hawthorne Conference organized by Thomas Woodson at Bowdoin College in Brunswick, Maine, allowed us to meet each other for the first time and lay plans for this book. Then a week-long meeting among the three coauthors on the campus of Texas A&M University helped us make the idea a reality. For this we thank the Department of English, the Interdisciplinary Group for Historical Literary Study, and the Study Abroad Office, as well as the individuals who offered their support: Jeffrey Cox, Katherine O'Brien O'Keeffe, Larry Reynolds, Mona Rizk-Finne, and, once more, Hamlin Hill.

HAWTHORNE'S
AMERICAN TRAVEL SKETCHES

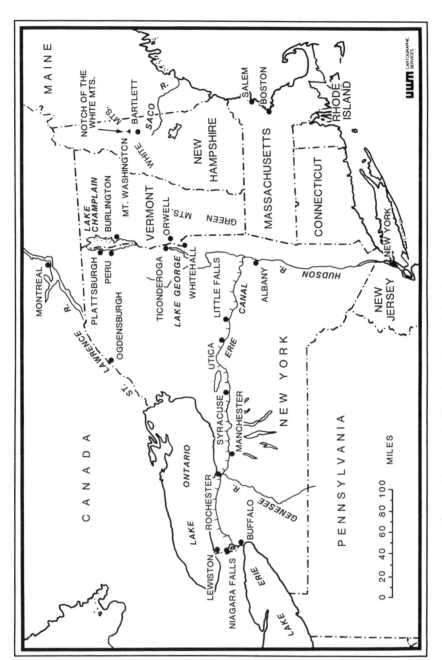

Places of interest in Hawthorne's travel sketches. UWM Cartographic Services Laboratory.

Please substitute for the map on page xvi.

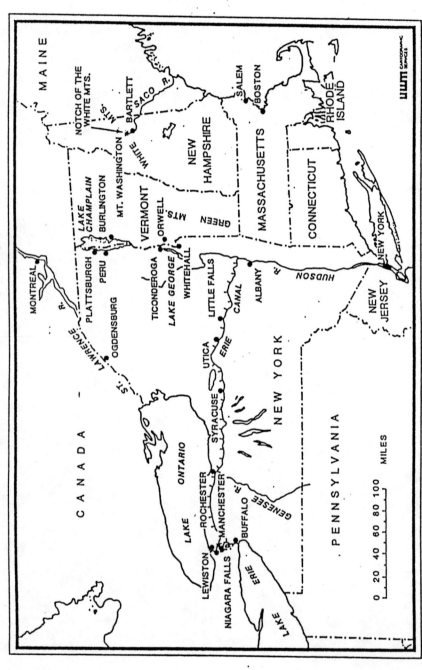

Places of interest in Hawthorne's travel sketches. UWM Cartographic
Services Laboratory.

HAWTHORNE'S TOUR OF 1832 THROUGH NEW ENGLAND AND UPSTATE NEW YORK

Alfred Weber

Hawthorne's work does not limit itself to romances of the legendary and historical past of New England, to a presentation of problems of moral psychology, and to allegorical narratives; it also includes authentic and critical descriptions of American cities, landscapes, and people. Many of these descriptions resulted from travels that led Hawthorne, even as a young man, to explore a wide range of American nature and American life. Arlin Turner speaks of Hawthorne's

lifelong efforts to know the land and the people of his region, to understand the nature and the meaning of the American experience, from the first settlement onward, and in the full diversity of the people. . . . Prepared by observations recorded in his mind and in his notebook during repeated travels in New England and New York, and by an intimate familiarity with American history, he undertook to know the character of the new nation, and to foresee its future. His findings and his conclusions are woven into his sketches, tales, and romances.[1]

Hawthorne himself commented on the significance which his youthful travels and "excursions" had for him. In an autobiographical fragment written in 1853, he looked back to his earlier years of solitude in Salem:

I had always had a natural tendency . . . toward seclusion; and this I now [after returning from college in 1825] indulged to the utmost, so, that, for months together, I scarcely held human intercourse outside of my own family. . . . Once a year, or thereabouts, I used to make an excursion of a

1

few weeks, in which I enjoyed as much of life as other people do in the whole year's round.[2]

He seems to have experienced his rambles and trips with great intensity, judging by the traces they left in his works. In these solitary years, he also became a lover of travel books, so much so that this kind of literature formed at the time a major "reading pattern" for him.[3]

*

In 1832 Hawthorne undertook his first long trip alone, a journey through New England and upstate New York. There is still disagreement among scholars about the route Hawthorne took[4] because there exists only scanty information about the author's early life. He saw to it that most of his letters to the family were destroyed after they had served their purpose. Only a few remain to document early trips to New Haven and other parts of Connecticut, and to Concord and Canterbury in New Hampshire, trips in company with his uncle, Samuel Manning, who owned a stagecoach-line and was often on the road to buy new horses. Two of these family letters, along with a third document, provide all the first-hand information available about his northern tour of 1832. In a letter of 28 June 1832 to Franklin Pierce, Hawthorne described his plan for the journey in the following words:

I was making preparations for a northern tour, when this accursed Cholera broke out in Canada. It was my intention to go by way of New-York and Albany to Niagara, from thence to Montreal and Quebec, and home through Vermont and New-Hampshire. I am very desirous of making this journey on account of a book by which I intend to acquire an (undoubtedly) immense literary reputation, but which I cannot commence writing till I have visited Canada. (CE, XV, 224)[5]

He went on to say that he hoped to depart in August or September, as soon as the cholera had disappeared.[6] In fact, he departed about two-and-a-half months later. Another letter, written to his mother on 16 September 1832, from Burlington, Vermont, shows that he had indeed left Salem about the end of August or the beginning of September, but he had changed his itinerary. He had not gone from Salem to New York and Albany, as originally planned, but had started out north to the White Mountains of New Hampshire and from there had turned west to Burlington. He wrote:

I have arrived in health and safety at this place, and have so much to do and to see, that I cannot find time to tell you all my adventures. I passed through the White Hills and stayed two nights and part of three days in Ethan Crawford's house. Moreover, I mounted what the people called a "plaguey high-lifed crittur" and rode with four gentlemen and a guide six miles to the foot of Mt. Washington. It was but four °clock A.M. when we started, and a showery morning, and we had to ride through the very worst road that ever was seen, mud and mire, and several rivers to be forded, and trees to be jumped over (fallen trees, I mean) through all which I galloped and trotted and tript and stumbled, and arrived without breaking my neck at last. The other particulars, how I climbed three miles into the air, and how it snowed all the way, and how, when I got up the mountain on one side, the wind carried me a great distance off my feet and almost blew me down the other, and how the thermometer stood at twelve degrees below the freezing point, I shall have time enough to tell you when I return.

I do not know exactly the course which I shall take from here. I might be in Canada tomorrow if I thought proper, but I have no sort of intention of going there. I see that there have been five new cases of the Cholera in Boston, and shall be impatient for further intelligence, which is very slow in getting to this part of the world. (CE, XV, 226)

The last extant document relating to this journey is a printed certification that Nathaniel Hawthorne had "passed behind the Great Falling Sheet of Water to Termination Rock" at Niagara Falls, on 28 September 1832.[7] It proves that Hawthorne, after his stay at Burlington, continued his wanderings for at least twelve more days and actually reached Niagara Falls.

It was the first extensive tour which Hawthorne planned and undertook on his own, and it led him far beyond the region he knew from his earlier travels. It occurred in a period of his life when he spent most of his time in solitary study and writing in his Salem chamber. Most important, it marked a turning point in his writings, away from the study of history to an exploration of the present, and away from Gothic and historical romances to more realistic sketches of contemporary life.

*

The journey was planned and undertaken "on account of a book" that Hawthorne intended to write, a book intended to be different from the three unsuccessful works he had written before: the "Seven Tales of My Native Land," written in the Gothic manner; the "Provincial Tales," a collection of historical tales about the co- lonial past of New England; and *Fanshawe,* a romance about the death of a young intellectual, based on Hawthorne's own college experiences. This new book, which he entitled "The Story Teller," was to be a work by which he might at last achieve, almost unknown as he was at that time, literary success.[8]

He actually wrote "The Story Teller" between the winter of 1832 and the summer of 1834. It amounted to two manuscript volumes and was the largest and most ambitious work he had yet composed. In its introduction, the protagonist and narrator, looking back on his youthful life as an itinerant storyteller, describes the plan for the book:

> The following pages will contain a picture of my vagrant life, intermixed with specimens, generally brief and slight, of that great mass of fiction to which I gave existence, and which has vanished like cloud-shapes. Besides the occasions when I sought a pecuniary reward, I was accustomed to exercise my narrative faculty, wherever chance had collected a little audi- ence, idle enough to listen. These rehearsals were useful in testing the strong points of my stories; and, indeed, the flow of fancy soon came upon me so abundantly, that its indulgence was its own reward; though the hope of praise, also, became a powerful incitement. Since I shall never feel the warm gush of new thought, as I did then, let me beseech the reader to believe, that my tales were not always so cold as he may find them now. With each specimen will be given a sketch of the circumstances in which the story was told. Thus my air-drawn pictures will be set in frames, per- haps more valuable than the pictures themselves, since they will be em- bossed with groups of characteristic figures, amid the lake and mountain scenery, the villages and fertile fields, of our native land. . . . [the book] is the experience of a wandering story teller. (CE, X, 408–9)

It has the structure of a framed story-cycle and the scope of an *Entwicklungsroman*: the framing story presents the whole life and the destiny of an American storyteller, and it describes at the same time his inner moral and artistic development. He is a persona of young Nathaniel Hawthorne, and many details of the narrative can be related to Hawthorne's own life. Oberon, as he is called, is a fanciful and eccentric young man who has become aware of his poetical tastes and talents and thus revolts against the uncomprehending and oppressive environment of his native New England village. His imagination passionately longs for employment and a free unfolding of its powers. He casts off all burdensome ties and goes into the world as a wandering storyteller to make his fortune and to enjoy the free life of an artist. During this time, in which he produces a great many stories, he comes to know life and the world, and he inwardly matures. His hope of happiness and his longing for love, however, remain unfulfilled. After a severe illness far away from home, he resolves to give up his wanderings. Disillusioned but wiser, he returns to his native village. Here, secluded and lonely, he dies young.

The largest part of "The Story Teller" frame is taken up by the descriptions of Oberon's wanderings through the northeastern United States. This frame narrative develops a central motif of travel that combines two types of travel literature, the book of real travels and the presentation of a "spiritual journey" or *voyage imaginaire*. "The Story Teller," remarkable for its wide thematic range and structural complexity, must be regarded as the major work, however ill-fated, of Hawthorne's early literary career.[9]

Hawthorne sent the manuscript to Samuel G. Goodrich, the editor of *The Token*, who then passed it on to Park Benjamin, the editor of first the *New-England Magazine* and then the *American Monthly Magazine*. The opening sections of "The Story Teller," in their original form and under the original title, appeared in the *New-England Magazine* of November and December 1834.[10] After two installments, however, publication was discontinued. Parts and fragments of the manuscript were published piecemeal in later numbers of the *New-England Magazine*, then in the *American Monthly Magazine* and perhaps also in other publications. Park Benjamin, who in an 1836 review of *The Token* celebrated Hawthorne as the best living

American author after Washington Irving, is responsible for cutting up the work. As late as July 1837 he published anonymously the "Fragments from the Journal of a Solitary Man." Close analysis shows that Benjamin meddled with Hawthorne's text and composed these "Fragments" out of the concluding parts of the frame and some of the remaining unpublished fragments.[11] The young author resigned himself to the failure of this ambitious work, and it was never published in the form he intended. However, the established facts that the opening sections of "The Story Teller" appeared in their original form, and that a part of the "Fragments from the Journal of a Solitary Man" formed the book's conclusion, provide a basis for a hypothetical reconstruction of the work's original outlines.[12]

Quite a few fragments of the frame were published as separate travel sketches, most of them as "Sketches from Memory." They were integral parts of this fictional work, but they also contained authentic delineations of routes and places that really exist. Their descriptions of landscapes, of towns, and of people in New England and upstate New York are so detailed and graphic, that they surely must have been based on personal observations. It is likely that they were taken down in a notebook and perhaps even transcribed in family letters that have been lost. So these travel sketches, discussed in the essays in this volume, can be taken as additional sources for the reconstruction of the trip. However, they must be used carefully: they were written as integral parts of a larger work of fiction, and the itinerary of its protagonist need not be identical with the route taken by Hawthorne in 1832. While the fictional journey certainly was much longer in time, it may have also included places and experiences from Hawthorne's travels before 1832, and the sketches may have been arranged by the author not in the order of his real journey, but according to a thematic or dramatic pattern he had in mind. Still, their factual core comes from Hawthorne's 1832 journey, which obviously formed the groundwork for the frame of "The Story Teller."

*

Hawthorne's love of travel and his great interest in travel literature not only afford revealing glimpses of the young, solitary writer in his formative years, but they also mirror the social, intellectual, and cultural history of the period. In the 1820s and early 1830s in America, the time had come for travel. The frontier was moving further west and civilization was progressing into formerly unsettled parts of the country. Earlier, tours from the East to the West had been difficult because of poor roads. But with the development of steamboat traffic on the Great Lakes and with the building of canals and railroads, the means for travel and commerce had greatly improved. Waves of immigrants poured into the United States, and a host of English and European tourists were seen on the stagecoach lines and waterways, especially in New York and southern Canada. Documenting these developments, Roger Haydon finds that the majority of British travelers between 1815 and 1845 were governed by an aesthetic interest that had two main concerns: the literary and the pictorial. In 1835, the two American authors most popular in Europe were New Yorkers—Washington Irving and James Fenimore Cooper. But, according to Haydon, "New York was preeminent not merely for its literary associations but also for its 'pictorial' interest." He goes on to explain:

The Hudson River Valley was ever being compared with the valley of the Rhine for picturesqueness . . . [while] at the other end of the state, Niagara Falls encompassed the very essence of the word "sublime." . . .

Niagara was for many visitors their journey's culmination, and there is a sense in which crossing the state from the Hudson to Niagara is traveling through the categories of landscape—from the picturesque through the beautiful to the sublime.[13]

The time had also come for Americans to tour and sketch the picturesque and sublime beauties of nature in their own country. Alongside travelers of the American leisure class one could see a growing number of writers and artists such as Washington Irving and William Cullen Bryant, and early landscape painters such as Thomas Cole, Henry Cheever Pratt, and Asher B. Durand. They had a nationalistic motive for their travels: "Convinced that art must be based on American subjects to avoid being derivative, they looked for what was special about America and found it in the land."[14] In the introduction to his *Sketch Book* of 1819–1820, Irving describes his American travel experiences thus:

I visited various parts of my own country; and had I been merely a lover
of fine scenery, I should have felt little desire to seek elsewhere its gratification, for on no other country have the charms of nature been more
prodigally lavished. Her mighty lakes, like oceans of liquid silver; her
mountains, with their bright aerial tints; her valleys, teeming with wild
fertility; her tremendous cataracts, thundering in their solitudes; her
boundless plains, waving with spontaneous verdure; her broad deep rivers,
rolling in solemn silence to the ocean; her trackless forests, where vegetation puts forth all its magnificence; her skies, kindling with the magic of
summer clouds and glorious sunshine;—no, never need an American look
beyond his own country for the sublime and beautiful of natural scenery.[15]

Both Hawthorne's 1832 tour and "The Story Teller" were in part
motivated by these concerns. Hawthorne certainly knew Irving's
Sketch Book, and he borrowed his *Tales of a Traveller* between 1 and
7 February 1832,[16] around the time when he was planning his own
journey.

Travel fiction such as Irving's and narratives such as Basil Hall's
Travels in North America or Theodore Dwight's *Sketches of Scenery and
Manners in the United States* had become very popular at this time.[17]
The growing number of European and American tourists also
created the market for another genre of travel literature: the tourist
guides, early American "Baedekers." They contained everything a
traveler of the period should know for planning and making a trip:
descriptions of tours and special sights, facts and figures on historical developments and commercial life, information on the stagecoach, steamboat, and canal-boat lines with their distances, prices,
and schedules; and even the names of recommended hotels. When
they describe the landscape along the recommended routes, these
tourist guides quote from the travel books, retelling such local stories as the death of the Willey family in a White Mountain landslide
or the final jump of Sam Patch at the Genesee Falls.[18] Within a
short time, most of them went through several editions and were
considerably revised and enlarged.[19]

The Traveller's Directory through the United States by John Melish may
have been the earliest American tourist guide. It first appeared in
1814, and in this and subsequent editions offered a description of

the most important commercial and tourist routes by water and by land within the United States. Another guide was the anonymous *Traveller's Guide, or, a few weeks tour in the New-England States* (1823). Its introduction emphasizes the increasing demand for tourist information:

> The Northern part of this country is annually visited by so many travellers, and the roads, taverns, and stages offer so many conveniences, that it is to be regretted there should as yet have been no measures taken for supplying the stranger with such local information as is necessary for his pleasure and convenience. A general remark or two concerning the quality of the road he is to travel, the distances between towns, and the names of the best inns might often be of essential benefit.[20]

In the introduction to *The Traveller's Guide: through the middle and northern states, and the provinces of Canada* (1834), Gideon Miner Davison provides a capsule description of American tourism in the twenties and early thirties:

> The oppressive heat of summer in the southern sections of the United States, and the consequent exposure to illness, have long induced the wealthy part of the population to seek, at that season of the year, the more salubrious climate of the north. But the recent gigantic internal improvements in the northern and middle states, and the development of new and highly interesting natural scenery, together with the increased facilities of travelling, have greatly augmented the number of tourists within a short period. The rail roads, canals, coal mines, the Springs, the Falls, the Lakes, the fortifications of Quebec, the sublime mountain scenery in New York and New England, with the various attractions presented in the large commercial cities, cannot fail of insuring to a traveller a rich compensation for the toils incident to a journey.[21]

The book also presents a particular set of tours that were fashionable at the time, such as those indicated in the title of another successful travel guide, Theodore Dwight's *The Northern Traveller: containing the routes to Niagara, Quebec, and the Springs: with descriptions of the principal scenes, and useful hints to strangers.*[22]

The tours described in these tourist guides are more or less limited to the northeastern United States: New England, upstate New

York, and Lakes Ontario and Erie. A comparison of what these books present as the most interesting, most attractive, most comfortable, and most popular routes of travel discloses a pattern of four principal routes on which they all agree. Among them are three of special interest for Hawthorne's 1832 tour: One explores part of New England and runs from Boston through the White Mountains of New Hampshire either to Burlington, Vermont, or to Montreal, Canada; another leaves New York City and leads north, along the Hudson River, through the Champlain canal and Lake Champlain to Montreal, with a branch line along Lake George and through Saratoga Springs; a third goes up the Hudson River to Albany, and from there west on the Erie Canal to Niagara Falls.[23] These were standard routes not only for tourists, but also for commercial traffic. They form part of a network on which the main traffic moved in the early 1830s, shortly before the railroads further facilitated and enlarged the possibilities for commerce and travel.

*

The tourist guides and their documentation of the principal routes of travel help reconstruct Hawthorne's itinerary. When he wrote to his friend Pierce that he had been making preparations for a "northern tour," he used a key term introduced by the guide-books; and when he mentioned in the same letter his "intention to go by way of New York and Albany to Niagara, from thence to Montreal and Quebec," he echoed the recommended route of *The Tourist* (1830) by Robert J. Vandewater, who, as the subtitle of the third edition of his book indicates, described a tour "on the Hudson River, the Western Canal and Stage Road to Niagara Falls down Lake Ontario and the St. Lawrence to Montreal and Quebec."[24] Most important, all the places and itineraries mentioned by Hawthorne both in his two letters and in the relevant travel sketches lie, without exception, on one of the three routes described in the tourist guides. So Hawthorne, while planning in 1832 his journey through upstate New York and New England, must have consulted one or more of these guidebooks. When he set out on his trip, he traveled by stagecoach, on the steamboats and packet boats and, over shorter distances, on foot. He was not a wandering storyteller, but a traveling writer in search of the picturesque, the beautiful, and the sublime—standard terms in all the tourist guides—and he was only one of the many such American and European tourists of the time. As his travel sketches show, he consciously recognized this role by making tourism one of their central themes.

A final set of facts helpful in reconstructing the 1832 journey is suggested by Hawthorne's references to cholera in his letters to his mother and to Pierce. Cholera was the classic epidemic disease of the nineteenth century, as were yellow fever and smallpox during the previous two centuries. It came through Europe from India. When it first appeared in Southern Canada and the state of New York in June and July 1832, people were helpless and frightened. Similarly alarmed, the medical profession began desperately searching —in a great number of conferences and publications—for remedies and cures. The causes of the cholera were still unknown, and its progress was fast and fatal.[25] It was a highly dramatic epidemic disease, which arrived in America at a time when the frontier had reached the Mississippi region and when a great number of new land and water routes had been created, especially in the St. Lawrence and Great Lakes regions and in the state of New York. A study of a number of medical publications of the time[26] shows that the cholera of 1832 traveled on three principal routes: (1) from Quebec west, along the St. Lawrence River and the Great Lakes to Buffalo, Detroit, and Chicago; (2) from the St. Lawrence River south, along Lakes Champlain and George and the Hudson River to New York City; and (3) from Albany along the Erie Canal, to Utica, Syracuse, Rochester, and Buffalo. These were also the main routes of commerce, immigration, and tourism.

The cholera prevailed in southeastern Canada and the north-eastern United States from the middle of June 1832 until the beginning of September, with two notable exceptions: (1) New York City was particularly severely hit, and here the cholera lasted longest, from the end of June until about the middle of October; (2) while there were indeed some short-lived appearances of the cholera in Boston and Portsmouth, New England as a whole remained free from any severe visitations of this disease.

The sudden appearance and the dramatic spread of the epidemic had of course an influence on Hawthorne's journey, not only on the postponement of his departure until the end of August or the beginning of September, but also on his final itinerary. The cholera was, it seems, on his mind from June, when he wrote to Pierce, until September, when he wrote to his mother from Burlington. He badly wanted to travel because of his projected book, but he was also careful to avoid the epidemic. He wanted to visit Canada, but in Burlington, Vermont, after having traveled through healthy New England and just before entering the cholera zones of Southern Canada and upstate New York, he was undecided where to go. The thought of the cholera must have been a leitmotiv in all his further decisions, and the way the disease spread explains why he cancelled New York City from his itinerary and why, when the cholera had spent its force, he set out north to the White Mountains, into a part of New England which had been free from all cholera dangers.

On the basis of all the evidence found in Hawthorne's own letters and travel sketches, in the tourist guides, and in the cholera documents, his 1832 journey can be reconstructed with more certainty than ever before. The following narrative of his tour will be illustrated by selected reproductions of oil paintings, lithographs, and engravings done by early nineteenth-century artists. They had traveled on some of the same routes as Hawthorne, and their pictures show how some of the memorable sights Hawthorne saw looked to them at the time.

*

Hawthorne's point of departure was, of course, Salem, Massachusetts, from which he could take a stagecoach along a route recommended in Theodore Dwight's *The Northern Traveller*.[27] On his way north he may have revisited Concord, New Hampshire, on the Merrimack River, a center of the stagecoach business. This was the same route taken by Thomas Cole, who in October 1828, together with his friend Henry Cheever Pratt, set out from Concord on an arduous trip by coach and on foot to the White Mountains.[28] Hawthorne may have then passed Lake Winnipesaukee, where, according to Theodore Dwight's *The Northern Traveller,* the country begins to assume the features of bold and mountain scenery. Even before arriving at the lake, the prospect is varied with many of those noble elevations which rise to such a height of grandeur and sublimity as the traveller proceeds; and the frequent glimpses afforded between the sloping hills, over the beautiful lake below, by a happy contrast increase the effect.[29]

He certainly went on to Conway, and from there the shortest road into the White Mountains led up north to Bartlett and through the valley of the Saco River (ill. 4).[30] In 1826, six years before Hawthorne visited this area, a catastrophe occurred which was reported nationwide in the newspapers and which is mentioned in all the tourist guides.[31] Gideon Miner Davison puts it thus:

A tremendous catastrophe occurred among the White Mountains on the night of Aug. 28th, 1826. A storm of rain, unprecedented within the memory of the oldest inhabitants, deluged the principal peaks of the mountains, and poured such an inundation upon the valleys and plains below, that it is commonly attributed to the "bursting of a cloud [.]". . .

The inundation was so great and so sudden, that the channels of the streams were totally insufficient to admit of the passage of the water, which consequently overflowed the little level valleys at the feet of the mountains. Innumerable torrents immediately formed on all sides; and such deep trenches were cut by the rushing water, that vast bodies of earth and stones fell from the mountains, bearing with them the forests that had covered them for ages [ill. 3]. Some of these "slides" . . . are supposed to have been half a mile in breadth, and from one to five miles in length. Scarcely any natural occurrence can be imagined more sublime; and among the devastation which it has left to testify the power of the elements, the traveller will be filled with awe at the thought of that Being by whom they are controlled and directed. . . .

The *Willey House* [ill. 4] was the scene of a most melancholy tragedy on the night above mentioned, when this inundation occurred. Several days previously, a large "slide" came down from the mountains behind it, and passed so near as to cause great alarm, without any injury to the inmates. The house was occupied by Mr. Calvin Willey, whose wife was a young woman of a very interesting character, and of an education not to be looked for in so wild a region. They had a number of young children, and their family at the time included several other persons, amounting in all to eleven. They were waked in the night by the noise of the storm, or more probably, by the second descent of avalanches from the neighbouring mountains; and fled in their night clothes from the house to seek their safety, but thus threw themselves in the way of destruction. One of the slides, 100 feet high, stopped within 3 feet of the house. Another took away the barn, and overwhelmed the family. . . . [T]hey had all been crushed on leaving the door, or borne away with the water that overflowed the meadow. The bodies of several of them were never found. A catastrophe so melancholy, and at the same time so singular in its circumstances, has hardly ever occurred. It will always furnish the traveller with a melancholy subject of reflection.[32]

This event inspired "The Ambitious Guest," one of the stories in "The Story Teller." From the Willey house the road winds up north, along the Saco River, between the narrowing mountains. It leads up to the famous Notch of the White Mountains, which "is so narrow as to allow only room enough for the path and the Saco, which is here a mere brook only four feet in breadth."[33] In its narrowest part it is only twenty-two feet wide. Behind the Notch the valley widens and presents a level surface: the "Notch Meadow," where the Crawford Inn (or Notch House) stood (ill. 5), offering food and shelter for all kinds of travelers.[34] Here Hawthorne spent parts of three days and two nights.

From their inn, the Crawfords led guests up to the top of Mount Washington. "The ascent of the mountain," Dwight says,

was formerly a most arduous undertaking, and was very rarely performed, but several ladies have lately been enumerated among those who have gained the summit [ill. 6]. . . . In a clear atmosphere the view is sublime, and almost boundless. . . . [T]he eye ranges over an extent of surface, which quite bewilders the mind. Mountains, hills, and valleys, farm houses, villages, and towns, add their variety to the natural features of the country. . . ."[35]

The Crawford House was the center of early White Mountain tourism, and the Crawfords were for many of their guests the guides of a quite strenuous tour up to the peak of Mount Washington.[36] By taking this trip in 1832, Hawthorne was part of a pioneering band of travelers, for as R. Stuart Wallace has observed, prior to 1840 "tourism [in this area] was conducted on a limited scale. Writers, scientists, artists, and a few curious and daring souls visited the White Mountains to experience firsthand the wonders of a little-known region."[37] For years this mountain range represented "the archetypal American wilderness."[38] Thomas Cole, who devoted many of his paintings to this region, found, as he says in his "Essay on American Scenery" (1836), "in the mountains of New Hampshire . . . a union of the picturesque, the sublime, and the magnificent; there the bare peaks of granite, broken and desolate, cradle the clouds; while the vallies and broad bases of the mountains rest under the shadow of noble and varied forests."[39]

From Crawford's House, Hawthorne traveled through the Green Hills of Vermont to Burlington, Vermont, on the eastern shore of Lake Champlain, a flourishing inland port of thirty-five hundred inhabitants and a center of commercial and tourist traffic.[40] Lake Champlain, connected by a canal with the Hudson River, is an important waterway between Canada and New York. According to Davison's tourist guide, a

great proportion of the lands on the margin of the lake are still unredeemed from a state of nature, and in some places, particularly at the north end, are low and marshy. After entering the territories of the United States, the country is more populous, and under a better state of improvement. The villages seen from the lake all exhibit a cheerful and thriving appearance. . . . The history of Champlain involves many interesting events associated with the French and Revolutionary wars. During those periods several fortifications were constructed, which have since undergone some repairs, but are now in a state of decay. The ruins of the ancient fortresses at Ticonderoga and Crown Point are still visible.[41]

Hawthorne may well have made a one-day steamboat excursion to the northern part of the lake in order to assess the cholera situation. He may even have gone as far as Montreal, because the narrator in "The Inland Port" mentions that he had taken a little skiff in Peru, on the west side of the lake and nine miles south of Plattsburgh, to return to Burlington on the eastern shore.[42]

Hawthorne's further itinerary can only be inferred from the

sketches in "The Story Teller" and from the fact that he was heading for Niagara and took twelve days to reach it from Burlington.[43]
He must have gone south, by coach and by steamboat, and he must
have passed Fort Ticonderoga (ills. 23–26), viewing it either from
the eastern side of Lake Champlain or from one of the boats on
the lake. He probably visited it later, on his way home, after his stay
at Niagara Falls, as indicated in the first paragraph of "Old Ticonderoga": "In returning once to New England, from a visit to Niagara, I found myself, one summer's day, before noon, at Orwell
. . . on the Vermont shore, with a ferry, of less than a mile wide,
between us and the town of Ti, in New York."[44] This old fort, built
by the French in 1756, had been occupied in turn by French, British, and American troops before it was abandoned after the Revolutionary War. It had been left to decay, and presented at the time
"one of the most interesting ruins of the kind" and an attraction
for a great number of tourists.[45] For an American romancer who
complained that America had no ruins and treasures of the past,
this sight had a special significance.

On his way south Hawthorne may have traveled along Lake
George. "The wild and romantic scenery of this lake," so one of
the travel guides explains, "is unrivalled in the United States, and
stands pre-eminent for its charming beauties."[46] From there he may
have gone to Saratoga Springs, a town "justly celebrated as being
the most noted watering place in the United States, there being
here found a large number of mineral springs, possessing great
medicinal properties" which attracted crowds of tourists in the summer months.[47] In the "Canal-Boat" sketch the traveler reaches the
Erie Canal at "about thirty miles below Utica," that is, Little Falls
at the Mohawk River, and Hawthorne may indeed have taken the
morning stage from Saratoga Springs, passing through Ballston,
Galway, and Johnston, and arriving at Little Falls (ill. 9) in the afternoon.[48]

The canal, the most impressive feat of American engineering of
the day, was one of the major sights many tourists wanted to see
(ills. 8–11, 13–14). It was completed in 1825, and united the waters
of the Hudson River at Albany with those of Lake Erie at Buffalo.

Stretching 363 miles, it was by far the longest and most important canal in the United States. It made an immediate impact on commerce and tourism, as Ralph K. Andrist notes:

> From the moment the Erie Canal opened, its waters were thronged with lines of vessels moving in opposite directions. . . . The major east-west transport of goods and people moved along the Erie Canal, and each year the traffic increased. There was a constant bustle of emigrants going west to find new homes; of European visitors coming to see the sights they had read about.[49]

Patricia Anderson describes the effect a canal journey through the wilderness had on these early tourists:

> visions of broad valleys, lone lakes, and vast forests greeted those who made the once impossible journey across New York State in the Canal's first packet boats. As changing scenery rolled by them at a speed of five miles per hour, passengers could contemplate the many and various wonders with which God had favored this region in particular. . . . As Willis pointed out in *American Scenery* (1840), "romantic raptures" awaited those who made the delightful excursion from Schenectady to Buffalo.
>
> To experience nature in this way—as a continual scenic display—was the privilege of . . . a new leisure class following upon the country's new commercialism.[50]

In "The Canal-Boat," Hawthorne's narrator describes his passage through Utica (ill. 12) and "the long level," a dead flat between Utica and Syracuse, and his departure from the boat at night shortly before Syracuse (ill. 13). It is reasonable to assume that this sketch is based on Hawthorne's personal experiences, and that he actually traveled eighty miles and spent about twenty hours, one whole day and part of the following night, on a packet boat like the one Theodore Dwight described in *The Northern Traveller*:

> The length is 60 or 70 feet, a large part of which is devoted to the dining room, where the two rows of tables are set. At night, mattresses are spread on the seats at each side, and in another row above them on cots suspended from the roof. The ladies are accommodated with berths in the cabin, which is usually carpeted, hung with curtains, and in other respects more handsomely furnished. The kitchen and bar are conveniently situated; and

the tables are spread with an abundance, and often a delicacy which may well surprise those not accustomed to the cheapness of travelling in this part of the country.

A small library, a number of newspapers, will serve to make the time pass agreeably, even if the traveller be a stranger, or the weather not inviting. In many places, the view from the deck is highly interesting; but it cannot be too often recommended to the stranger to beware of standing on deck when approaching a bridge, and never to expose the head and hands out of a window.[51]

Such a boat moved day and night at four to five miles per hour, with stops only to use the locks or exchange the horses that towed the boats. The canal was forty feet wide at the top and twenty-eight feet wide at the bottom. The tow path was about four feet above the surface of the water and was ten feet wide. At the time, the canal offered a radically new way of traveling that, despite its discomforts, improved considerably upon stage travel, as Dwight realized:

In the hot season, when most travellers are on their journies, stage coaches are often found uncomfortable, and hotels and inns too often furnish little real repose to the way-worn stranger . . . so that, after all, it may be questioned whether the canal boats, with their monotony, their comparative sluggishness, and the republican equality with which they reduce different grades of society, ought not to be more generally in good repute, than they are.[52]

After a trip of about eighty miles, Hawthorne very probably left the packet boat at Syracuse (ill. 14).[53] From there he had the choice of two possible routes to Rochester. He could have taken a well-known stagecoach line and traveled, in about three days, north to the Thousand Islands (a scenic attraction of seventeen hundred small islands in the mouth of the St. Lawrence River, right at the Canadian border) and then, at Ogdensburg (ill. 15), embarked on a steamboat across Lake Ontario to Rochester;[54] or, he could have gone directly, by stage or boat, to this thriving young city. Rochester (ill. 16), according to Vandewater, was the most extensive, populous, and important place in the western country. It has been termed the "Western New-York." The *Genesee river* passes through the village, and the Great Falls, 97 feet in height, are about 80 rods below [see ills. 17 and 18]. From the centre of these falls the celebrated *Sam Patch,* of immortal memory, made his "last jump," in the autumn of 1829. . . . His body was not found until the ensuing spring. In 1812 Rochester was a wilderness; and in the short space of 18 years its growth has been unprecedented, as will be perceived by a slight glance at its present statistics. It contains 2000 buildings, and a population of about 13,000.[55]

Because the town "had sprung up like a mushroom" (see p. 46), Rochester became a symbol of the American rush toward western development. Horatio Gates Spafford's *Pocket Guide* points to the changes that had taken place in Rochester:

But a few years since, this whole region was a wilderness: not a house, in 1797, from Genesee river to this place, and here only a few huts for Indian traders. . . . [The author remembers perfectly well, when the Genesee river was] considered the very end, the extreme limit of 'the westward' . . . into which the stream of emigration has long been pouring its almost countless numbers, and yet that stream is not exhausted, nor is 'the westward' half full of people. . . . Here are passing, as I should suppose, 500 persons, each day, all going *west,* and that in July, a season of the year rather early for the pouring out of the full stream.[56]

Rochester was a center of traffic in upstate New York and Canada. Its steamboat landing was a convenient point of embarkation for all ports on Lake Ontario and the St. Lawrence River; Erie Canal packet boats left the city every morning for Buffalo and Albany; and the stage, which Hawthorne probably took, left daily for Buffalo via Lewiston, Manchester, and Niagara Falls. Manchester, as the map shows (see page xvi), was a small village just north of the falls, not the present western New York town of that name. In "My Visit to Niagara," the narrator follows this latter itinerary, taking the famous and scenic "ridge road," one of the best in the state, for 104 miles along the shore of Lake Erie.[57]

About ten to twelve days after his stay in Burlington, Hawthorne arrived at Niagara Falls, obviously the culmination of his journey, and, according to Patricia Anderson, the aim of many romantic pilgrimages and the undisputed climax of North American tourism in the 1820s and 1830s (ills. 19–22):

Certainly it was the falls at Niagara which lured visitors to upstate New York in increasing numbers after 1825. "Niagara! that wonder of the world!," Cole exclaimed in his "Essay on American Scenery." . . . Americans adopted the falls as something of a New World symbol: in their immensity and power they might be a metaphor for the great developing nation itself. A visit to the falls was a must for travelers.[58]

Robert D. Vandewater's description in *The Tourist* may be taken as an example of the extensive passages on the Niagara Falls that Hawthorne would have found in every travel guide:

The cataract of Niagara, the grandest spectacle in the world, suddenly bursting upon the sight of its first visit[o]rs [such as Father Hennepin in 1679], who could contemplate nature in her wild native dress, must have struck their senses more potently, and excited their feelings more intensely than it can now do of those who see it surrounded by cultivated fields, and monuments of art. What can we imagine more beautiful, more truly sublime, than a majestic river suddenly contracted into less than half its former width, after tumbling over a bed of loose rocks, precipitated, roaring as it were, with very terror, into a dark caldron below, maddened and lashed into foam white as the driven snow, and throwing up a thick column of spray towering to the very arch of heaven,—a cloud that is seen to hang over the Falls by those navigating Erie and Ontario—by spectators a hundred miles distant from each other. Add to this impression on the eye, that made upon the ear, and our own senses partake of the wild tumult of the scene. Confused, we leave the spot with a true idea of the vast, the grand, the sublime.[59]

"My Visit to Niagara" makes it clear that the narrator had read extensively about the sublimity of the Falls before he finally reached them, and that his "treasury of anticipated enjoyments, comprising all the wonders of the world, had nothing else so magnificent" (see p. 55).

Some final inferences may be drawn about the last stages of Hawthorne's tour. In "A Night Scene," the narrator takes passage in a steamboat on Lake Erie, suggesting that Hawthorne may have traveled this way from Buffalo to Detroit,[60] another fast-growing city on the Great Lakes. However, there is no way of knowing whether he really traveled farther west. He may have simply returned to Albany from Buffalo via an Erie Canal packet boat, a steamboat, or one of the regular stagecoaches. From Albany he may have gone down the Hudson River to New York City (reversing his original plan) or, from fear of the cholera still lingering there, he may have taken the stagecoach to Boston and back to Salem.[61] The whole journey probably took him at least a month, a longer time than any of his earlier trips.

*

This is the outline of the probable itinerary of the journey Hawthorne undertook in September of 1832. A complete reconstruction in which the exact route could be retraced with absolute certainty remains unattainable as long as any notebook that Hawthorne might have written on this trip and the letters he very likely wrote home remain lost. Nevertheless, the degree of probability that can be reached with the evidence at hand is high enough to attempt a final assessment of the journey's significance in Hawthorne's career.

It was Hawthorne's first and probably his only extensive journey beyond his home region of New England and through a larger part of the United States. Because, as Roger Haydon notes, "New York State was for the early nineteenth century the very image of the United States,"[62] Hawthorne's tour of the region revealed to him a wider and more representative dimension of American life than he had previously seen. As the many parallels between this journey and the stories and sketches of "The Story Teller" suggest, there is no question that it was undertaken with the express intention of discovering materials for a work that could make a contribution to the literature of the young American nation.

Furthermore, with this journey Hawthorne became a member of the first group of American artists and writers who, like Irving, Bryant, Cole, Pratt, and Durand, traveled in the United States in order to explore the American landscape, describe its natural beauties, and give their creative work a genuine American setting. He experienced the picturesque, the beautiful, and the sublime of the natural scenery which his own country could abundantly provide.

It was a romantic American journey with two major natural attractions: The White Mountains with Mount Washington, and Niagara Falls, one of the famous wonders of the New World. But this is not all. He who had measured out in his previous studies and works the American past of the seventeenth and eighteenth centuries now changed the focus of his interest and turned to the American present and to contemporary American life around him. He observed the dynamics of the frontier, the destruction of nature on the Erie Canal and at Rochester and the Genesee Falls, the advance of technical civilization, the expansion of traffic and commerce, the waves of immigration, and the bustle of tourism. He also saw firsthand the scenes of such sensational contemporary events as the landslide and the Willey disaster in the White Mountains and the last jump of Sam Patch at Genesee Falls, events that had grown into local legends and added romance and moral value to the American scene. He studied American life and the American society of his time critically by drawing, in his travel sketches and stories of "The Story Teller," a whole series of contemporary, realistic, representative American figures.

Hawthorne undertook this journey in preparation for "The Story Teller," which was so important to him that the dangers of the cholera could not make him cancel the trip, but only postpone it. Apart from a few early short stories and sketches, "The Story Teller" was Hawthorne's first work to deal with contemporary life and to integrate elements of the romance with those of the novel. His northern tour of 1832 provided the factual basis for the frame of this story-cycle, and most if not all of the travel sketches reprinted here have their place in this work of fiction. These sketches give "The Story Teller" the character of a fictionalized American travel book, comparable perhaps to *Our Old Home*, Hawthorne's later series of English sketches, or to *The Marble Faun*, the romance based on his Italian travel notebook. They also introduce into Hawthorne's prose the landscape materials that, in 1850, prompted Herman Melville to praise Hawthorne with a significant travel metaphor: "if you travel away inland into his deep and noble nature, you will hear the far roar of his Niagara."[63]

Hawthorne was in 1832 one of the many tourists who traveled through New England and upstate New York, obviously using the early American Baedekers that had been published for their convenience and their sight-seeing. But it was more than a "fashionable tour," to use an expression of his time. It was important to him for his own writing and, as is shown in the other essays in this volume, had a significant influence on his artistic development.

AN EDITION OF HAWTHORNE'S AMERICAN TRAVEL SKETCHES WITH TEXTUAL INTRODUCTIONS

Alfred Weber

This edition of Hawthorne's travel sketches uses the first publication in periodicals as copy-text and arranges them in geographical order according to the probable itinerary of Hawthorne's 1832 journey. Except for "An Ontario Steam-Boat," the sketches were all edited and published by Park Benjamin, editor of the *New-England Magazine* and later *The American Monthly Magazine.* He took them out of the two-volume manuscript of "The Story Teller" which Hawthorne had given him for publication. The sketches were originally links in the frame of this work, but the order in which Benjamin published them in the two magazines does not necessarily reflect the order in which they occurred in Hawthorne's original manuscript. Benjamin selected and trimmed passages for independent publication and in a number of the sketches indicated his deletions from the manuscript by asterisks between paragraphs. In the two installments of "Sketches from Memory," Benjamin even added introductory paragraphs of his own.

When some of these sketches were republished in a later collection, Hawthorne left the task of searching them out and selecting them to his publishers, even though they were widely scattered and published anonymously. Ticknor and Fields planned to publish a second and enlarged edition of *Mosses from an Old Manse* and asked the writer for further material. He answered Ticknor in a letter of 7 June 1854:

It has just occurred to me, moreover, that, in the New England Magazine, when published by Park Benjamin, many of the Stories appeared which

are now collected in the "Twice-told Tales"; and the publication of them
was commenced with about ten or more pages of introductory matter,
which, I think, will do very well to publish as an article in the "Mosses." It
should be separated from all extraneous stuff (which, if I recollect rightly,
may be done easy enough,) and may be called "passages from a relinquished work"—or something of that kind. I believe the title was "The
Itinerant Storyteller." There are other detached passages of mine, scattered
through Park Benjamin's volumes of that magazine; and Fields would
readily recognize them. Let him do as he pleases about inserting any or
all of them;—only being careful to put in nothing that he does not feel
absolutely certain about. . . .

P.S. All that I now recollect of my articles in the New England Magazine
are,—The Storyteller aforesaid, begun in an early number and concluded
long afterwards, I think, under some other title; and a description of an
evening at the mountain-house, among the White Hills. These passages
formed part of a work, the whole of which was never published. Do not
print any more of it than will be sufficient to meet the exigency of the
case; though really, as far as I can remember, it is no bad stuff. (CE, XVII,
225, 227)

For "Passages From a Relinquished Work," Fields selected only the
first two installments of "The Story Teller," omitting "Mr. Higginbotham's Catastrophe" because it had already appeared in 1837 in
the *Twice-told Tales*. He also neglected three "Sketches from Memory" ("The Notch of the White Mountains," "Our Evening Party
Among the Mountains," and "The Canal-Boat"), a cohesive group
of travel sketches that is reprinted here in full in their original form
and order.

Obvious printing errors of the copy-text are emended. Each
emendation is listed after the introductory textual note as follows:

Page. Line   Emended text > Original text in the periodical.

SKETCHES FROM MEMORY.
BY A PEDESTRIAN.
NO. I.

This was published anonymously in the *New-England Magazine* 9 (November
1835): 321–26.

"The Notch" and "Our Evening Party Among the Mountains" were reprinted by Fields in the second edition of *Mosses from an Old Manse* (1854) as
two of the three "Sketches from Memory." He used the text of the first publication, but changed the title of the first sketch to "The Notch of the White
Mountains," and he deleted the three asterisks after the second paragraph of
"The Notch," replacing them with a larger space between the paragraphs. CE
takes the 1854 *Mosses* as its copy-text and reprints the two sketches in X, 422–
38.

The editorial introduction, written by Park Benjamin, was omitted from
Mosses by Fields and was never collected. It appears only in the historical col-
lation of CE, X, 648 and in the notes to the Library of America edition of
Hawthorne's *Tales and Sketches*, 1487–88.

Emendations: 33. 5 poetical than that> poetical that that
                33. 33–34 have been looking> have been lookgin

We are so fortunate as to have in our possession the portfolio of
a friend, who traveled on foot in search of the picturesque over
New-England and New-York. It contains many loose scraps and
random sketches, which appear to have been thrown off at different
intervals, as the scenes once observed were recalled to the mind of
the writer by recent events or associations. He kept no journal nor
set down any notes during his tour; but his recollection seems to
have been faithful, and his powers of description as fresh and effective as if they had been tasked on the very spot which he describes. Some of his quiet delineations deserve rather to be called
pictures than sketches, so lively are the colors shed over them. The
first which we select, is a reminiscence of a day and night spent
among the White Mountains, and will revive agreeable thoughts in
the minds of those tourists who have but just returned from a visit
to their sublime scenery.

THE NOTCH.

It was now the middle of September. We had come since sunrise
from Bartlett, passing up through the valley of the Saco, which
extends between mountainous walls, sometimes with a steep ascent,
but often as level as a church-aisle. All that day and two preceding

ones, we had been loitering towards the heart of the White Mountains—those old crystal hills, whose mysterious brilliancy had gleamed upon our distant wanderings before we thought of visiting them. Height after height had risen and towered one above another, till the clouds began to hang below the peaks. Down their slopes, were the red path-ways of the Slides, those avalanches of earth, stones and trees, which descend into the hollows, leaving vestiges of their track, hardly to be effaced by the vegetation of ages. We had mountains behind us and mountains on each side, and a group of mightier ones ahead. Still our road went up along the Saco, right towards the centre of that group, as if to climb above the clouds, in its passage to the farther region.

In old times, the settlers used to be astounded by the inroads of the northern Indians, coming down upon them from this mountain rampart, through some defile known only to themselves. It is indeed a wondrous path. A demon, it might be fancied, or one of the Titans, was traveling up the valley, elbowing the heights carelessly aside as he passed, till at length a great mountain took its stand directly across his intended road. He tarries not for such an obstacle, but rending it asunder, a thousand feet from peak to base, discloses its treasures of hidden minerals, its sunless waters, all the secrets of the mountain's inmost heart, with a mighty fracture of rugged precipices on each side. This is the Notch of the White Hills. Shame on me, that I have attempted to describe it by so mean an image—feeling, as I do, that it is one of those symbolic scenes, which lead the mind to the sentiment, though not to the conception, of Omnipotence.

* * * * *

We had now reached a narrow passage, which showed almost the appearance of having been cut by human strength and artifice in the solid rock. There was a wall of granite on each side, high and precipitous, especially on our right, and so smooth that a few evergreens could hardly find foothold enough to grow there. This is the entrance, or, in the direction we were going, the extremity of the romantic defile of the Notch. Before emerging from it, the rattling of wheels approached behind us, and a stage-coach rumbled out of the mountain, with seats on top and trunks behind, and a smart driver, in a drab great-coat, touching the wheel horses with the whip-stock, and reining in the leaders. To my mind, there was a sort of poetry in such an incident, hardly inferior to what would have accompanied the painted array of an Indian war-party, gliding forth from the same wild chasm. All the passengers, except a very fat lady on the back seat, had alighted. One was a mineralogist, a scientific, green-spectacled figure in black, bearing a heavy hammer, with which he did great damage to the precipices, and put the fragments in his pocket. Another was a well-dressed young man, who carried an opera-glass set in gold, and seemed to be making a quotation from some of Byron's rhapsodies on mountain scenery. There was also a trader, returning from Portland to the upper part of Vermont; and a fair young girl, with a very faint bloom, like one of those pale and delicate flowers, which sometimes occur among Alpine cliffs.

They disappeared, and we followed them, passing through a deep pine forest, which, for some miles, allowed us to see nothing but its own dismal shade. Towards night-fall, we reached a level amphitheatre, surrounded by a great rampart of hills, which shut out the sunshine long before it left the external world. It was here that we obtained our first view, except at a distance, of the principal group of mountains. They are majestic, and even awful, when contemplated in a proper mood; yet, by their breadth of base, and the long ridges which support them, give the idea of immense bulk, rather than of towering height. Mount Washington, indeed, looked near to Heaven; he was white with snow a mile downward, and had caught the only cloud that was sailing through the atmosphere, to veil his head. Let us forget the other names of American statesmen, that have been stamped upon these hills, but still call the loftiest— WASHINGTON. Mountains are Earth's undecaying monuments. They must stand while she endures, and never should be consecrated to the mere great men of their own age and country, but to the mighty ones alone, whose glory is universal, and whom all time will render illustrious.

The air, not often sultry in this elevated region, nearly two thousand feet above the sea, was now sharp and cold, like that of a clear November evening in the low-lands. By morning, probably, there would be a frost, if not a snow-fall, on the grass and rye, and an icy surface over the standing water. I was glad to perceive a prospect of comfortable quarters, in a house which we were approaching, and of pleasant company in the guests who were assembled at the door.

OUR EVENING PARTY AMONG THE MOUNTAINS.

We stood in front of a good substantial farm-house, of old date in that wild country. A sign over the door denoted it to be the White Mountain Post-Office, an establishment which distributes letters and newspapers to perhaps a score of persons, comprising the population of two or three townships among the hills. The broad and weighty antlers of a deer, 'a stag of ten,' were fastened at a corner of the house; a fox's bushy tail was nailed beneath them; and a huge black paw lay on the ground, newly severed and still bleeding—the trophy of a bear-hunt. Among several persons collected about the door-steps, the most remarkable was a sturdy mountaineer, of six feet two and corresponding bulk, with a heavy set of features, such as might be moulded on his own blacksmith's anvil, but yet indicative of mother-wit and rough humor. As we appeared, he uplifted a tin trumpet, four or five feet long, and blew a tremendous blast, either in honor of our arrival, or to awaken an echo from the opposite hill.

Ethan Crawford's guests were of such a motley description as to form quite a picturesque group, seldom seen together, except at some place like this, at once the pleasure-house of fashionable tourists, and the homely inn of country travelers. Among the company at the door, were the mineralogist and the owner of the gold opera-glass, whom we had encountered in the Notch; two Georgian gentlemen, who had chilled their southern blood, that morning, on the top of Mount Washington; a physician and his wife, from Conway; a trader, of Burlington, and an old 'Squire, of the Green Mountains; and two young married couples, all the way from Massachusetts, on the matrimonial jaunt. Besides these strangers, the rugged county of Coos, in which we were, was represented by half a dozen wood-cutters, who had slain a bear in the forest and smitten off his paw.

I had joined the party, and had a moment's leisure to examine them, before the echo of Ethan's blast returned from the hill. Not one, but many echoes had caught up the harsh and tuneless sound, untwisted its complicated threads, and found a thousand aerial harmonies in one stern trumpet-tone. It was a distinct, yet distant and dreamlike symphony of melodious instruments, as if an airy band had been hidden on the hill-side, and made faint music at the summons. No subsequent trial produced so clear, delicate, and spiritual a concert as the first. A field-piece was then discharged from the top of a neighboring hill, and gave birth to one long reverberation, which ran round the circle of mountains in an unbroken chain of sound, and rolled away without a separate echo. After these experiments, the cold atmosphere drove us all into the house, with the keenest appetites for supper.

It did one's heart good to see the great fires that were kindled in the parlor and bar-room, especially the latter, where the fireplace was built of rough stone, and might have contained the trunk of an old tree for a back-log. A man keeps a comfortable hearth when his own forest is at his very door. In the parlor, when the evening was fairly set in, we held our hands before our eyes, to shield them from the ruddy glow, and began a pleasant variety of conversation. The mineralogist and the physician talked about the invigorating qualities of the mountain air, and its excellent effect on Ethan Crawford's father, an old man of seventy-five, with the unbroken frame of middle life. The two brides and the doctor's wife held a whispered discussion, which, by their frequent titterings and a blush or two, seemed to have reference to the trials or enjoyments of the matrimonial state. The bridegrooms sat together in a corner, rigidly silent, like quakers whom the spirit moveth not, being still in the odd predicament of bashfulness towards their own young wives. The Green Mountain 'Squire chose me for his companion, and described the difficulties he had met with, half a cen-

tury ago, in traveling from the Connecticut river through the Notch
to Conway, now a single day's journey, though it had cost him eighteen. The Georgians held the album between them, and favored us
with the few specimens of its contents, which they considered ridiculous enough to be worth hearing. One extract met with de-
served applause. It was a 'Sonnet to the snow on Mount Washington,' and had been contributed that very afternoon, bearing a
signature of great distinction in magazines and annuals. The lines
were elegant and full of fancy, but too remote from familiar sentiment, and cold as their subject, resembling those curious specimens of crystallized vapor, which I observed next day on the
mountain-top. The poet was understood to be the young gentleman
of the gold opera-glass, who heard our laudatory remarks with the
composure of a veteran.

Such was our party, and such their ways of amusement. But, on
a winter evening, another set of guests assembled at the hearth,
where these summer travelers were now sitting. I once had it in
contemplation to spend a month hereabouts, in sleighing-time, for
the sake of studying the yeomen of New-England, who then elbow
each other through the Notch by hundreds, on their way to Portland. There could be no better school for such a purpose than
Ethan Crawford's inn. Let the student go thither in December, sit
down with the teamsters at their meals, share their evening merriment, and repose with them at night, when every bed has its three
occupants, and parlor, bar-room and kitchen are strewn with slumberers around the fire. Then let him rise before daylight, button
his great-coat, muffle up his ears, and stride with the departing
caravan a mile or two, to see how sturdily they make head against
the blast. A treasure of characteristic traits will repay all inconve-
niences, even should a frozen nose be of the number.

The conversation of our party soon became more animated and
sincere, and we recounted some traditions of the Indians, who believed that the father and mother of their race were saved from a
deluge by ascending the peak of Mount Washington. The children
of that pair have been overwhelmed, and found no such refuge. In
the mythology of the savage, these mountains were afterwards con-

sidered sacred and inaccessible, full of unearthly wonders, illuminated at lofty heights by the blaze of precious stones, and inhabited
by deities, who sometimes shrouded themselves in the snow-storm,
and came down on the lower world. There are few legends more
poetical than that of the 'Great Carbuncle' of the White Mountains.
The belief was communicated to the English settlers, and is hardly
yet extinct, that a gem, of such immense size as to be seen shining
miles away, hangs from a rock over a clear, deep lake, high up
among the hills. They who had once beheld its splendor, were en-
thralled with an unutterable yearning to possess it. But a spirit
guarded that inestimable jewel, and bewildered the adventurer with
a dark mist from the enchanted lake. Thus, life was worn away in
the vain search for an unearthly treasure, till at length the deluded
one went up the mountain, still sanguine as in youth, but returned
no more. On this theme, methinks I could frame a tale with a deep
moral.

The hearts of the pale-faces would not thrill to these superstitions
of the red men, though we spoke of them in the centre of their
haunted region. The habits and sentiments of that departed people
were too distinct from those of their successors to find much real
sympathy. It has often been a matter of regret to me, that I was
shut out from the most peculiar field of American fiction, by an
inability to see any romance, or poetry, or grandeur, or beauty in
the Indian character, at least, till such traits were pointed out by
others. I do abhor an Indian story. Yet no writer can be more secure
of a permanent place in our literature, than the biographer of the
Indian chiefs. His subject, as referring to tribes which have mostly
vanished from the earth, gives him a right to be placed on a classic
shelf, apart from the merits which will sustain him there.

I made inquiries whether, in his researches about these parts, our
mineralogist had found the three 'Silver Hills,' which an Indian
sachem sold to an Englishman, nearly two hundred years ago, and
the treasure of which the posterity of the purchaser have been
looking for ever since. But the man of science had ransacked every
hill along the Saco, and knew nothing of these prodigious piles of
wealth. By this time, as usual with men on the eve of great adven-

ture, we had prolonged our session deep into the night, considering how early we were to set out on our six miles' ride to the foot of Mount Washington. There was now a general breaking-up. I scrutinized the faces of the two bridegrooms, and saw but little probability of their leaving the bosom of earthly bliss, in the first week of the honey-moon, and at the frosty hour of three, to climb above the clouds. Nor, when I felt how sharp the wind was, as it rushed through a broken pane, and eddied between the chinks of my unplastered chamber, did I anticipate much alacrity on my own part, though we were to seek for the 'Great Carbuncle.'

SKETCHES FROM MEMORY.
BY A PEDESTRIAN.
NO. II.

This was published anonymously in the *New-England Magazine* 9 (December 1835): 398–409.

"The Canal-Boat" was reprinted by Fields as one of the three "Sketches From Memory" in the second edition of *Mosses from an Old Manse* (1854). He used the text of the first publication without any notable textual changes: he deleted the asterisks after the fifth and ninth paragraphs and replaced them with larger spaces between these and the following paragraphs. CE, X, 429–38, reprints the sketch using *Mosses* (1854) as copy-text.

Park Benjamin's editorial introduction was never reprinted. It appears only in the historical collation of CE, X, 648–49 and the textual notes in the Library of America *Tales and Sketches*, 1488.

The other four sketches never appeared in any collection of Hawthorne's short fiction published during his lifetime. They were identified and collected only later: "The Inland Port," "Rochester," and "A Night Scene" were first republished by George Parsons Lathrop under the title "Sketches from Memory. [Second Series]." Lathrop erroneously commented that the "first series was added to the revised edition of the *Mosses from an Old Manse*." See SLE, XII, 13–22. Lathrop's edition was the copy-text for CE, XI, 298–305, where it is reprinted under "Uncollected Tales." CE again omits the asterisks in "Rochester" after the second and fourth paragraphs, although Lathrop ended these paragraphs with three dots.

"An Afternoon Scene" was taken by Benjamin from the first paragraph of "My Home Return" (CE, XI, 322–23) and published by him later in the *Amer-*

ican Monthly Magazine n.s. 4 (July 1837) under the title "Fragments from the Journal of a Solitary Man." It was never republished in this form.

Emendations: 39. 18 Schenectady> Schnectady
            40. 2 shrinking> skrinking
            40. 21 when others ceased> when others cease
            44. 3 analogy> analagy

We present to our readers a few more of the loose sketches from our friend's portfolio, which, we think, will, more clearly than those of the last month, shew the truth of our remark, that, like the careless drawings of a master-hand, they shadow forth a power and beauty, that might be visibly embodied into life-like forms on the canvass. 'The Afternoon Scene' and 'The Night Scene' will, we trust, suggest subjects to our landscape painters. The former, which has the mellow richness of a Claude, might be exquisitely done by Doughty; and young Brown, whose promise is as great as the hopes of his friends, could employ his glowing pencil upon no subject better adapted to call forth all his genius, than the latter.

THE CANAL-BOAT.

I was inclined to be poetical about the Grand Canal. In my imagination, De Witt Clinton was an enchanter, who had waved his magic wand from the Hudson to lake Erie, and united them by a watery highway, crowded with the commerce of two worlds, till then inaccessible to each other. This simple and mighty conception had conferred inestimable value on spots which nature seemed to have thrown carelessly into the great body of the earth, without foreseeing that they could ever attain importance. I pictured the surprise of the sleepy Dutchmen when the new river first glittered by their doors, bringing them hard cash or foreign commodities, in exchange for their hitherto unmarketable produce. Surely, the water of this canal must be the most fertilizing of all fluids; for it causes towns—with their masses of brick and stone, their churches and theatres, their business and hubbub, their luxury and refinement, their gay dames and polished citizens—to spring up, till, in time, the wondrous stream may flow between two continuous lines of buildings, through one thronged street, from Buffalo to Albany. I embarked about thirty miles below Utica, determining to voyage along the whole extent of the canal, at least twice in the course of the summer.

Behold us, then, fairly afloat, with three horses harnessed to our vessel, like the steeds of Neptune to a huge scallop-shell, in mythological pictures. Bound to a distant port, we had neither chart nor compass, nor cared about the wind, nor felt the heaving of a billow, nor dreaded shipwreck, however fierce the tempest, in our adventurous navigation of an interminable mud-puddle—for a mud-puddle it seemed, and as dark and turbid as if every kennel in the land paid contribution to it. With an imperceptible current, it holds its drowsy way through all the dismal swamps and unimpressive scenery, that could be found between the great lakes and the sea-coast. Yet there is variety enough, both on the surface of the canal and along its banks, to amuse the traveler, if an overpowering tedium did not deaden his perceptions.

Sometimes we met a black and rusty-looking vessel, laden with lumber, salt from Syracuse, or Genessee flour, and shaped at both ends like a square-toed boot, as if it had two sterns, and were fated always to advance backward. On its deck would be a square hut, and a woman seen through the window at her house-hold work, with a little tribe of children, who perhaps had been born in this strange dwelling and knew no other home. Thus, while the husband smoked his pipe at the helm, and the eldest son rode one of the horses, on went the family, traveling hundreds of miles in their own house, and carrying their fireside with them. The most frequent species of craft were the 'line boats,' which had a cabin at each end, and a great bulk of barrels, bales, and boxes in the midst; or light packets, like our own, decked all over, with a row of curtained windows from stem to stern, and a drowsy face at every one. Once, we encountered a boat, of rude construction, painted all in gloomy black, and manned by three Indians, who gazed at us in silence and with a singular fixedness of eye. Perhaps these three alone, among the ancient possessors of the land, had attempted to derive benefit from the white man's mighty projects, and float along the current of his enterprise. Not long after, in the midst of a swamp and beneath a clouded sky, we overtook a vessel that seemed full of mirth and sunshine. It contained a little colony of Swiss, on their way to Michigan, clad in garments of strange fashion and gay colors, scarlet, yellow and bright blue, singing, laughing, and making merry, in odd tones and a babble of outlandish words. One pretty damsel, with a beautiful pair of naked white arms, addressed a mirthful remark to me; she spoke in her native tongue, and I retorted in good English, both of us laughing heartily at each other's unintelligible wit. I cannot describe how pleasantly this incident affected me. These honest Swiss were an itinerant community of jest and fun, journeying through a gloomy land and among a dull race of money-getting drudges, meeting none to understand their mirth and only one to sympathize with it, yet still retaining the happy lightness of their own spirit.

Had I been on my feet at the time, instead of sailing slowly along in a dirty canal-boat, I should often have paused to contemplate the diversified panorama along the banks of the canal. Sometimes the scene was a forest, dark, dense, and impervious, breaking away occasionally and receding from a lonely tract, covered with dismal black stumps, where, on the verge of the canal, might be seen a log-cottage, and a sallow-faced woman at the window. Lean and aguish, she looked like Poverty personified, half clothed, half fed, and dwelling in a desert, while a tide of wealth was sweeping by her door. Two or three miles further would bring us to a lock, where the slight impediment to navigation had created a little mart of trade. Here would be found commodities of all sorts, enumerated in yellow letters on the window-shutters of a small grocery-store, the owner of which had set his soul to the gathering of coppers and small change, buying and selling through the week, and counting his gains on the blessed Sabbath. The next scene might be the dwelling-houses and stores of a thriving village, built of wood or small gray stones, a church-spire rising in the midst, and generally two taverns, bearing over their piazzas the pompous titles of 'hotel,' 'exchange,' 'tontine,' or 'coffee-house.' Passing on, we glide now into the unquiet heart of an inland city—of Utica, for instance—and find ourselves amid piles of brick, crowded docks and quays, rich warehouses and a busy population. We feel the eager and hurrying spirit of the place, like a stream and eddy whirling us along with it. Through the thickest of the tumult goes the canal, flowing between lofty rows of buildings and arched bridges of hewn stone. Onward, also, go we, till the hum and bustle of struggling enterprise die away behind us, and we are threading an avenue of the ancient woods again.

This sounds not amiss in description, but was so tiresome in reality, that we were driven to the most childish expedients for amusement. An English traveler paraded the deck with a rifle in his walking-stick, and waged war on squirrels and woodpeckers, sometimes sending an unsuccessful bullet among flocks of tame ducks and geese, which abound in the dirty water of the canal. I, also, pelted these foolish birds with apples, and smiled at the ridiculous earnestness of their scrambles for the prize, while the apple bobbed about like a thing of life. Several little accidents afforded us good-natured diversion. At the moment of changing horses, the tow-rope caught a Massachusetts farmer by the leg, and threw him down in a very indescribable posture, leaving a purple mark around his sturdy limb. A new passenger fell flat on his back, in attempting to step on deck, as the boat emerged from under a bridge. Another, in his Sunday clothes, as good luck would have it, being told to leap aboard from the bank, forthwith plunged up to his third waistcoat button in the canal, and was fished out in a very pitiable plight, not at all amended by our three rounds of applause. Anon, a Virginia schoolmaster, too intent on a pocket Virgil to heed the helmsman's warning—'bridge! bridge!'—was saluted by the said bridge on his knowledge-box. I had prostrated myself, like a pagan before his idol, but heard the dull leaden sound of the contact, and fully expected to see the treasures of the poor man's cranium scattered about the deck. However, as there was no harm done, except a large bump on the head, and probably a corresponding dent in the bridge, the rest of us exchanged glances and laughed quietly. Oh, how pitiless are idle people! * * *

The table being now lengthened through the cabin, and spread for supper, the next twenty minutes were the pleasantest I had spent on the canal—the same space at dinner excepted. At the close of the meal, it had become dusky enough for lamplight. The rain pattered unceasingly on the deck, and sometimes came with a sullen rush against the windows, driven by the wind, as it stirred through an opening of the forest. The intolerable dullness of the scene engendered an evil spirit in me. Perceiving that the Englishman was taking notes in a memorandum-book, with occasional glances round the cabin, I presumed that we were all to figure in a future volume of travels, and amused my ill-humor by falling into the probable vein of his remarks. He would hold up an imaginary mirror, wherein our reflected faces would appear ugly and ridiculous, yet still retain an undeniable likeness to the originals. Then, with more sweeping malice, he would make these caricatures the representatives of great classes of my countrymen.

He glanced at the Virginia schoolmaster, a Yankee by birth, who, to recreate himself, was examining a freshman from Schenectady college, in the conjugation of a Greek verb. Him, the Englishman would portray as the scholar of America, and compare his erudition to a schoolboy's Latin theme, made up of scraps, ill-selected and worse put together. Next, the tourist looked at the Massachusetts farmer, who was delivering a dogmatic harangue on the iniquity of Sunday mails. Here was the far-famed yeoman of New-England; his religion, writes the Englishman, is gloom on the Sabbath, long prayers every morning and eventide, and illiberality at all times; his boasted information is merely an abstract and compound of newspaper paragraphs, Congress debates, caucus harangues, and the argument and judge's charge in his own lawsuits. The bookmonger cast his eye at a Detroit merchant, and began scribbling faster than ever. In this sharp-eyed man, this lean man, of wrinkled brow, we see daring enterprise and close-fisted avarice combined; here is the worshipper of Mammon at noonday; here is the three-times bankrupt, richer after every ruin; here, in one word, (Oh, wicked Englishman to say it!) here is the American! He lifted his eye-glass to inspect a western lady, who at once became aware of the glance, reddened, and retired deeper into the female part of the cabin. Here was the pure, modest, sensitive, and shrinking woman of America; shrinking when no evil is intended; and sensitive like diseased flesh, that thrills if you but point at it; and strangely modest, without confidence in the modesty of other people; and admirably pure, with such a quick apprehension of all impurity.

In this manner, I went all through the cabin, hitting everybody as hard a lash as I could, and laying the whole blame on the infernal Englishman. At length, I caught the eyes of my own image in the looking-glass, where a number of the party were likewise reflected, and among them the Englishman, who, at that moment, was intently observing myself. * * *

The crimson curtain being let down between the ladies and gentlemen, the cabin became a bed-chamber for twenty persons, who were laid on shelves, one above another. For a long time, our various incommodities kept us all awake, except five or six, who were accustomed to sleep nightly amid the uproar of their own snoring, and had little to dread from any other species of disturbance. It is a curious fact, that these snorers had been the most quiet people in the boat, while awake, and became peace-breakers only when others ceased to be so, breathing tumult out of their repose. Would it were possible to affix a wind instrument to the nose, and thus make melody of a snore, so that a sleeping lover might serenade his mistress, or a congregation snore a psalm-tune! Other, though fainter sounds than these, contributed to my restlessness. My head was close to the crimson curtain—the sexual division of the boat—behind which I continually heard whispers and stealthy footsteps; the noise of a comb laid on the table, or a slipper dropt on the floor; the twang, like a broken harp-string, caused by loosening a tight belt; the rustling of a gown in its descent; and the unlacing of a pair of stays. My ear seemed to have the properties of an eye; a visible image pestered my fancy in the darkness; the curtain was withdrawn between me and the western lady, who yet disrobed herself without a blush.

Finally, all was hushed in that quarter. Still, I was more broad awake than through the whole preceding day, and felt a feverish impulse to toss my limbs miles apart, and appease the unquietness of mind by that of matter. Forgetting that my berth was hardly so wide as a coffin, I turned suddenly over, and fell like an avalanche on the floor, to the disturbance of the whole community of sleepers. As there were no bones broken, I blessed the accident, and went on deck. A lantern was burning at each end of the boat, and one of the crew was stationed at the bows, keeping watch, as mariners do on the ocean. Though the rain had ceased, the sky was all one cloud, and the darkness so intense, that there seemed to be no world, except the little space on which our lanterns glimmered. Yet, it was an impressive scene.

We were traversing the 'long level,' a dead flat between Utica and Syracuse, where the canal has not rise or fall enough to require a lock for nearly seventy miles. There can hardly be a more dismal tract of country. The forest which covers it, consisting chiefly of white cedar, black ash, and other trees that live in excessive mois- ture, is now decayed and death-struck, by the partial draining of the swamp into the great ditch of the canal. Sometimes, indeed, our lights were reflected from pools of stagnant water, which stretched far in among the trunks of the trees, beneath dense masses of dark foliage. But generally, the tall stems and intermin- gled branches were naked, and brought into strong relief, amid the surrounding gloom, by the whiteness of their decay. Often, we be- held the prostrate form of some old sylvan giant, which had fallen, and crushed down smaller trees under its immense ruin. In spots, where destruction had been riotous, the lanterns showed perhaps a hundred trunks, erect, half overthrown, extended along the ground, resting on their shattered limbs, or tossing them desper- ately into the darkness, but all of one ashy-white, all naked together, in desolate confusion. Thus growing out of the night as we drew nigh, and vanishing as we glided on, based on obscurity, and ov- erhung and bounded by it, the scene was ghost-like—the very land of unsubstantial things, whither dreams might betake themselves, when they quit the slumberer's brain.

My fancy found another emblem. The wild Nature of America had been driven to this desert-place by the encroachments of civilized man. And even here, where the savage queen was throned on the ruins of her empire, did we penetrate, a vulgar and worldly throng, intruding on her latest solitude. In other lands, Decay sits among fallen palaces; but here, her home is in the forests.

Looking ahead, I discerned a distant light, announcing the approach of another boat, which soon passed us, and proved to be a rusty old scow—just such a craft as the 'Flying Dutchman' would navigate on the canal. Perhaps it was that celebrated personage himself, whom I imperfectly distinguished at the helm, in a glazed hat and rough great-coat, with a pipe in his mouth, leaving the fumes of tobacco a hundred yards behind. Shortly after, our boat-man blew a horn, sending a long and melancholy note through the forest-avenue, as a signal for some watcher in the wilderness to be ready with a change of horses. We had proceeded a mile or two with our fresh team, when the tow-rope got entangled in a fallen branch on the edge of the canal, and caused a momentary delay, during which I went to examine the phosphoric light of an old tree, a little within the forest. It was not the first delusive radiance that I had followed.

The tree lay along the ground, and was wholly converted into a mass of diseased splendor, which threw a ghastliness around. Being full of conceits that night, I called it a frigid fire: a funeral light, illumining decay and death: an emblem of fame, that gleams around the dead man without warming him; or of genius, when it owes its brilliancy to moral rottenness; and was thinking that such ghost-like torches were just fit to light up this dead forest, or to blaze coldly in tombs, when, starting from my abstraction, I looked up the canal. I recollected myself, and discovered the lanterns glimmering far away.

'Boat ahoy!' shouted I, making a trumpet of my closed fists.

Though the cry must have rung for miles along that hollow passage of the woods, it produced no effect. These packet-boats make up for their snail-like pace by never loitering day nor night, especially for those who have paid their fare. Indeed, the captain had an interest in getting rid of me, for I was his creditor for a breakfast.

'They are gone! Heaven be praised!' ejaculated I, 'for I cannot possibly overtake them! Here am I, on the 'long level,' at midnight, with the comfortable prospect of a walk to Syracuse, where my baggage will be left; and now to find a house or shed, wherein to pass the night.' So thinking aloud, I took a flambeau from the old tree, burning, but consuming not, to light my steps withal, and, like a Jack-o'-the-lantern, set out on my midnight tour.

THE INLAND PORT.

It was a bright forenoon, when I set foot on the beach at Burlington, and took leave of the two boatmen, in whose little skiff I had voyaged since daylight from Peru. Not that we had come that morning from South America, but only from the New-York shore of lake Champlain. The highlands of the coast behind us stretched north and south, in a double range of bold, blue peaks, gazing over each other's shoulders at the Green Mountains of Vermont. The latter are far the loftiest, and, from the opposite side of the lake, had displayed a more striking outline. We were now almost at their feet, and could see only a sandy beach, sweeping beneath a woody bank, around the semi-circular bay of Burlington. The painted light-house, on a small green island, the wharves and warehouses, with sloops and schooners moored alongside, or at anchor, or spreading their canvass to the wind, and boats rowing from point to point, reminded me of some fishing town on the sea-coast.

But I had no need of tasting the water to convince myself that lake Champlain was not an arm of the sea; its quality was evident, both by its silvery surface, when unruffled, and a faint, but unpleasant and sickly smell, forever steaming up in the sunshine. One breeze from the Atlantic, with its briny fragrance, would be worth more to these inland people than all the perfumes of Arabia. On closer inspection, the vessels at the wharves looked hardly sea-worthy—there being a great lack of tar about the seams and rigging, and perhaps other deficiencies, quite as much to the purpose. I observed not a single sailor in the port. There were men, indeed, in blue jackets and trowsers, but not of the true nautical fashion, such as dangle before slop-shops; others wore tight pantaloons and coats preponderously long-tailed—cutting very queer figures at the mast-head; and, in short, these freshwater fellows had about the same analogy to the real 'old salt,' with his tarpaulin, pea-jacket and sailor-cloth trowsers, as a lake fish to a Newfoundland cod.

Nothing struck me more, in Burlington, than the great number of Irish emigrants. They have filled the British provinces to the brim, and still continue to ascend the St. Lawrence, in infinite tribes, overflowing by every outlet into the States. At Burlington, they swarm in huts and mean dwellings near the lake, lounge about the wharves, and elbow the native citizens entirely out of competition in their own line. Every species of mere bodily labor is the prerogative of these Irish. Such is their multitude, in comparison with any possible demand for their services, that it is difficult to conceive how a third part of them should earn even a daily glass of whiskey, which is doubtless their first necessary of life—daily bread being only the second. Some were angling in the lake, but had caught only a few perch, which little fishes, without a miracle, would be nothing among so many. A miracle there certainly must have been, and a daily one, for the subsistence of these wandering hordes. The men exhibit a lazy strength and careless merriment, as if they had fed well hitherto, and meant to feed better hereafter; the women strode about, uncovered in the open air, with far plumper waists and brawnier limbs, as well as bolder faces, than our shy and slender females; and their progeny, which was innumerable, had the reddest and the roundest cheeks of any children in America.

While we stood at the wharf, the bell of a steamboat gave two preliminary peals, and she dashed away for Plattsburgh, leaving a trail of smoky breath behind, and breaking the glassy surface of the lake before her. Our next movement brought us into a handsome and busy square, the sides of which were filled up with white houses, brick stores, a church, a court-house, and a bank. Some of these edifices had roofs of tin, in the fashion of Montreal, and glittered in the sun with cheerful splendor, imparting a lively effect to the whole square. One brick building, designated in large letters as the custom-house, reminded us that this inland village is a port of entry, largely concerned in foreign trade, and holding daily intercourse with the British empire. In this border country, the Canadian bank-notes circulate as freely as our own, and British and American coin are jumbled into the same pocket, the effigies of the king of England being made to kiss those of the goddess of liberty. Perhaps there was an emblem in the involuntary contact. There was a pleasant mixture of people in the square of Burlington, such as cannot be seen elsewhere, at one view: merchants from Montreal, British officers from the frontier garrisons, French Canadians, wandering Irish, Scotchmen of a better class, gentlemen of the south on a pleasure-tour, country 'squires on business; and a great throng of Green Mountain boys, with their horse-wagons and ox-teams, true Yankees in aspect, and looking more superlatively so, by contrast with such a variety of foreigners.

ROCHESTER.

The gray, but transparent evening, rather shaded than obscured the scene—leaving its stronger features visible, and even improved, by the medium through which I beheld them. The volume of water is not very great, nor the roar deep enough to be termed grand, though such praise might have been appropriate before the good people of Rochester had abstracted a part of the unprofitable sublimity of the cascade. The Genessee has contributed so bountifully to their canals and mill-dams, that it approaches the precipice with diminished pomp, and rushes over it in foamy streams of various width, leaving a broad face of the rock insulated and unwashed, between the two main branches of the falling river. Still it was an impressive sight, to one who had not seen Niagara. I confess, however, that my chief interest arose from a legend, connected with these falls, which will become poetical in the lapse of years, and was already so to me, as I pictured the catastrophe out of dusk and solitude. It was from a platform, raised over the naked island of the cliff, in the middle of the cataract, that Sam Patch took his last leap, and alighted in the other world. Strange as it may appear— that any uncertainty should rest upon his fate, which was consummated in the sight of thousands—many will tell you that the illus-

trious Patch concealed himself in a cave under the falls, and has
continued to enjoy posthumous renown, without foregoing the
comforts of this present life. But the poor fellow prized the shout
of the multitude too much not to have claimed it at the instant, had
he survived. He will not be seen again, unless his ghost, in such a
twilight as when I was there, should emerge from the foam, and
vanish among the shadows that fall from cliff to cliff. How stern a
moral may be drawn from the story of poor Sam Patch! Why do
we call him a madman or a fool, when he has left his memory
around the falls of the Genessee, more permanently than if the
letters of his name had been hewn into the forehead of the precipice? Was the leaper of cataracts more mad or foolish than other
men who throw away life, or misspend it in pursuit of empty fame,
and seldom so triumphantly as he? That which he won is as invaluable as any, except the unsought glory, spreading, like the rich
perfume of richer fruit, from virtuous and useful deeds.

Thus musing, wise in theory, but practically as great a fool as
Sam, I lifted my eyes and beheld the spires, warehouses, and dwellings of Rochester, half a mile distant on both sides of the river,
indistinctly cheerful, with the twinkling of many lights amid the
fall of evening. * * * *

The town had sprung up like a mushroom, but no presage of
decay could be drawn from its hasty growth. Its edifices are of
dusky brick, and of stone that will not be grayer in a hundred years
than now; its churches are Gothic; it is impossible to look at its
worn pavements, and conceive how lately the forest-leaves have
been swept away. The most ancient town in Massachusetts appears
quite like an affair of yesterday, compared with Rochester. Its attributes of youth are the activity and eager life with which it is
redundant. The whole street, sidewalks and centre, was crowded
with pedestrians, horsemen, stage-coaches, gigs, light wagons, and
heavy ox-teams, all hurrying, trotting, rattling, and rumbling, in a
throng that passed continually, but never passed away. Here, a
country wife was selecting a churn, from several gaily-painted ones
on the sunny sidewalk; there, a farmer was bartering his produce;
and, in two or three places, a crowd of people were showering bids

on a vociferous auctioneer. I saw a great wagon and an ox-chain knocked off to a very pretty woman. Numerous were the lottery-offices—those true temples of Mammon—where red and yellow bills offered splendid fortunes to the world at large, and banners of painted cloth gave notice that the 'lottery draws next Wednesday.' At the ringing of a bell, judges, jurymen, lawyers, and clients, elbowed each other to the court-house, to busy themselves with cases that would doubtless illustrate the state of society, had I the means of reporting them. The number of public houses benefitted the flow of temporary population; some were farmers' taverns—cheap, homely, and comfortable; others were magnificent hotels, with negro waiters, gentlemanly landlords in black broadcloth, and foppish bar-keepers in Broadway coats, with chased gold watches in their waistcoat pockets. I caught one of these fellows quizzing me through an eye-glass. The porters were lumbering up the steps with baggage from the packet-boats, while waiters plied the brush on dusty travelers, who, meanwhile, glanced over the innumerable advertisements in the daily papers.

In short, everybody seemed to be there, and all had something to do, and were doing it with all their might, except a party of drunken recruits for the western military posts, principally Irish and Scotch, though they wore uncle Sam's gray jacket and trowsers. I noticed one other idle man. He carried a rifle on his shoulder and a powder-horn across his breast, and appeared to stare about him with confused wonder, as if, while he was listening to the wind among the forest boughs, the hum and bustle of an instantaneous city had surrounded him. * * *

AN AFTERNOON SCENE.

There had not been a more delicious afternoon than this, in all the train of summer—the air being a sunny perfume, made up of balm and warmth and gentle brightness. The oak and walnut trees, over my head, retained their deep masses of foliage, and the grass, though for months the pasturage of stray cattle, had been revived with the freshness of early June, by the autumnal rains of the preceding week. The garb of Autumn indeed resembled that of Spring. Dandelions and buttercups were sprinkled along the roadside, like drops of brightest gold in greenest grass; and a starshaped little flower, with a golden centre. In a rocky spot, and rooted under the stone-wall, there was one wild rose-bush, bearing three roses, very faintly tinted, but blessed with a spicy fragrance. The same tokens would have announced that the year was brightening into the glow of summer. There were violets, too, though few and pale ones. But the breath of September was diffused through the mild air, whenever a little breeze shook out the latent coolness.

A NIGHT SCENE.

The steamboat in which I was passenger for Detroit, had put into the mouth of a small river, where the greater part of the night would be spent in repairing some damages of the machinery. As the evening was warm, though cloudy and very dark, I stood on deck, watching a scene that would not have attracted a second glance in the day-time, but became picturesque by the magic of strong light and deep shade. Some wild Irishmen were replenishing our stock of wood, and had kindled a great fire on the bank, to illuminate their labors. It was composed of large logs and dry brushwood, heaped together with careless profusion, blazing fiercely, spouting showers of sparks into the darkness, and gleaming wide over lake Erie—a beacon for perplexed voyagers, leagues from land. All around and above the furnace, there was total obscurity. No trees, or other objects, caught and reflected any portion of the brightness, which thus wasted itself in the immense void of night, as if it quivered from the expiring embers of the world, after the final conflagration. But the Irishmen were continually emerging from the dense gloom, passing through the lurid glow, and vanishing into the gloom on the other side. Sometimes a whole figure would be made visible, by the shirt-sleeves and light-colored dress; others were but half seen, like imperfect creatures; many flitted, shadow-like, along the skirts of darkness, tempting fancy to a vain pursuit; and often, a face alone was reddened by the fire, and stared strangely distinct, with no traces of a body. In short, these wild Irish, distorted and exaggerated by the blaze, now lost in deep shadow, now bursting into sudden splendor, and now struggling between light and darkness, formed a picture which might have been transferred, almost unaltered, to a tale of the supernatural. As they all carried lanterns of wood, and often flung sticks upon the fire, the least imaginative spectator would at once compare them to devils, condemned to keep alive the flame of their own torment.

AN ONTARIO STEAM-BOAT.

This sketch was first published anonymously in the *American Magazine of Useful and Entertaining Knowledge* 2 (March 1836): 270–72. It never appeared in any collection of Hawthorne's during his lifetime, and was not included in George Parsons Lathrop's editions or in CE. It was reprinted by Arlin Turner in *Hawthorne as Editor,* pages 58–64, and Alfred Weber in *Die Entwicklung der Rahmenerzählungen Nathaniel Hawthornes,* pages 337–41.

There is no final proof that this sketch was, like all the others in this edition, part of "The Story Teller"; but it seems certain that it was based on the 1832 trip through upstate New York.

The Steam-boats on the Canadian lakes, afford opportunities for a varied observation of society. In the spacious one, on board which I had embarked at Ogdensburgh, and was voyaging westward, to the other extremity of Lake Ontario, there were three different orders of passengers;—an aristocracy, in the grand cabin and ladies' saloon; a commonalty in the forward cabin; and, lastly, a male and female multitude on the forward deck, constituting as veritable a Mob, as could be found in any country. These latter did not belong to that proud and independent class, among our native citizens, who chance, in the present generation, to be at the bottom of the body politic; they were the exiles of another clime—the scum which every wind blows off the Irish shores—the pauper-dregs which England flings out upon America. Thus, within the precincts of our Steam-boat—which indeed was ample enough, being about two hundred feet from stem to stern—there were materials for studying the characteristics of different nations, and the peculiarities of different castes. And the study was simplified, in comparison to what it might have been in a wider sphere, by the strongly marked distinctions of rank that were constituted by the regulations of the vessel. In our country at large, the different ranks melt and mingle into one another, so that it is as impossible to draw a decided line between any two contiguous classes, as to divide a rainbow accurately into its various hues. But here, the high, the middling, and the low, had classified themselves, and the laws of the vessel rigidly kept each inferiour from stepping beyond his proper limits. The mob of the deck would have infringed these immutable laws, had they ventured abaft the wheels, or into the forward cabin; while the honest yeomen, or other thrifty citizens, who were the rightful occupants of that portion of the boat, would have incurred both the rebuke of the captain and the haughty stare of the gentry, had they thrust themselves into the department of the latter. Here, therefore, was something analogous to that picturesque state of society, in other countries and earlier times, when each upper class excluded every lower one from its privileges, and when each individual was content with his allotted position, because there was no possibility of bettering it.

I, by paying ten dollars instead of six or four, had entitled myself to the aristocratic privileges of our floating community. But, to confess the truth, I would as willingly have been any where else, as in the grand cabin. There was good company, assuredly;—among others, a Canadian judge, with his two daughters, whose stately beauty and bright complexions made me proud to feel that they were my countrywomen; though I doubt whether these lovely girls would have acknowledged that their country was the same as mine. The inhabitants of the British provinces have not yet acquired the sentiment of brotherhood or sisterhood, towards their neighbours of the States. Besides these, there was a Scotch gentleman, the agent of some land company in England; a Frenchman, attached to the embassy at Washington; a major in the British army; and some dozen or two of our own fashionables, running their annual round of Quebec, Montreal, the Lakes and Springs.—All were very gentlemanly and ladylike people, but too much alike to be made portraits of, and affording few strong points for a general picture. Much of their time was spent at cards and backgammon, or in promenading from end to end of the cabin, numbering the burnished mahogany panels as they passed, and viewing their own figures in one or other of the tall mirrors, which, at each end of the long apartment, appeared to lengthen out the scene. Then came the dinner, with its successive courses, soup, fish, meat, pastry, and a dessert, all attended with a somewhat affected punctuality of ceremonies. Lastly, the slow sipping of their wine kept them at the table, till it was well nigh time to spread it again for supper. On the whole, the time passed wearily, and left little but a blank behind it.

What was the state of affairs in the forward cabin, I cannot positively say. There the passengers of the second class feasted on the relics of the original banquet, in company with the steward, waiters, and ladies' maids. A pleasant sketch, I think, might be made of the permanent household of a steam-boat, from the captain downward; though it is observable, that people in this and similar situations have little variety of character, and seldom much depth of intelligence. Their ideas and sentiments are confined within a narrow sphere; so far as that extends, they are sufficiently acute, but not a step beyond it. They see, it is true, many different figures of men and women, but scarcely any thing of human nature; for the continually varying crowd, which is brought into temporary connexion with them, always turns the same surface to their view, and shows nothing beneath that surface. And the circumstances of their daily life, in spite of much seeming variety, are nevertheless arranged in so strict a routine, that their minds and characters are moulded by it. But this is not what I particularly meant to write about.

The scene on the forward deck interested my mind more than any thing else that was connected with our voyage. On this occasion, it chanced that an unusual number of passengers were congregated there.—All were expected to find their own provisions; several, of a somewhat more respectable rank in life, had brought their beds and bedding, all the way from England or Ireland; and for the rest, as night came on, some sort of litter was supplied by the officers of the boat. The decks, where they were to sleep, was not, it must be understood, open to the sky, but was sufficiently roofed over by the promenade-deck. On each side of the vessel was a pair of folding doors, extending between the wheels and the ladies' saloon; and when these were shut, the deck became in reality a cabin. I shall not soon forget the view which I took of it, after it had been arranged as a sleeping apartment for at least, fifty people, male and female.

A single lamp shed a dim ray over the scene, and there was also a dusky light from the boat's furnaces, which enabled me to distinguish quite as much as it was allowable to look upon, and a good deal more than it would be decorous to describe. In one corner, a bed was spread out on the deck, and a family had already taken up their night's quarters; the father and mother, with their faces turned towards each other on the pillow, were talking of their private affairs; while three or four children, whose heads protruded from the foot of the bed, were already asleep. Others, both men and women, were putting on their night-caps, or enveloping their heads in handkerchiefs, and laying aside their upper garments. Some were strewn at random about the deck, as if they had dropped down, just where they had happened to be standing. Two men, seeing nothing softer than the oak-plank to stretch themselves upon, had sat down back to back, and thus mutually supporting each other, were beginning to nod. Slender girls were preparing to repose their maiden-like forms on the wide, promiscuous couch of the deck. A young woman, who had a babe at her bosom, but whose husband was nowhere to be seen, was wrangling with the steward for some better accommodation than the rug which he had assigned her. In short, to dwell no longer upon the particulars of the scene, it was, to my unaccustomed eye, a strange and sad one—and so much the more sad, because it seemed entirely a matter of course, and a thing of established custom, to men, women, and children. I know not what their habits might have been, in their native land; but since they quitted it, these poor people had led such a life in the steerages of the vessels, that brought them across the Atlantic, that they probably stept ashore, far ruder and wilder beings than they had embarked; and afterwards, thrown homeless upon the wharves of Quebec and Montreal, and left to wander whither they might, and subsist how they could, it was impossible for their moral natures not to have become wofully deranged and debased. I was grieved, also, to discern a want of fellow-feeling among them. They appeared, it is true, to form one community, but connected by no other bond than that which pervades a flock of wild geese in the sky, or a herd of wild horses in the desert. They were all going the same way, by a sort of instinct—some laws of mutual aid and fellowship had necessarily been established—yet each individual was lonely and selfish. Even domestic ties did not invariably retain their hallowed strength.

But there was one group, that had attracted my notice several times, in the course of the day; and it did me good to look at them. They were a father and mother, and two or three children, evidently in very straightened circumstances, yet preserving a decency of aspect, that told of better days gone by, and was also a sure prophecy of better days to come. It was a token of moral strength, that would assuredly bear them through all their troubles, and bring them at length to a good end. This family now sat together near one of the furnaces, the light of which was thrown upon their sober, yet not uncheerful faces, so that they looked precisely like the members of a comfortable household, sitting in the glow of their own fireside. And so it was their own fireside. In one sense, they were homeless, but in another, they were always at home; for domestic love, the remembrance of joys and sorrows shared together, the mutual anxieties and hopes, the united trust in Heaven, these gave them a home in one another's hearts; and whatever sky might be above them, that sky was the roof of their home.

Still, the general impression that I had received from the scene, here so slightly sketched, was a very painful one. Turning away, I ascended to the promenade deck, and there paced to and fro, in the solitude of wild Ontario at nightfall. The steersman sat in a small square apartment, at the forward extremity of the deck; but I soon forgot his presence, and ceased to hear the voices of two or three Canadian boatmen, who were chatting French in the fore-castle. The stars were now brightening, as the twilight withdrew. The breeze had been strong throughout the day, and was still ris-ing; while the billows whitened around us, and rolled short and sharp, so as to give the vessel a most uneasy motion; indeed, the peculiar tossing of the waves, on the lakes, often turns the stomachs of old seamen. No land was visible; for a head-wind had compelled us to keep farther seaward than in the ordinary passage. Far astern of us, I saw the faint gleam of a white sail, which we were fast leaving; and it was singular, how much the sight of that distant sail increased my sense of the loneliness of our situation.

For an hour or more, I paced the promenade, meditating on the varied congregation of human life that was beneath me. I was trou-bled on account of the poor vagabonds of the deck. It seemed as if a particular Providence were more necessary, for the guidance of this mob of desperate individuals, than for people of better reg-ulated lives; yet it was difficult to conceive how they were not lost from that guidance, drifting at large along the stream of existence. What was to become of them all, when not a single one had the certainty of food or shelter, from one day to the next? And the women! Had they been guarded by fond fathers, counselled by watchful mothers, and wooed with chaste and honourable love? And if so, must not all these good influences have been done away, by the disordered habits of their more recent life? Amid such re-flections, I found no better comfort than in the hope and trust, that it might be with these homeless exiles, in their passage through the world, as it was with them and all of us, in the voyage on which we had embarked together. As we had all our destined port, and the skill of the steersman would suffice to bring us thither, so had each of these poor wanderers a home in futurity—and the God above them knew where to find it.

It was cheering, also, to reflect, that nothing short of settled de-pravity could resist the strength of moral influences, diffused throughout our native land;—that the stock of home-bred virtue is large enough to absorb and neutralize so much of foreign vice;—

and that the outcasts of Europe, if not by their own choice, yet by an almost inevitable necessity, promote the welfare of the country that receives them to its bosom.

MY VISIT TO NIAGARA.

This sketch was first published anonymously, "by the author of 'The Gray Champion,'" in the *New-England Magazine* 8 (February 1835): 91–96. It never reappeared in any collection of Hawthorne's fiction published during his lifetime.

It was identified and collected only later by George Parsons Lathrop in his editions of Hawthorne's works (see SLE, 42–50) without any notable changes but one: In its first publication the sixth paragraph closing with "beholding them again" ends with five asterisks. They were omitted by Lathrop in the later reprintings and replaced by a larger space between the sixth and the seventh paragraphs. CE, XI, 281–88, reprints this sketch under "Uncollected Tales" with asterisks silently omitted.

See also "Fragments from the Journal of a Solitary Man. [Two Extracts]." In Hawthorne's original manuscript of "The Story Teller" these two fragments were obviously closely related to the Niagara sketch. Extract two possibly followed the paragraph ending with asterisks, and extract one possibly followed the last paragraph and closed the narrator's description of his visit to Niagara.

Never did a pilgrim approach Niagara with deeper enthusiasm, than mine. I had lingered away from it, and wandered to other scenes, because my treasury of anticipated enjoyments, comprising all the wonders of the world, had nothing else so magnificent, and I was loth to exchange the pleasures of hope for those of memory so soon. At length, the day came. The stage-coach, with a Frenchman and myself on the back seat, had already left Lewiston, and in less than an hour would set us down in Manchester. I began to listen for the roar of the cataract, and trembled with a sensation like dread, as the moment drew nigh, when its voice of ages must roll, for the first time, on my ear. The French gentleman stretched himself from the window, and expressed loud admiration, while, by a sudden impulse, I threw myself back and closed my eyes. When the scene shut in, I was glad to think, that for me the whole burst of Niagara was yet in futurity. We rolled on, and entered the village of Manchester, bordering on the falls.

I am quite ashamed of myself here. Not that I ran, like a madman, to the falls, and plunged into the thickest of the spray—never stopping to breathe, till breathing was impossible: not that I committed this, or any other suitable extravagance. On the contrary, I alighted with perfect decency and composure, gave my cloak to the black waiter, pointed out my baggage, and inquired, not the nearest way to the cataract, but about the dinner-hour. The interval was spent in arranging my dress. Within the last fifteen minutes, my mind had grown strangely benumbed, and my spirits apathetic, with a slight depression, not decided enough to be termed sadness. My enthusiasm was in a deathlike slumber. Without aspiring to immortality, as he did, I could have imitated that English traveler, who turned back from the point where he first heard the thunder of Niagara, after crossing the ocean to behold it. Many a western trader, by-the-by, has performed a similar act of heroism with more heroic simplicity, deeming it no such wonderful feat to dine at the hotel and resume his route to Buffalo or Lewiston, while the cataract was roaring unseen.

Such has often been my apathy, when objects, long sought, and earnestly desired, were placed within my reach. After dinner—at which, an unwonted and perverse epicurism detained me longer than usual—I lighted a ciger and paced the piazza, minutely attentive to the aspect and business of a very ordinary village. Finally, with reluctant step, and the feeling of an intruder, I walked towards Goat island. At the toll-house, there were further excuses for delaying the inevitable moment. My signature was required in a huge leger, containing similar records innumerable, many of which I read. The skin of a great sturgeon, and other fishes, beasts, and reptiles; a collection of minerals, such as lie in heaps near the falls; some Indian moccasins, and other trifles, made of deer-skin and embroidered with beads; several newspapers from Montreal, New-York, and Boston; all attracted me in turn. Out of a number of twisted sticks, the manufacture of a Tuscarora Indian, I selected one of curled maple, curiously convoluted, and adorned with the carved images of a snake and a fish. Using this as my pilgrim's staff, I crossed the bridge. Above and below me were the rapids, a river of impetuous snow, with here and there a dark rock amid its whiteness, resisting all the physical fury, as any cold spirit did the moral influences of the scene. On reaching Goat island, which separates the two great segments of the falls, I chose the righthand path, and followed it to the edge of the American cascade. There, while the falling sheet was yet invisible, I saw the vapor that never vanishes, and the Eternal Rainbow of Niagara.

It was an afternoon of glorious sunshine, without a cloud, save those of the cataracts. I gained an insulated rock, and beheld a broad sheet of brilliant and unbroken foam, not shooting in a curved line from the top of the precipice, but falling headlong down from height to depth. A narrow stream diverged from the main branch, and hurried over the crag by a channel of its own, leaving a little pine-clad island and a streak of precipice, between itself and the larger sheet. Below arose the mist, on which was painted a dazzling sun-bow, with two concentric shadows—one, almost as perfect as the original brightness; and the other, drawn faintly round the broken edge of the cloud.

Still, I had not half seen Niagara. Following the verge of the island, the path led me to the Horse-shoe, where the real, broad St. Lawrence, rushing along on a level with its banks, pours its whole breadth over a concave line of precipice, and thence pursues its course between lofty crags towards Ontario. A sort of bridge, two or three feet wide, stretches out along the edge of the descending sheet, and hangs upon the rising mist, as if that were the foundation of the frail structure. Here I stationed myself, in the blast of wind, which the rushing river bore along with it. The bridge was tremulous beneath me, and marked the tremor of the solid earth. I looked along the whitening rapids, and endeavored to distinguish a mass of water far above the falls, to follow it to their verge, and go down with it, in fancy, to the abyss of clouds and storm. Casting my eyes across the river, and every side, I took in the whole scene at a glance, and tried to comprehend it in one vast idea. After an hour thus spent, I left the bridge, and, by a staircase, winding almost interminably round a post, descended to the base of the precipice. From that point, my path lay over slippery stones, and among great fragments of the cliff, to the edge of the cataract, where the wind at once enveloped me in spray, and perhaps dashed the rainbow round me. Were my long desires fulfilled? And had I seen Niagara?

Oh, that I had never heard of Niagara till I beheld it! Blessed were the wanderers of old, who heard its deep roar, sounding through the woods, as the summons to an unknown wonder, and approached its awful brink, in all the freshness of native feeling. Had its own mysterious voice been the first to warn me of its existence, then, indeed, I might have knelt down and worshipped. But I had come thither, haunted with a vision of foam and fury, and dizzy cliffs, and an ocean tumbling down out of the sky—a scene, in short, which nature had too much good taste and calm simplicity to realize. My mind had struggled to adapt these false conceptions to the reality, and finding the effort vain, a wretched sense of disappointment weighed me down. I climbed the precipice, and threw myself on the earth—feeling that I was unworthy to look at the Great Falls, and careless about beholding them again. * * * * *

All that night, as there has been and will be, for ages past and to come, a rushing sound was heard, as if a great tempest were sweeping through the air. It mingled with my dreams, and made them full of storm and whirlwind. Whenever I awoke, and heard this dread sound in the air, and the windows rattling as with a mighty blast, I could not rest again, till, looking forth, I saw how bright the stars were, and that every leaf in the garden was motionless. Never was a summer-night more calm to the eye, nor a gale of autumn louder to the ear. The rushing sound proceeds from the rapids, and the rattling of the casements is but an effect of the vibration of the whole house, shaken by the jar of the cataract. The noise of the rapids draws the attention from the true voice of Niagara, which is a dull, muffled thunder, resounding between the cliffs. I spent a wakeful hour at midnight, in distinguishing its reverberations, and rejoiced to find that my former awe and enthusiasm were reviving.

Gradually, and after much contemplation, I came to know, by my own feelings, that Niagara is indeed a wonder of the world, and not the less wonderful, because time and thought must be employed in comprehending it. Casting aside all pre-conceived notions, and preparation to be dire-struck or delighted, the beholder must stand beside it in the simplicity of his heart, suffering the mighty scene to work its own impression. Night after night, I dreamed of it, and was gladdened every morning by the consciousness of a growing capacity to enjoy it. Yet I will not pretend to the all-absorbing enthusiasm of some more fortunate spectators, nor deny, that very trifling causes would draw my eyes and thoughts from the cataract.

The last day that I was to spend at Niagara, before my departure for the far west, I sat upon the Table Rock. This celebrated station did not now, as of old, project fifty feet beyond the line of the precipice, but was shattered by the fall of an immense fragment, which lay distant on the shore below. Still, on the utmost verge of the rock, with my feet hanging over it, I felt as if suspended in the open air. Never before had my mind been in such perfect unison with the scene. There were intervals, when I was conscious of nothing but the great river, rolling calmly into the abyss, rather descending than precipitating itself, and acquiring tenfold majesty from its unhurried motion. It came like the march of Destiny. It was not taken by surprise, but seemed to have anticipated, in all its course through the broad lakes, that it must pour their collected waters down this height. The perfect foam of the river, after its descent, and the ever varying shapes of mist, rising up, to become clouds in the sky, would be the very picture of confusion, were it merely transient, like the rage of a tempest. But when the beholder has stood awhile, and perceives no lull in the storm, and considers that the vapor and the foam are as everlasting as the rocks which produce them, all this turmoil assumes a sort of calmness. It soothes, while it awes the mind.

Leaning over the cliff, I saw the guide conducting two adventurers behind the falls. It was pleasant, from that high seat in the

sunshine, to observe them struggling against the eternal storm of
the lower regions, with heads bent down, now faltering, now press-
ing forward, and finally swallowed up in their victory. After their
disappearance, a blast rushed out with an old hat, which it had
swept from one of their heads. The rock, to which they were di-
recting their unseen course, is marked, at a fearful distance on the
exterior of the sheet, by a jet of foam. The attempt to reach it,
appears both poetical and perilous, to a looker-on, but may be
accomplished without much more difficulty or hazard, than in
stemming a violent northeaster. In a few moments, forth came the
children of the mist. Dripping and breathless, they crept along the
base of the cliff, ascended to the guide's cottage, and received, I
presume, a certificate of their achievement, with three verses of
sublime poetry on the back.

My contemplations were often interrupted by strangers, who
came down from Forsyth's to take their first view of the falls. A
short, ruddy, middle-aged gentleman, fresh from old England,
peeped over the rock, and evinced his approbation by a broad grin.
His spouse, a very robust lady, afforded a sweet example of maternal solicitude, being so intent on the safety of her little boy that she
did not even glance at Niagara. As for the child, he gave himself
wholly to the enjoyment of a stick of candy. Another traveler, a
native American, and no rare character among us, produced a
volume of captain Hall's tour, and labored earnestly to adjust Niagara to the captain's description, departing, at last, without one
new idea or sensation of his own. The next comer was provided,
not with a printed book, but with a blank sheet of foolscap, from
top to bottom of which, by means of an ever pointed pencil, the
cataract was made to thunder. In a little talk, which we had together,
he awarded his approbation to the general view, but censured the
position of Goat island, observing that it should have been thrown
farther to the right, so as to widen the American falls, and contract
those of the Horse-shoe. Next appeared two traders of Michigan,
who declared, that, upon the whole, the sight was worth looking at;
there certainly was an immense water-power here; but that, after
all, they would go twice as far to see the noble stone-works of Lockport, where the Grand Canal is locked down a descent of sixty feet.

They were succeeded by a young fellow, in a home-spun cotton dress, with a staff in his hand, and a pack over his shoulders. He advanced close to the edge of the rock, where his attention, at first wavering among the different components of the scene, finally became fixed in the angle of the Horse-shoe falls, which is, indeed, the central point of interest. His whole soul seemed to go forth and be transported thither, till the staff slipped from his relaxed grasp, and falling down—down—down—struck upon the fragment of the Table Rock.

In this manner, I spent some hours, watching the varied impression, made by the cataract, on those who disturbed me, and returning to unwearied contemplation, when left alone. At length, my time came to depart. There is a grassy foot-path, through the woods, along the summit of the bank, to a point whence a causeway, hewn in the side of the precipice, goes winding down to the ferry, about half a mile below the Table Rock. The sun was near setting, when I emerged from the shadow of the trees, and began the descent. The indirectness of my downward road continually changed the point of view, and shewed me, in rich and repeated succession— now, the whitening rapids and the majestic leap of the main river, which appeared more deeply massive as the light departed; now, the lovelier picture, yet still sublime, of Goat island with its rocks and grove, and the lesser falls, tumbling over the right bank of the St. Lawrence, like a tributary stream; now, the long vista of the river, as it eddied and whirled between the cliffs, to pass through Ontario towards the sea, and everywhere to be wondered at, for this one unrivalled scene. The golden sunshine tinged the sheet of the American cascade, and painted on its heaving spray the broken semicircle of a rainbow, Heaven's own beauty crowning earth's sublimity. My steps were slow, and I paused long at every turn of the descent, as one lingers and pauses, who discerns a brighter and brightening excellence in what he must soon behold no more. The solitude of the old wilderness now reigned over the whole vicinity of the falls. My enjoyment became the more rapturous, because no poet shared it—nor wretch, devoid of poetry, profaned it: but the spot, so famous through the world, was all my own!

FRAGMENTS FROM THE JOURNAL OF
A SOLITARY MAN.
[Two Extracts]

These fragments consist of an editor's report describing the life and early death of his solitary friend Oberon interspersed with a series of six fragments given as direct quotes from Oberon's journal. The two extracts reprinted here are the third and fourth fragments. This entire article was published anonymously in the *American Monthly Magazine* n.s. 4 (July 1837): 45–56. It must be the concluding part of "The Story Teller" mentioned by Hawthorne in his letter to Ticknor (see pp. 25–26). Close analysis shows that it was assembled and edited by Park Benjamin from the remaining parts of the "Story Teller" manuscript (see Weber, *Entwicklung*, 344–49, and note 11 to "Hawthorne's Tour," page 183).

The article never appeared in any collection of Hawthorne's fiction published during his lifetime. It was identified only later by George Parsons Lathrop and included in his editions of Hawthorne's works (see SLE, XII, 23–41). It is included under the "Uncollected Tales" in CE, XI, 312–28 and the Library of America *Tales and Sketches*, 493–95.

[1]

"On reaching the ferry-house, a rude structure of boards at the foot of the cliff, I found several of these wretches devoid of poetry, and lost some of my own poetry by contact with them. The hut was crowded by a party of provincials—a simple and merry set, who had spent the afternoon fishing near the Falls, and were bartering black and white bass and eels for the ferryman's whiskey. A greyhound and three spaniels, brutes of much more grace and decorous demeanor than their masters, sat at the door. A few yards off, yet wholly unnoticed by the dogs, was a beautiful fox, whose countenance betokened all the sagacity attributed to him in ancient fable. He had a comfortable bed of straw in an old barrel, whither he retreated, flourishing his bushy tail as I made a step towards him, but soon came forth and surveyed me with a keen and intelligent eye. The Canadians bartered their fish and drank their whiskey, and were loquacious on trifling subjects, and merry at simple jests, with as little regard to the scenery as they could have shown to the flattest part of the Grand Canal. Nor was I entitled to despise them; for I amused myself with all those foolish matters of fishermen, and dogs, and fox, just as if Sublimity and Beauty were not married at that place and moment; as if their nuptial band were not the brightest of all rainbows on the opposite shore; as if the gray precipice were not frowning above my head and Niagara thundering around me.

The grim ferryman, a black-whiskered giant, half drunk withal, now thrust the Canadians by main force out of his door, launched a boat, and bade me sit down in the stern-sheets. Where we crossed the river was white with foam, yet did not offer much resistance to a straight passage, which brought us close to the outer edge of the American falls. The rainbow vanished as we neared its misty base, and when I leaped ashore, the sun had left all Niagara in shadow."

[2]

"A sound of merriment, sweet voices and girlish laughter, came dancing through the solemn roar of waters. In old times, when the French and afterwards the English, held garrisons near Niagara, it used to be deemed a feat worthy of a soldier, a frontier man, or an Indian, to cross the rapids to Goat Island. As the country became less rude and warlike, a long space intervened, in which it was but half believed, by a faint and doubtful tradition, that mortal foot had ever trod this wild spot of precipice and forest clinging between two cataracts. The island is no longer a tangled forest, but a grove of stately trees, with grassy intervals about their roots and woodland paths among their trunks. There was neither soldier nor Indian here now, but a vision of three lovely girls, running brief races through the broken sunshine of the grove, hiding behind the trees, and pelting each other with the cones of the pine. When their sport had brought them near me, it so happened that one of the party ran up and shook me by the hand—a greeting which I heartily returned, and would have done the same had it been tenderer. I had known this wild little black-eyed lass in my youth and her childhood, before I had commenced my rambles.

We met on terms of freedom and kindness, which elder ladies might have thought unsuitable with a gentleman of my description. When I alluded to the two fair strangers, she shouted after them by their Christian names, at which summons, with grave dignity, they drew near, and honored me with a distant curtsey. They were from the upper part of Vermont. Whether sisters, or cousins, or at all related to each other, I cannot tell; but they are planted in my memory like 'two twin roses on one stem,' with the fresh dew in both their bosoms; and when I would have pure and pleasant thoughts, I think of them. Neither of them could have seen seventeen years. They both were of a height, and that a moderate one. The rose-bloom of their cheeks could hardly be called bright in her who was the rosiest, nor faint, though a shade less deep, in her companion. Both had delicate eye-brows, not strongly defined, yet somewhat darker than their hair; both had small sweet mouths, maiden mouths, of not so warm and deep a tint as ruby, but only red as the reddest rose; each had those gems, the rarest, the most precious, a pair of clear, soft, bright blue eyes. Their style of dress was similar; one had on a black silk gown, with a stomacher of velvet, and scalloped cuffs of the same from the wrist to the elbow; the other wore cuffs and stomacher of the like pattern and material, over a gown of crimson silk. The dress was rather heavy for their slight figures, but suited to September. They and the darker beauty all carried their straw bonnets in their hands."

OLD TICONDEROGA.
A PICTURE OF THE PAST.

This was first published anonymously in the *American Monthly Magazine*, n.s. 1 (February 1836): 138–42, and reprinted in *The Snow-Image and Other Tales* (London, 1851) and *The Snow-Image, and Other Twice-Told Tales* (Boston, 1852). In these and all later editions including CE, XI, 185–91, the first two paragraphs were omitted. They are, however, included in the textual notes to the

Library of America *Tales and Sketches*, 1488, and the historical collation in CE, XI, 470. There were no other notable textual changes.

In returning once to New England, from a visit to Niagara, I found myself, one summer's day, before noon, at Orwell, about forty miles from the southern extremity of Lake Champlain, which has here the aspect of a river or a creek. We were on the Vermont shore, with a ferry, of less than a mile wide, between us and the town of Ti, in New-York.

On the bank of the lake, within ten yards of the water, stood a pretty white tavern, with a piazza along its front. A wharf and one or two stores were close at hand, and appeared to have a good run of trade, foreign as well as domestic; the latter with Vermont farmers, the former with vessels plying between Whitehall and the British dominions. Altogether, this was a pleasant and lively spot. I delighted in it, among other reasons, on account of the continual succession of travellers, who spent an idle quarter of an hour in waiting for the ferry-boat; affording me just time enough to make their acquaintance, penetrate their mysteries, and be rid of them without the risk of tediousness on either part.

The greatest attraction, in this vicinity, is the famous old fortress of Ticonderoga; the remains of which are visible from the piazza of the tavern, on a swell of land that shuts in the prospect of the lake. Those celebrated heights, Mount Defiance and Mount Independence, familiar to all Americans in history, stand too prominent not to be recognised, though neither of them precisely correspond to the images excited by their names. In truth, the whole scene, except the interior of the fortress, disappointed me. Mount Defiance, which one pictures as a steep, lofty, and rugged hill, of most formidable aspect, frowning down with the grim visage of a precipice on old Ticonderoga, is merely a long and wooded ridge; and bore, at some former period, the gentle name of Sugar Hill. The brow is certainly difficult to climb, and high enough to look into every corner of the fortress. St. Clair's most probable reason, however, for neglecting to occupy it, was the deficiency of troops to man the works already constructed, rather than the supposed inacces-

sibility of Mount Defiance. It is singular that the French never fortified this height, standing, as it does, in the quarter whence they
must have looked for the advance of a British army.

In my first view of the ruins I was favored with the scientific
guidance of a young lieutenant of engineers, recently from West
Point, where he had gained credit for great military genius. I saw
nothing but confusion in what chiefly interested him; straight lines
and zig-zags, defence within defence, wall opposed to wall, and
ditch intersecting ditch; oblong squares of masonry below the surface of the earth, and huge mounds, or turf-covered hills of stone,
above it. On one of these artificial hillocks, a pine tree has rooted
itself, and grown tall and strong, since the banner-staff was levelled.
But where my unmilitary glance could trace no regularity, the
young lieutenant was perfectly at home. He fathomed the meaning
of every ditch, and formed an entire plan of the fortress from its
half-obliterated lines. His description of Ticonderoga would be as
accurate as a geometrical theorem, and as barren of the poetry that
has clustered round its decay. I viewed Ticonderoga as a place of
ancient strength, in ruins for half a century; where the flags of
three nations had successively waved, and none waved now; where
armies had struggled, so long ago that the bones of the slain were
mouldered; where Peace had found a heritage in the forsaken
haunts of War. Now the young West Pointer, with his lectures on
ravelins, counterscarps, angles, and covered ways, made it an affair
of brick and mortar and hewn stone, arranged on certain regular
principles, having a good deal to do with mathematics but nothing
at all with poetry.

I should have been glad of a hoary veteran to totter by my side,
and tell me, perhaps, of the French garrisons and their Indian
allies—of Abercrombie, Lord Howe, and Amherst—of Ethan Allen's triumph and St. Clair's surrender. The old soldier and the old
fortress would be emblems of each other. His reminiscences, though
vivid as the image of Ticonderoga in the lake, would harmonize
with the gray influence of the scene. A survivor of the long-dis-
banded garrisons, though but a private soldier, might have mustered his dead chiefs and comrades—some from Westminster

Abbey, and English churchyards, and battle-fields in Europe—others from their graves here in America—others, not a few, who lie sleeping round the fortress; he might have mustered them all, and bid them march through the ruined gateway, turning their old historic faces on me as they passed. Next to such a companion, the best is one's own fancy.

At another visit I was alone, and, after rambling all over the ramparts, sat down to rest myself in one of the roofless barracks. These are old French structures, and appear to have occupied three sides of a large area, now overgrown with grass, nettles, and thistles. The one, in which I sat, was long and narrow, as all the rest had been, with peaked gables. The exterior walls were nearly entire, constructed of gray, flat, unpicked stones, the aged strength of which promised long to resist the elements, if no other violence should precipitate their fall. The roof, floors, partitions, and the rest of the wood-work, had probably been burnt, except some bars of stanch old oak, which were blackened with fire but still remained embedded into the window-sills and over the doors. There were a few particles of plastering near the chimney, scratched with rude figures, perhaps by a soldier's hand. A most luxuriant crop of weeds had sprung up within the edifice and hid the scattered fragments of the wall. Grass and weeds grew in the windows, and in all the crevices of the stone, climbing, step by step, till a tuft of yellow flowers was waving on the highest peak of the gable. Some spicy herb diffused a pleasant odor through the ruin. A verdant heap of vegetation had covered the hearth of the second floor, clustering on the very spot where the huge logs had mouldered to glowing coals, and flourished beneath the broad flue, which had so often puffed the smoke over a circle of French or English soldiers. I felt that there was no other token of decay so impressive as that bed of weeds in the place of the back-log.

Here I sat, with those roofless walls about me, the clear sky over my head, and the afternoon sunshine falling gently bright through the window-frames and doorway. I heard the tinkling of a cow-bell, the twittering of birds, and the pleasant hum of insects. Once a gay butterfly, with four gold-speckled wings, came and fluttered about

my head, then flew up and lighted on the highest tuft of yellow
flowers, and at last took wing across the lake. Next a bee buzzed
through the sunshine, and found much sweetness among the weeds.
After watching him till he went off to his distant hive, I closed my
eyes on Ticonderoga in ruins, and cast a dream-like glance over
pictures of the past, and scenes of which this spot had been the
theatre.

At first, my fancy saw only the stern hills, lonely lakes, and venerable woods. Not a tree, since their seeds were first scattered over
the infant soil, had felt the axe, but had grown up and flourished
through its long generation, had fallen beneath the weight of years,
been buried in green moss, and nourished the roots of others as
gigantic. Hark! A light paddle dips into the lake, a birch canoe
glides round the point, and an Indian chief has passed, painted
and feather-crested, armed with a bow of hickory, a stone toma-
hawk, and flint-headed arrows. But the ripple had hardly vanished
from the water, when a white flag caught the breeze, over a castle
in the wilderness with frowning ramparts and a hundred cannon.
There stood a French chevalier, commandant of the fortress, paying
court to a copper-colored lady, the princess of the land, and win-
ning her wild love by the arts which had been successful with Pa-
risian dames. A war-party of French and Indians were issuing from
the gate to lay waste some village of New England. Near the fortress
there was a group of dancers. The merry soldiers footing it with
the swart savage maids; deeper in the wood, some red men were
growing frantic around a keg of the fire-water; and elsewhere a
Jesuit preached the faith of high cathedrals beneath a canopy of
forest boughs, and distributed crucifixes to be worn beside English
scalps.

I tried to make a series of pictures from the old French war,
when fleets were on the lake and armies in the woods, and especially
of Abercrombie's disastrous repulse, where thousands of lives were
utterly thrown away; but being at a loss how to order the battle, I
chose an evening scene in the barracks after the fortress had sur-
rendered to Sir Jeffrey Amherst. What an immense fire blazes on
that hearth, gleaming on swords, bayonets, and musket barrels, and

blending with the hue of the scarlet coats till the whole barrack-room is quivering with ruddy light! One soldier has thrown himself down to rest, after a deer-hunt, or perhaps a long run through the woods, with Indians on his trail. Two stand up to wrestle, and are on the point of coming to blows. A fifer plays a shrill accompaniment to a drummer's song—a strain of light love and bloody war, with a chorus thundered forth by twenty voices. Mean time a veteran in the corner is prosing about Dettingen and Fontenoye, and relates camp-traditions of Marlborough's battles; till his pipe, having been roguishly charged with gun-powder, makes a terrible explosion under his nose. And now they all vanish in a puff of smoke from the chimney.

I merely glanced at the ensuing twenty years, which glided peacefully over the frontier fortress, till Ethan Allen's shout was heard, summoning it to surrender "in the name of the great Jehovah and of the Continental Congress." Strange allies! thought the British captain. Next came the hurried muster of the soldiers of liberty, when the cannon of Burgoyne, pointing down upon their stronghold from the brow of Mount Defiance, announced a new conqueror of Ticonderoga. No virgin fortress, this! Forth rushed the motley throng from the barracks, one man wearing the blue and buff of the Union, another the red coat of Britain, a third a dragoon's jacket, and a fourth a cotton frock; here was a pair of leather breeches, and striped trowsers there; a grenadier's cap on one head, and a broad-brimmed hat, with a tall feather, on the next; this fellow shouldering a king's arm, that might throw a bullet to Crown Point, and his comrade a long fowling piece, admirable to shoot ducks on the lake. In the midst of the bustle, when the fortress was all alive with its last warlike scene, the ringing of a bell on the lake made me suddenly unclose my eyes, and behold only the gray and weed-grown ruins. They were as peaceful in the sun as a warrior's grave.

Hastening to the rampart, I perceived that the signal had been given by the steam-boat Franklin, which landed a passenger from Whitehall at the tavern, and resumed its progress northward, to reach Canada the next morning. A sloop was pursuing the same track; a little skiff had just crossed the ferry; while a scow, laden with lumber, spread its huge square sail and went up the lake. The whole country was a cultivated farm. Within musket shot of the ramparts lay the neat villa of Mr. Pell, who, since the revolution, has become proprietor of a spot for which France, England, and America have so often struggled. How forcibly the lapse of time and change of circumstances came home to my apprehension! Banner would never wave again, nor cannon roar, nor blood be shed, nor trumpet stir up a soldier's heart, in this old fort of Ticonderoga. Tall trees had grown upon its ramparts, since the last garrison marched out, to return no more, or only at some dreamer's summons, gliding from the twilight past to vanish among realities.

THE NORTHERN TOUR IN
CONTEMPORARY PAINTINGS AND ENGRAVINGS

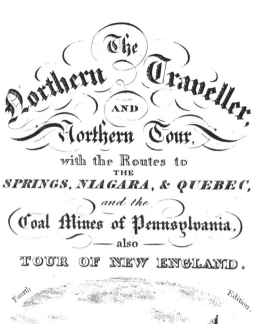

The Northern Traveller, AND Northern Tour,

with the Routes to
THE
SPRINGS, NIAGARA, & QUEBEC,
and the
(Coal Mines of Pennsylvania,)
— also —
TOUR OF NEW ENGLAND.

Fourth

Edition.

NEW YORK.
J & J. HARPER.
1830.

[1]

Title page, fourth edition of Theodore Dwight's popular tourist guide. The vignette shows a view of the Battery at the foot of Manhattan, the starting point for steamboat trips up the Hudson and the first leg of the northern tour. Evidence suggests this is the guidebook Hawthorne may have used, although several others were available. Dwight's book went through six editions between 1825 and 1841.

[2]

Thomas Cole, *View of the White Mountains,* oil on canvas, 1827, Wadsworth Atheneum, Hartford. Bequest of Daniel Wadsworth. In reply to a query by the painting's purchaser, Daniel Wadsworth, Cole wrote, "The view of M Washington is taken about nine miles from Crawfords, on the road to Franconia . . . the river you see in the valley is the Amonasuc [Ammonoosuc]" (8 December 1827; *The Correspondence of Thomas Cole and Daniel Wadsworth,* 26). This is nine miles north of the Notch House, looking east from near the present-day village of Bretton Woods. Hawthorne's tale "The Great Carbuncle" opens in the valley of the Ammonoosuc.

74

[3]

Anonymous, *One of the White Hills, Stripped of Forest and Soil by the Storm of 1826*, ca. 1827, engraving from Theodore Dwight, *Things As They Are* (1834), facing 158. Similar illustrations also appeared in the tourist guides of the time. Hawthorne memorialized this event in "The Ambitious Guest" (1835).

[4]

William Henry Bartlett, *The Willey House*, ca. 1837; engraved by E. Benjamin for N. P. Willis's *American Scenery*, 1, 1840, facing 76. Bartlett was an English artist who visited the United States three times between 1836 and 1841, sketching and traveling extensively throughout Canada and the Northeast. The Willey House is in the center, surrounded by the rubble of the landslide that narrowly missed it. The house stood in the heart of the Notch, on the west side of the Saco River, which can be seen rushing past on the right.

[5]

William Henry Bartlett, *The Notch-House, White Mountains,* ca. 1837; engraved by J. Cousen for N. P. Willis's *American Scenery,* 1, 1840, facing 192. This engraving was reproduced as a Currier and Ives lithograph after 1857 and offered one of the most popular views of the Notch. Thomas Cole, William Trost Richards, and John Kensett all painted this scene as well. It looks south into the narrowest part of the Notch from a point about two miles north of the Willey House. Hawthorne spent two nights at this inn, also known as the Crawford House, in 1832.

[6]

William Henry Bartlett, *Mount Jefferson (from Mount Washington)*, ca. 1837; engraved by R. Brandard for N. P. Willis's *American Scenery*, 2, 1840, facing 243. Ascents of Mount Washington, the highest peak in the eastern United States (6,288 feet), were commonplace by the time of Bartlett's visits in 1836–1838. This view looks north toward the towns of Lancaster and Jefferson.

[7]

William Henry Bartlett, *Mount Washington and the White Hills,* ca. 1837; engraved by S. T. Davies for N. P. Willis's *American Scenery,* 1, 1840, facing 100. The size of the river suggests that it is the Ammonoosuc, and that the view is taken from a spot not far from that of Cole's *View of the White Mountains* (ill. 2)—about ten miles north of the Notch House.

[8]

Henry Inman, *Travelling on the Erie Canal,* engraved by Peter Maverick for Theodore Dwight's *The Northern Traveller* (1830), facing 57. According to Dwight's description, this depicts a spot twenty-five miles east of Little Falls known as "Anthony's Nose," evidently the name of the sloping mountain in the left background. The Mohawk River follows the canal at the left.

[9]

William Henry Bartlett, *Village of Little Falls*, ca. 1837; engraved by S. Brad-
shaw for N. P. Willis's *American Scenery*, 2, 1840, facing 40. Hawthorne may
have begun his canal trip at this point. The tourist guidebooks considered
Little Falls one of the most scenic and best-engineered spots along the Erie
Canal. The dramatically elevated waterway contrasted sharply with the
rapids of the Mohawk River and the pastoral village itself. Gideon Miner
Davison advised travelers "to spend some time at this place, in viewing its
great natural and artificial works" (*Traveller's Guide*, 5th ed., 1833, 199).

[10]

John William Hill, *Erie Canal, 1831*, watercolor, ca. 1829–30. Courtesy of
The New-York Historical Society, New York City. According to Patricia
Anderson in *The Course of Empire*, 63, Hill wanted to depict human activity
along the new waterway for a portfolio of aquatints, but the intended collection was never published. This view also appears to be in the area
around Little Falls.

82

[11]

John William Hill, *[View of the Erie Canal]*, watercolor, ca. 1829–30. I. N.
Phelps Stokes Collection. Miriam & Ira D. Wallach Division of Art, Prints
and Photographs. The New York Public Library. Astor, Lenox and Tilden
Foundations. Like illustration 10, this is one of the few topographical drawings of the canal from the period of Hawthorne's tour. The locale is uncertain.

[12]

William Henry Bartlett, *Utica*, ca. 1837; engraved by R. Brandard for N. P. Willis's *American Scenery*, 1, 1840, facing 94. This busy scene mirrors "the hum and bustle of struggling enterprise" that Hawthorne's tourist observed from a canal boat.

[13]
John William Hill, *[Scene of Night-Time Traffic on the Erie Canal]*, watercolor, ca. 1829–30. I. N. Phelps Stokes Collection. Miriam & Ira D. Wallach Division of Art, Prints and Photographs. The New York Public Library. Astor, Lenox and Tilden Foundations. This unusual, eerie scene may depict the "long level," the flat and swampy stretch of canal between Utica and Syracuse. This was the least scenic and interesting part of the journey, as Hawthorne's traveler discovers.

85

[14]

John W. Barber and Henry Howe, *Western view in the central part of Syracuse*, ca. 1840; engraving in *Historical collections of the state of New York,* 395. In 1830 Robert J. Vandewater described Syracuse as "the most important place between Utica and Rochester," with a skyline that gave it "the appearance of New-York in miniature" (*The Tourist*, 1st. ed., 40).

[15]

John W. Barber and Henry Howe, *View of Ogdensburg*, ca. 1840; engraving in *Historical collections of the state of New York*, 486. Ogdensburg was an important railhead and port on the St. Lawrence River, connecting steamboat traffic from Montreal to Rochester via the St. Lawrence River and Lake Ontario. Hawthorne may have embarked from here on the trip described in "An Ontario Steam-Boat."

[16]

John W. Barber and Henry Howe, *Central Part of Buffalo Street, Rochester, N.Y.*, ca. 1840; engraving in *Historical collections of the state of New York*, facing 269. Rochester was strategically located at the confluence of the Genesee River, Lake Ontario, and the Erie Canal. It was the fastest-growing city in western New York.

[17]
J. H. Bufford, *The Upper Falls of the Genesee at Rochester, N.Y.,* lithograph, ca. 1835. Courtesy of The New-York Historical Society, New York City. This view was taken from the east bank looking northwest. Sam Patch leaped to his death at these falls in 1829, an event Hawthorne mentions in his sketch "Rochester."

[18]
Anonymous, *Falls of the Genesee, N.Y.,* ca. 1838, engraving in *Settlement in the West.* Courtesy of the New-York Historical Society, New York City. This appears to be taken from a perspective opposite to that in illustration 17. In addition to their scenic beauty, the Genesee Falls were the primary source of power for the burgeoning industry of Rochester.

[19]

William James Bennett, *View of the British Fall Taken From Goat Island,* aquatint, 1830, engraved by William James Bennett. Courtesy of The New-York Historical Society, New York City. Bennett, an Englishman, sketched numerous views of the falls between 1829 and 1840. This print appeared in a collection of Niagara prints that enjoyed widespread popularity.

[20]

George Catlin, *View of Niagara: No. 6, Table Rock from Below,* lithograph, 1831. Courtesy of The New-York Historical Society, New York City. Although more famous for his portraits of American Indians, Catlin began his artistic career as a topographical artist. This is one of the earliest drawings of the famous sidetrip behind Niagara's Horseshoe Falls. Tourists who made the trip—Hawthorne was one—received a certificate recording their accomplishment.

[21]

John F. Vanderlyn, *Niagara Falls from Table Rock,* oil painting, 1835. Bequest of Martha C. Karolik for the Karolik Collection of American Paintings, 1815–1865. Courtesy, Museum of Fine Arts, Boston. This famous panoramic view of the Horseshoe Falls is taken from the Canadian side. Goat Island is on the far left.

[22]

William Henry Bartlett, *Ferry Landing on the American Side,* ca. 1837, lithograph by Hall and Mooney, *Steele's Niagara Falls Portfolio.* The wooden stairway down the side of the Niagara gorge was one of the earliest improvements at the falls. The first one was constructed in 1818, replacing an Indian ladder. It was rebuilt and enlarged several times in subsequent years.

[23]

Henry Reinagle, *View of the Ruins of Ticonderoga Forts on Lake Champlain*, ca.
1817, engraved by Gideon Fairman. I. N. Phelps Stokes Collection. Miriam
& Ira D. Wallach Division of Art, Prints and Photographs. The New York
Public Library. Astor, Lenox and Tilden Foundations. This was reproduced
in aquatint for the *Analectic*, 11 (April 1818), facing 323. Accompanying
the plate is a short article describing the fort's tumultuous history, an emphasis that suggests the importance attached to events rather than aesthetics at this time.

[24]

Anonymous, *Ticonderoga From Mount Independence*, 1830, engraved by C. H. Throop for Theodore Dwight, *The Northern Traveller* (1830), facing 179. Although Dwight recognized that "the hand of cultivation has been gradually levelling the forest that once covered the valley," he still believed that "There are few sites in our country that can be compared with this for a combination of natural and moral interest" (*The Northern Traveller,* 1st ed., 1825, 127–28).

[25]

Thomas Cole, *Ruins of Fort Ticonderoga, New York,* engraving, 1831, accession no. 39.559.35. Courtesy The Detroit Institute of Arts, Founders Society Purchase, William H. Murphy Fund. This was based on one of Cole's earliest landscapes, painted ca. 1826.

[26]

William Henry Bartlett, *View of the Ruins of Fort Ticonderoga*, ca. 1837; engraved by E. Benjamin for N. P. Willis's *American Scenery*, 1, 1840, facing 38. The letterpress accompanying this engraving recounts Ethan Allen's bold capture of the fort during the American Revolution.

A LITERARY AND PICTORIAL ICONOGRAPHY OF HAWTHORNE'S TOUR

Dennis Berthold

Nineteenth-century readers expected travel writers to supply vivid word pictures or "sketches" of the actual scenes visited and observed. Although this expectation grew out of a long tradition of British travel books, in the 1820s the best-known work of this kind was an American volume, Washington Irving's *The Sketch Book* (1819), a genial collection of rich and varied pictures of life in England that set a new standard for travel description. When Park Benjamin chose the title "Sketches from Memory" for the six Hawthorne travel essays in the *American Monthly Magazine* of 1836, he was simply acknowledging this standard. Benjamin's two prefaces emphasize the pictorial quality of the essays: found in "the portfolio of a friend," they consist of "random sketches" so accurate that the author's "powers of description" appear to have been "tasked on the very spot." Some "deserve rather to be called pictures than sketches, so lively are the colors shed over them," while others merit comparison with the landscapes of Claude Lorraine, Thomas Doughty, and George Loring Brown.

While some of Benjamin's rhetoric is clearly overdone—few passages in the sketches are as richly wrought as a Claude painting— there are larger truths in Benjamin's contentions. What E. H. Gombrich realized about painters is also true of travel writers: one never sees a scene afresh.[1] Observers carry with them images seen or read about in previous travel books, paintings, engravings, magazine illustrations, even embellishments on stationery, maps, or public buildings. Responses are preconditioned and constrained by the iconography of the time, and actual scenes are rendered according to popular visual formulas and habits of viewing.

What is described in a travel sketch, then, must not be considered as "reality" any more than a contemporary critic would consider the persona to be the author. In both cases, that of narrative and narrator, conventions intervene and affect perceptions and descriptions in ways that reflect values and experiences far beyond those of any one individual. Examining the pictorial conventions in the illustrations of the places Hawthorne visited will reveal his debt to contemporary visual representations of scenery and will define the iconographic motifs common to American culture of the 1820s and 1830s.

While on the broadest level the precise sources of pictorial conventions are unimportant, on a historical and biographical level, closer connections between the writer and the pictures should exist. There is no record of particular paintings or engravings Hawthorne saw before or during his American travels. Yet, given his omnivorous reading, the rising popularity of sketches of American scenery, and his later interest in art, he probably saw several of the pictures discussed in this essay. Magazines he read, annuals and gift-books to which he contributed, and travel guides he might have used all contained engravings replete with a characteristic and conventionalized iconography. Combined with what Jean Normand has called a "cinematographic" vision already highly developed at the time of his travels,[2] his milieu provided Hawthorne with a rich supply of pictorial resources that made him a sophisticated observer of both art and nature. For example, when he was editor of the *American Magazine of Useful and Entertaining Knowledge* in 1836, he complained to his sister Elizabeth about the wretched woodcuts he was forced to use to illustrate articles (CE, XV, 232); and in his earliest extant journal description of scenery, a walk through North Salem in 1835, he commented on the landscape in aesthetic terms: "quite a picture of beauty, gently picturesque" (CE, VIII, 5). The travel sketches are therefore written by a sensitive observer and recorder of the American scene well versed in the pictorial conventions of his time. They both derive from and comment upon these conventions, and represent visual as well as verbal habits of description that reveal, once more, how extensively their author was immersed in the rapidly developing culture that surrounded him.

*

Perhaps the best nineteenth-century example of culturally preconditioned perceptions of landscape was New Hampshire's White
Mountains. According to Robert L. McGrath, visitors to the famous
Notch in 1832 had preconceived notions of what they would see:
"For the nineteenth century, the White Mountains were an idea
before they were a reality. Popular consciousness of the region was
formed by artifacts rather than facts. Images and words rather than
experience served to structure the place in the American imagination."[3] In the 1820s, during the time Hawthorne would have
formed his ideas about the mountains, they, like much of the American landscape, were predominantly considered in terms of the sublime. Along with Niagara Falls, they were emblems of the vastness
and immensity of America, and like Niagara Falls their true size
was often exaggerated to conform to the ideal of sublimity. Mc-
Grath cites the embellishments to Philip Carrigain's 1816 map that
give the hills truly Andean proportions, depicting them in fierce
and distant profile as if from a vast plain. More like Kilimanjaro
or the Himalayas, they thrust snow-clad peaks sharply upward
against a backdrop of thin clouds, threatening to tumble down on
any traveler foolish enough to dare their majesty.[4]

When Thomas Cole first visited the White Mountains with Henry
Cheever Pratt in 1827, he too was caught up in the quest for sublimity and reproduced it in such paintings as *View of the White Mountains* (ill. 2). Donald D. Keyes, who has studied the genesis of this
painting from on-the-spot sketches to finished oil, believes that, "In
the transition between the drawings and the painting, Cole adjusted
elements in order to produce an ideal vision that conformed to the
Burkeian concept of the Sublime."[5] While no painting is likely to
correspond to every point in Burke's formula, Cole's landscape does
emphasize ponderous masses of darkness, rugged terrain, vast
heights and distances, and human isolation. The figure in the foreground indicates nature's immensity, especially when compared to
the enormous and exaggerated height of the nearby tree. And the
sharp peak in the background, swathed in heavenly light, appears
impossibly beyond human touch. By carefully arranging the three
planes of foreground, middle ground, and background, Cole adds

depth to his painting and draws the spectator uneasily through alternating areas of light and shadow. One wants to move beyond the threat of landslides suggested by the rocks at the lower left and join the two travelers at the edge of the woods; but the path is long and dark, and mountain sublimity remains a distant pleasure.

Hawthorne was keenly aware of the sublime terrors associated with the White Mountains. When a truly terrifying event occurred there, the famous Willey tragedy of 1826, he probably heard about it immediately and pondered its meaning for several years afterward.[6] The true story of an entire family's destruction by a landslide reinforced the sublime image of the mountains and provided guidebook writers with a romantic legend as dreadful as the peaks themselves. In Hawthorne's fictional version of the Willey disaster, "The Ambitious Guest" (1835), the sublime image of the region predominates. The little family, we are told, lives "in the bleakest spot of all New-England . . . the Notch of the White Hills, where the wind was sharp throughout the year, and pitilessly cold in the winter" (CE, IX, 324). Echoing the iconography of both the Carrigain map and the Cole painting, the story stresses the danger and darkness of the place: "They dwelt in a cold spot and a dangerous one; for a mountain towered above their heads, so steep, that the stones would often rumble down its sides, and startle them at midnight" (CE, IX, 324). Rockslides, of course, could occur at any hour of the day or night; but by emphasizing frightening sounds at "midnight," Hawthorne gains that atmosphere of darkness necessary to the sublime. Shortly after the young stranger arrives, a premonitory stone noisily tumbles past the cottage, conjoining expectation with reality and prompting the innkeeper to mention his "sure place of refuge" from landslides. But as the vast emptiness in the Cole painting implies, there are no sure places of refuge in these regions. Mountaintops, a traditional place of safety, are in reality too distant and inhospitable to offer succor. In an ironic verbal parallel to the cold and distant peak in Cole's painting, the ambitious guest himself humorously accuses the eldest daughter of belittling his desires for fame: "You think my ambition as nonsensical as if I were to freeze myself to death on the top of Mount Washington, only that people might spy at me from the country roundabout" (CE, IX, 328). The story's gruesome conclusion—an entire family is destroyed—demonstrates the irrational power and random destructive potential of wild nature.

In the story, Hawthorne was self-consciously competing with writers such as Lydia H. Sigourney who had appropriated the tragedy of the Willey family. Like Cole returning to the studio to compose a finished picture, Hawthorne deliberately arranged "The Ambitious Guest" to conform to popular notions of terror and sublimity. In his travel sketches of the area, however, Hawthorne offered a less credulous view of the mountains' sublimity. The sketches bear the same relationship to "The Ambitious Guest" as Cole's initial drawings bear to his completed painting, and suggest how carefully Hawthorne distinguished his travel writing from his fiction.

Neither Cole nor Hawthorne would have visited the White Mountains had the region not been made accessible to visitors who could find there ample food and comfortable lodging. Even while cartographers, painters, and storytellers purveyed the sublime terrors of the region, innkeepers were encouraging tourism. In order to succeed, they knew they would have to satisfy expectations of sublimity, and none was more successful than the Crawford family. A father and two sons, the Crawfords ran three inns in the vicinity of the Notch and were as renowned for their theatricality as their hospitality. They kept deer, wolves, bears, and a moose to display to visitors, and Ethan Allen Crawford, known for his bulk as "the Giant of the Mountains," fired a cannon so tourists could enjoy the "spectacular echo."[7] His showmanship did not go unnoticed. In *American Scenery* (1840), N. P. Willis compares Crawford to a "Titan," but then goes on to quote a friend who had, in fact, found nothing remarkable in Crawford's size and noticed in the mountaineer "an apparent consciousness that something original is expected of him."[8] Although a far cry from P. T. Barnum, Ethan Crawford knew how to live up to his guests' lofty expectations.

Sharing the cool eye of Willis and his friend, Hawthorne's tourist pays due homage to the sublime ideal even while he records actual events that undercut it. At first, he seems awed by the natural power evident in the mountains' size and ruggedness, as he verbally echoes the imagery of an illustration in Theodore Dwight's *Things As They Are* (ill. 3). The crude woodcut Dwight selected depicts the mountains just after the famous storm that killed the Willey family in 1826. Denuded of vegetation, terrifyingly huge in relation to the tiny house in the center foreground, and capable of vast destruction as shown by the deep gashes in their sides, the mountains dominate the horizon and loom like an insurmountable barrier before the two spectators. Following quite closely this iconography, Hawthorne's tourist remarks on the "red path-ways of the Slides" and acknowledges the vastness of the overall scene, seeing "mountains behind us and mountains on each side, and a group of mightier ones ahead" (see p. 28). His first descriptions of the Notch are metaphorical: the Titan tearing his way through the hills, and the stagecoach compared to an "Indian war-party." He immediately rejects the first metaphor as "trivial," and more subtly undercuts the second with his description of the ludicrous tourists actually riding in the stagecoach. Too sophisticated to mimic uncritically such amateurish attempts at sublimity as the guidebook engraving, and too self-conscious to accept straightforwardly his own sublime fancies, he recognizes how readily viewers turn the ordinary into the sublime and pulls himself up short precisely to draw attention to such artifices.

In fact, the very first simile for the region is distinctly civilized: the valley of the Saco, the traveler says, "extends between mountainous walls, sometimes with a steep ascent, but often as level as a church-aisle." The popular convention of the white-steepled New England landscape comes to mind, where piety and pastoralism go hand in hand. This humanization of the landscape continues in the third paragraph, which directly counters any notion of titanic intervention in carving out the notches: "We had now reached a narrow passage, which showed almost the appearance of having been cut by human strength and artifice in the solid rock." By the fourth paragraph of the sketch, the narrator seems bent on correcting erroneous sublime iconography of the mountains: "They are majestic, and even awful, when contemplated in a proper mood," he admits; "yet, by their breadth of base, and the long ridges which support them, give the idea of immense bulk, rather than of towering height." Such a reorientation of perspective robs the mountains of a chief claim to sublimity and lowers them literally and imaginatively. This frees the tourist to focus on people instead of landscape, to humanize the scene with its odd assortment of characters, and to enjoy the social rather than the sublime aspects of the region. The tourist, unlike the poetaster he observes carrying a gold opera-glass and mouthing "some of Byron's rhapsodies on mountain scenery," has detached himself from the conventions of sublime excess and subtly satirized them.

Hawthorne has cleared the path for an iconography more like that found in William H. Bartlett's views of the White Mountains published in *American Scenery* and sketched during Bartlett's two trips to the United States between 1836 and 1838.[9] Perhaps because he was born and trained in England, Bartlett portrays that blend of the civilized and wild characteristic of English scenery and associated with the picturesque rather than the sublime. He looks at scenery with the eye of the tourist, and represents it with a similar audience in mind. His view of the Notch House (ill. 5), sufficiently popular to become a Currier and Ives lithograph in 1857,[10] stresses the pastoral comforts of the Notch. Although Bartlett uses the same alternating patterns of light and dark as Cole, he chooses a perspective that makes the Notch House as large as the natural topography. The tree on the right, for example, is only about four times the height of the figure in the foreground, as opposed to the twelve-to-one ratio in Cole's painting. Using iconography similar to Hawthorne's, Bartlett fills the scene with domestic activity: a woodsman chops at a stump, a father and son walk a goat up the path, a small group of travelers returns from the Notch itself, and smoke puffs gently from the chimney. A woman in full Victorian dress waits in a carriage outside the inn, feminizing the rugged landscape. The mood of the approaching viewer is similar to that of Hawthorne's tourist: "I was glad to perceive a prospect of comfortable quarters, in a house which we were approaching, and of pleasant company in the guests who were assembled at the door."

The rest of Hawthorne's sketch introduces realistic imagery at an increasing rate and juxtaposes it with the theatrics of Ethan Crawford in order to show how contrived the sublime has become. The wild animals of the area, for instance, are not just tamed: they are dead. The tourist notices a bloody bear paw, a fox's tail, and deer antlers with the same mild regard he held for the stagecoach passengers. Such crude emblems of savagery interest him far less than the "picturesque group" of guests or Ethan Crawford's performance with a huge tin trumpet. The trumpet's echo inspires saccharine fancies of "an airy band . . . hidden on the hill-side," an image worthy of Joseph Rodman Drake's popular poem "The Culprit Fay" (1819). The tourist seems to understand that, in order to satisfy the expectations of sublimity encouraged by cartographers and romantic landscape painters, local innkeepers had to provide the thrills and terrors conventionally associated with a wilderness setting. The description in the sketch undercuts the sublimity of such antics and reveals them for what they are—manipulations of audiences for preconceived, artificial effects.

Once inside the inn, the sketch becomes a veritable genre scene of odd characters gathered around a roaring hearth displaying their characteristic eccentricities and traits. The intrusive paragraph imagining the place in winter, "when every bed has its three occupants, and parlor, bar-room and kitchen are strewn with slumberers around the fire," provides a bracing contrast to the milder evening enjoyed by the late summer visitors and again points to the artificiality of their experience. The tourist cannot stress the sublime because it has disappeared beneath an overlay of commerce and entertainment, two main ingredients of tourism. Hawthorne's visitors to the White Mountains seek comfort and pleasure, not sublime inspiration, and are most content when they feel most at home. They foreshadow the tourists in Bartlett's most famous painting of the region, *Mount Jefferson (from Mount Washington)* (ill. 6), a clear image of tourism predominating over the sublime. Bartlett offers a sublime panorama—vast scenes of distant mountain ranges, dark clouds, and nearby sharp peaks. But, as in the *Notch-House* illustration, the perspective chosen emphasizes persons in-

stead of place. A woman, again an emblem of the domestication of
wild nature, holds a parasol and is so unawed by the scene that she
looks away from it into her lap; one of her male companions reads,
while only the youngest tourist appears to feel any inspiration from
the sight, as he assumes the conventional pose of pointing to the
ostensible topic of the painting, Mount Jefferson. He is present
more to name than to inspire.

In Hawthorne's sketch, a similarly realistic descriptive strategy
may account for the absence of any reference to the Willey House,
even though the tourist-narrator must have walked past it earlier
in the day. Certainly its fame as an icon of sublimity was not yet
exhausted. The view of it in *American Scenery* (ill. 4) stresses such
images of natural destruction as shattered trees, piles of rubble,
and huge looming mountains that block the distant view. By neglecting the Willey House, Hawthorne's tourist avoids these sublime
images, while in the Bartlett engraving, tourism invades the sol-
emnity of the scene, much as it does in Hawthorne's sketch. A large
man reclines against the rocks opposite the blasted tree, while a
man and a woman, undoubtedly tourists, walk toward a man enthusiastically beckoning them to peer into a decrepit barn. The
Willey House itself sits atop a small rise on the left, swathed in light
and appearing, for all the ruggedness of its surroundings, like any
other rural cottage in America. All it lacks is smoke curling from
the chimney to complete its suggestion of domestic serenity. Like
the Notch, the Willey House has become a tourist shrine, a charming and safe place to visit on a sunny afternoon.

Another Bartlett painting, *Mount Washington and the White Hills*
(ill. 7), reveals how far the White Mountains had progressed as a
tourist spa. Analogous to the Cole in its sweeping view of the whole
range, it sharply differs in emphasis. Pastoral iconography fills the
foreground and softens the harshness of the sublime. Even Mount
Washington, the tallest peak, is blunter than in Cole's painting. A
stagecoach rolls across a picturesque wooden bridge, pedestrians
linger at one end of the structure, and a herdsman guides his flock
along the well-defined road that follows a gently curving, embow-
ered stream. Although the peaks themselves are barren, they do

not impend over the travelers as do the mountains in the Cole painting. To Bartlett, the White Mountains are accessible, even inviting. It is, to be sure, a region of great sublimity, but also a place congenial to humanity and its ordinary endeavors. Bartlett's engraving, like Hawthorne's sketch, reveals that popular perceptions of the region were moving into the stage Donald D. Keyes calls "the Jeffersonian picturesque," where "the wilderness and the savagery of nature were replaced by ordered fields and small towns that still preserved the land's beauty."[11] For Hawthorne, sublime iconography would be appropriate only for fiction, as in "The Ambitious Guest," not for the more realistic genre of travel writing.

*

City views presented peculiar problems to the painter. The essence of a city is trade, commerce, and people, not striking landscape features or topography. Honest portrayals of urban scenes thus ran the risk of pictorial uniformity—busy streets filled with wagons, coaches, merchants, and lined with banks, stores, churches. The topographical engravings by John Barber and Henry Howe of three cities Hawthorne visited on his tour—Syracuse, Ogdensburg, and Rochester (ills. 14, 15, 16)—display just such uniformity. Without captions, the viewer might be unable to distinguish the three towns. In order to remain true to the scene yet also individualize it, urban topographers had to exercise their ingenuity. They might focus on a particular historical event, a monument, or a beautiful landscape feature associated with the city. Joshua Shaw, whose *Picturesque Views of American Scenery* (1820) was one of the first American landscape books, characterized the city of Baltimore with an engraving of the spot where General Ross fell during the War of 1812, and portrayed Savannah, Georgia, as it appeared during the great fire of 1820. His depiction of Philadelphia borrows the convention of seascape painters and portrays the city in relation to its water environment, the beautiful Schuylkill River and nearby Wissahiccon Creek.[12]

The cities on Hawthorne's tour presented especially difficult subjects. They were too new to have either history or monuments. Ogdensburg and Rochester existed because of their commercial rather than scenic locations, and thus lacked settings to recommend them to the painter. But, since most of America's growth during the early nineteenth century was along waterways, the new towns did have the advantage of water views, and few urban landscape painters failed to include them whenever they could. In this respect, the towns on the northern tour were fortunate. They were on huge lakes, navigable rivers, or—because they had grown up as portages around rapids or waterfalls—were situated near the new technological wonder, the Erie Canal. Such cities required a contradictory iconography, at once commercial and natural; thus, painters and travel writers balanced images of urban progress with those of landscape beauty in their attempts to portray these new towns accurately. Sometimes, the two blended indistinguishably into a single landscape of great beauty, as at Canandaigua in the northern Finger Lakes district;[13] often, however, the honest observer recorded scenes of conflict between these two antagonistic forces familiar to twentieth-century tourists. The northern tour, because it provided the first standard itinerary for American travelers, became the testing-ground for descriptive strategies to resolve this conflict. And because the problem outran the abilities of observers to solve it, these strategies are all the more evident in both the pictorial record and Hawthorne's verbal imitation of it.

Hawthorne's sketch of Burlington illustrates the conflict well. The title, "The Inland Port," firmly marks the sketch as a waterscape, and the panoramic opening view mirrors the conventional descriptions of the Bay of Naples so popular in eighteenth-century travel books:[14] the lofty outline of the Green Mountains frames a "sandy beach, sweeping beneath a woody bank, around the semi-circular bay of Burlington" (see p. 43). Such beautiful natural scenery harmoniously blends with the emblems of the busy city itself in one of the most picturesque descriptions in the travel sketches: "The painted light-house, on a small green island, the wharves and warehouses, with sloops and schooners moored alongside, or at anchor, or spreading their canvass to the wind, and boats rowing from point to point, reminded me of some fishing town on the sea-coast." By appealing to popular tastes and exhausting the potential of the real scene, the traveler has created a nautical setting hundreds of miles from the ocean. But he is too honest to leave it there. The second paragraph directly undermines the impressions of the first by reminding readers that, in spite of appearances, Burlington is not a seaport. Compared to a coastal town, in fact, Burlington is rather unsavory. The air is still and steamy, and the lake water gives off such a "sickly smell" that "One breeze from the Atlantic, with its briny fragrance, would be worth more to these inland people than all the perfumes of Arabia." Even considered commercially, Burlington appears inferior to coastal cities: the ships look unseaworthy and poorly maintained, and the crews on the docks bear about as much resemblance to genuine "old salts" as does "a lake fish to a Newfoundland cod." As the rest of the sketch indicates, Burlington is best described in terms of its "pleasant mixture of people," the French, British, Scotch, Irish, and Yankees that crowd its busy square. The divided and even contradictory structure of this sketch demonstrates that a single, comprehensive view of Burlington is impossible. The city is at odds with its setting, and has failed to resolve the conflict between nature and commerce.

A similar pattern prevails at Rochester, where civic pride rested on the glory of the Genesee Falls. J. H. Bufford's 1835 lithograph of the falls (ill. 17) portrays them in sublime glory, complete with the conventional onlookers gazing in awe at the vast and turbulent scene. The mists and precipitous viewpoints rival Niagara's, and Bufford's de-emphasis on the factories and mills of the city clearly points to the power of nature over humanity. How different is the anonymous 1838 print of the falls (ill. 18). Although the conventional pair of sublime gazers remains, both they and the falls are diminished in comparison to the huge buildings that line the banks and rise above them. The smoke of manufactories replaces the mists of the river, and the quantity of water tumbling over the rocks is diminished to a comparative trickle. The straight lines and rigid geometrical patterns of industry that Charles Sheeler would celebrate in the twentieth century have begun to challenge the picturesque ruggedness of nature, as pipes and sluices channel and disperse the water into numerous small streams that look more like waste discharge than wild waterfalls. These two illustrations, painted at almost the same time, show warring impulses in the artistic imagination. One artist retains images of natural sublimity, while the other introduces images of commercial power. Both images are true in their portrayal of the transition from wilderness to civilization occurring so rapidly along America's rivers in the first great era of hydropower; but they cannot coexist, as later travel-book engravings of Rochester and the falls reveal. By the time of the massive illustrated travel guide to America's natural wonders, *Picturesque America* (1876), the mills are dilapidated and the falls are literally fragmented: the artist for the Genesee Falls chapter, Harry Fenn, actually divided his illustration of the waterfall into two halves. Meanwhile, the accompanying description says nothing about their beauty, but notes that the upper falls alone "equals forty thousand horsepower."[15] In less than forty years, commerce had triumphed over nature at Genesee Falls.

Hawthorne's sketch mirrors this uneasy transition in urban iconography. Although the traveler compares Genesee Falls to Niagara, he recognizes that technology, with its "canals and mill-dams," has diminished the "unprofitable sublimity of the cascade" (see p. 45). As in the 1838 print, the focus is on the decline of the sublime. The water view, which once established Rochester's claim to natural beauty, is fast disappearing and serving as an emblem more of growing commercialism than of natural beauty. As if structuring his perceptions around this transition, the tourist lifts his eyes from the falls and beholds "the spires, warehouses, and dwellings of Rochester, half a mile distant on both sides of the river, indistinctly cheerful, with the twinkling of many lights amid the fall of evening." One can no longer view the scene through the sublime froth of foaming waters. Rochester must be seen for what it is, a mushrooming city devoted to business, where lottery-offices—"those true temples of Mammon"—claim the attention and pocket books of visitors who once came to see the falls.

Hawthorne's sketch uses the same commercial iconography as Barber and Howe's rigidly geometrical illustration of Buffalo Street (ill. 16). As in other Barber and Howe engravings, little attention is given to nature. Churches, banks, stores, and public buildings (the edifice on the far right is the courthouse) lift their angular lines against a blank sky and an almost treeless avenue. The deep perspective afforded by the converging lines of the street implies the endlessness of human activity. The three different types of large commercial vehicles scattered irregularly across the foreground suggest both the variety and the chaos of city life in what appears to be a nineteenth-century traffic jam. As the organization of Hawthorne's sketch implies, Rochester is no longer a city known for its natural wonders, but for its commercial vigor and diverse populace.

Similarly, other illustrations by Barber and Howe reveal a new iconography of commerce, society, and busy human activity replacing the old iconography of nature. *View of Ogdensburg* (ill. 15) retains the convention of the water view and the gazing spectators, but their attention is directed toward an oversized steamboat churning through the very center of the engraving. If we would know Ogdensburg, the illustration seems to say, we should focus our gaze on the wonders of mechanized lake navigation. Ogdensburg *is* steamboats, buildings, bridges, wharves, and docks. The artists make no attempt to recall a wild natural setting; even the foreground is littered with huge cut blocks of stone, emblems of rapid progress in hewing nature into endlessly replicable geometric forms. *Western view in the central part of Syracuse* (ill. 14) is even more commercially inspired, for the water foreground itself has been rigidified into the straight lines and stone banks of the Erie Canal. Like some incipient Venice of the North, Syracuse is full of motion, with a series of huge canal boats gliding under a bridge which a carriage has just crossed to the left. On the right another carriage moves off the frame in the opposite direction, making the bridge and canal a metaphorical "crossroads" of the old and the new in travel. The pedestrians on either side of the canal further suggest movement within the scene, as they glance at the boats and then continue on their way. Busy, commonplace reality has replaced the sublime moment of static awe. Technological marvels command the attention once given to nature and blend with the daily activities of ordinary people, as the appropriate pictorial mode for depicting the American scene shifts from landscape to genre.

This shift is evident both in William Bartlett's painting of *Utica* (ill. 12) and in Hawthorne's brief description of the same city in "The Canal-Boat." The true center of pictorial interest has shifted from picturesque water views to busy town squares, what Hawthorne's tourist terms "the unquiet heart of an inland city" (see p. 38). Human beings and their daily occupations claim the attention once devoted to landscapes, and cities can be favorably depicted apart from their natural features and topography. Nothing in Bartlett's engraving suggests a distinctive natural setting. The composition carries the eye along streets and toward buildings, free of the associations and forms of nature. Similarly, Hawthorne includes Utica in his sketch precisely because its "hum and bustle of struggling enterprise" dramatically counterpoint the dismal forest scenery along other parts of the Erie Canal. Action has replaced contemplation as a motive for travel, and people now interact with each other rather than with nature. Bartlett paints conversationalists in the center foreground, and a gentleman doffing his top hat to a mother and daughter strolling along the sidewalk; Hawthorne too stresses movement, as his tourist feels "the eager and hurrying spirit of the place, like a stream and eddy whirling us along with it."

In this new iconography of travel, how one arrives at a place is as important as the place itself. After all, the point was to take a steamboat or canal boat trip, not just to visit a particular spot. This is the emphasis, of course, in the sketch "An Ontario Steam-Boat," which opens with the eager anticipation of "opportunities for a varied observation of society" afforded by steamboat travel (see p. 49). For the only time in the travel sketches, location is generalized—somewhere on "wild Ontario," beyond the sight of land, perhaps in Canada, perhaps in the United States, virtually as isolated as if at sea. The narrator even mentions that "a head-wind had compelled us to keep farther seaward," betraying in that last word his sense of dislocation. Like the passengers on Melville's Mississippi River steamboat *Fidèle* in *The Confidence-Man* (1857), Hawthorne's tourist is traveling on a form of modern transportation that has its own customs and social structures. If he comes to understand them, he has fulfilled one of the chief purposes of his voyage. The land-

scape is neutralized by sameness, and exists, like the vague mountain range in Bartlett's *Utica,* only as a backdrop for observing
society. And the focus, as in Barber and Howe's *Ogdensburg,* is on
the steamboat itself, not the surrounding landscape.

*

The most dramatic improvement in transportation in the region
covered by the northern tour was the Erie Canal. It opened up
previously inaccessible areas to commerce and trade, and provided
safe and easy travel to the most sublime wonder on the tour, Niagara
Falls. But the canal was more than a mode of transportation; it was
in itself a tourist attraction. Once again the journey became as much
a part of the tour as the destination. Perhaps the first technological
wonder in the United States, the Erie Canal quickly established an
iconography of bluff-bowed boats, curving towpaths, and steep
locks set against a landscape of small farms and villages. Even before the railroad, the more obtrusive and celebrated "machine in
the garden," the canal juxtaposed technology and nature in a con-
crete manifestation of the Jeffersonian dream and dramatically
foreshadowed the coming greatness of America.

The dominant visual mode of the Erie Canal was pastoral. As
Patricia Anderson has pointed out in her essay on "The Arcadian
or Pastoral State" of the waterway, "the Erie Canal, passing through
farmlands and quaint hamlets like a quiet, silver stream, was easily
assimilated into the American idyll."[16] Agrarian imagery predominates in the earliest attempts to portray the Erie Canal, a series of
aquatints painted by John William Hill around 1829–30. Intended
as a pictorial guide to the canal, something like William Guy Wall's
Hudson River Portfolio (1823–26), the series was never published and
only a few drawings were engraved. Nevertheless, it forms the most
complete record of Erie Canal iconography from the period of
Hawthorne's tour and establishes firmly the pastoral mode that
characterizes canal illustrations. In contrast to the White Mountains, the flat terrain around much of the canal freed the topog-
rapher and artist from the requirements of sublimity. Hill's view of
the Erie Canal (ill. 11) uses a low horizon and a blank sky to empty
the scene of all natural objects except a few smooth, deforested,

rolling hills in the distance. Farmhouses, barns, fences, tilled fields, domestic animals, and the broad sweep of the canal itself fill the busy middle ground. Finding no sure center of interest in the painting, the eye wanders among emblems of agricultural and commercial prosperity that, in their very disarray, imply hasty progress and abundance, two chief American traits. Hill makes no concessions to wildness. Across the entire foreground, where picturesque conventions would demand at least one blasted tree or craggy outcropping of rocks, stretches a spacious and straight farm road bridging the canal. A farmer, perhaps glancing at an unseen canal boat, drives a huge sow and her litter to market, in quiet testimony to the region's commercial wealth. Agrarianism has triumphed over wilderness, leaving a landscape where all is neatly fenced and ordered.

Yet expectations of sublimity remained in those who, like Hawthorne, had seen the White Mountains and were awaiting the vision of Niagara. The writers and painters who introduced tourists to the region recognized that a bland "pastoral sameness," to use Anderson's phrase, might disappoint experienced travelers. Consequently, they supplied the deficiency with words and pictures that focused on the more striking scenes along the canal such as Little Falls, where engineers had constructed a stone aqueduct 744 feet long and 30 feet high to carry boats past the turbulent rapids of the Mohawk. This stark contrast of natural wildness and human artifice, combined with the steep cliffs surrounding the river at this point, moved Gideon Miner Davison to construct one of the most florid rhetorical outbursts in his *Traveller's Guide*:

The view afforded from a packet boat of mountain scenery on either side, with a bare passage for the dashing waters of the Mohawk between, is highly interesting and sublime. Whichever way the eye is turned, it rests on huge masses of granite and limestone, piled in heaps. These rocks in some places rise to a great height, almost perpendicular, presenting a bleak dark surface, unbleached by the thousand storms which have beat upon them; others present a ragged and uneven face, crowned and overhung by dark evergreens, dropping their verdure into the foaming torrent below; the fissures between others of these huge piles produce hickory, maple, and other trees, which hang from them, and with their sombre shadow deepen the gloomy darkness of the rocks from which they spring; whilst the scanty soil upon others gives life and penurious nourishment to dwarf oaks and vegetation peculiar to similar inhospitable regions. In this scene, where the rude but magnificent works of nature are so profusely displayed, the imagination is overpowered, in their sublimity, and the proudest works of man, and man himself, lose their importance. Even the canal, cut upon the mighty and enduring precipice—the road entrenched upon the mountain side, and the substantial locks and gates, all sink into comparative insignificance under the mighty shadows of the everlasting hills.[17]

John William Hill caught something of Davison's mood in *Erie Canal, 1831* (ill. 10), where a steep rocky cliff fills the background, while wild evergreens cling to the sides and huge blocky rocks impend above the boat passing below. Similarly, William Bartlett's painting of Little Falls (ill. 9) displays sufficient tokens of the sublime to suggest how recently part of the canal's path was primitive wilderness. Dark masses of rocks form a Claudian *coulisse* (frame) on either side, and the water rushes impetuously into the foreground between steep, craggy cliffs. Although one large tree stump testifies to engineering might, the abundant vegetation seems bent on reclaiming the scene, or at least blurring sharp lines between civilization and nature. As the letterpress in *American Scenery* states, Little Falls sits "amid some of the most exquisite scenery of the world" and is renowned for combining "the picturesque and the hideous, the wildly beautiful and the merely useful."[18]

Yet both Hill's and Bartlett's engravings finally fail in their efforts to retain the American sublime along the Erie Canal. Hill places busy workmen in top hats in the foreground, implying that nature is little more than a backdrop for technological achievement, the real interest of the scene. Two buildings on the right sit firmly atop the rocky cliff, blending with it yet also literally dominating it. More subtly, Bartlett makes civilization—the churches, homes, and stores of Little Falls, plus a smoking locomotive—the backdrop for the whole scene. Most noticeably, both illustrations include women, sure emblems of domesticity. In Hill's sketch, a woman, perhaps the helmsman's wife, proffers a freshly cooked meal; in Bartlett's drawing, the women wear Victorian dresses and sport fashionable parasols, clearly intent on the pleasures of sightseeing.

This blend of human interest and natural sublimity is evident in Peter Maverick's engraving for *The Northern Traveller* (ill. 8), a tourist guide Hawthorne probably used. While retaining a broad contrast between spacious bright skies and massive dark hills, the painter Henry Inman nevertheless softens his outlines and centers the view on human activity—the canal boat, its six busy passengers, and the horses and riders alongside the canal. The serpentine lines of the towpath on the left and the gratuitous "worm fence" on the right provide order in the wilderness and keep nature within carefully engineered bounds. The two gazers atop the boat seem as much in awe of human achievement as of natural beauty.

Like these three illustrations, Hawthorne's verbal sketch of the canal emphasizes domestic and commercial activity while going even further in excluding sublimity. The narrator makes it plain that the landscape itself is not worth describing: the canal is "an interminable mud-puddle" that "holds its drowsy way through all the dismal swamps and unimpressive scenery, that could be found between the great lakes and the sea-coast" (see p. 36). In order to maintain his interest, therefore, he turns his attention to the boat and its passengers. Of course, Hawthorne's narrative concerns only that part of the canal between Utica and Syracuse, a stretch devoid of the rugged beauty around Little Falls. Nevertheless, it is just such a landscape that encourages the tourist, like the painters Hill and Bartlett, to portray the canal's busy pastoralism. Projecting the spirit of progress into the future, the tourist imagines the day when De Witt Clinton's "wondrous stream may flow between two continuous lines of buildings, through one thronged street, from Buffalo to Albany." This image parallels Bartlett's drawing of idle strollers and parasoled ladies making their way along the aqueduct at Little Falls, and recalls the motifs of progress in the busy workmen of Hill's sketch. Turning to the packet boats themselves, the narrator paints a picture as detailed as anything in the illustrations, describing various kinds of vessels along with their cargoes and their passengers. When his gaze occasionally wanders back to nature, he sees only "dismal black stumps" or decaying trees standing amidst "pools of stagnant water." Truly, nature is not worth describing. The greatest variety and visual interest in the sketch is concentrated in people, boats, and villages: the "little colony of Swiss, on their way to Michigan," the "black and rusty-looking vessel, laden with lumber," the "log-cottage" in the countryside, and the "piles of brick, crowded docks and quays, rich warehouses and a busy population" of Utica.

The most striking and original feature of Hawthorne's sketch is the description of the canal and surrounding forest at night. Although moonlight views of scenery were commonplace, and often recommended to picturesque travelers, very few such romanticized illustrations of the Erie Canal seem to exist. One that does, however, suggests the rightness of Hawthorne's descriptive strategy. John Hill's scene of nighttime traffic on the Erie Canal (ill. 13) has the same ghostlike and dreamy quality that Hawthorne's tourist attributes to the canal at midnight. But Hill draws no ominous moral from the scene, as does Hawthorne's somber tourist: the fenced wood on the right is parklike, not threatening, and the vegetation is vigorous and healthy, not dying and rotten as in Hawthorne's sketch. Characteristically, Hawthorne peers into the darker side of human achievements and finds emblems of death and "moral rottenness" that escape other observers of a similar scene. This difference indicates that the greatest value of "The Canal-Boat" lies in its bold juxtaposition of engineering accomplishment and primitive nighttime fears of mortality, the kind of paradoxical testimony to technological skill so commonplace today.

For Hawthorne, as for most Americans, the real interest of the Erie Canal lay in its social and commercial successes, not in its natural beauty or dim presage of the industrial wasteland. In the middle paragraphs of "The Canal-Boat," the narrator expanded his account of the interior life aboard by describing the guests around the dinner table. This, together with his famous fantasy about the "western lady" disrobing behind the crimson curtain and his derogation of the landscape, suggests that the people rather than the places associated with the Erie Canal endured longest in Hawthorne's imagination.

*

As Elizabeth McKinsey has recently demonstrated, no feature of
the American landscape was better known than Niagara Falls. Beginning around 1800, it was painted, engraved, sketched, and described more frequently than any other American view. Undoubtedly, Hawthorne knew many of these reproductions and their
conventional appropriation of the sublime. As his narrator says
after his first look at the falls, "I had come thither, haunted with a
vision of foam and fury, and dizzy cliffs, and an ocean tumbling
down out of the sky" (see p. 58). These were the exaggerated expectations that had been encouraged ever since Father Louis Hennepin first described the falls in 1697, nearly quadrupling its
height, exaggerating its loudness, and over-emphasizing its violence
and danger.[19]

A painting likely to have satisfied the tourist's imagination is John
Vanderlyn's *Niagara Falls from Table Rock* (ill. 21). As McKinsey says
of this work, "Its purpose is clearly to recreate the overwhelming
impact of the Falls for the viewer. . . . With the picture edge cutting
off the foreground ledge at the right side and along the bottom,
and the Falls flowing off the left edge of the picture, we feel the
prodigious power of the waterfall, uncontainable within the picture
frame."[20] Vanderlyn carefully includes all the icons of sublimity: a
rainbow arches across the left side of the falls, immense clouds scud
across the sky, mist and foam thunder up from the rapids almost
to the height of the falls themselves, Indians gesture in the right
foreground, and Table Rock juts out dangerously over the deepest
and blackest part of the river. This is the Niagara Falls of the romantic imagination, the sublime image that inspired unprecedented tourism.

Of course, Vanderlyn first saw the falls before they had been
developed as a tourist attraction, before construction of the footbridge to Goat Island, the stairway down the cliff on the American
side, and the grand hotels that lined the banks at the time of Hawthorne's visit. Vanderlyn, as his later paintings of the falls show, was
deliberately holding on to "that wilder image" of primordial Niagara in an effort to maintain a sublimity that, as at Genesee Falls,
was gradually diminishing. Some of the difficulties in dating this

particular painting, in fact, stem from Vanderlyn's insistence on painting and repainting the falls as he first saw them in 1801.[21]

Views of Niagara taken closer to the time when Hawthorne visited it introduce icons of civilization that modify and sometimes almost destroy the falls' sublimity. One of the most popular and influential of these prints was William James Bennett's *View of the British Fall Taken From Goat Island* (ill. 19). In sharp contrast to the Vanderlyn painting, the foreground dominates the picture, drawing the eye away from the falls and toward the brightly lighted group of picnickers on the left. The scene resembles a park more than a forest, and the tame goats suggest a fusion of animal and human mirrored in the trim, tame landscape itself. The background is similarly civilized. Instead of rolling waters and vast clouds, Bennett sketches the famous footbridge over the Horseshoe and, jutting out across the high horizon, two of the huge tourist hotels on the Canadian shore. Gone is the frisson of terror implied in Vanderlyn's awe-struck beholders. Here, as McKinsey has noticed, "people are absorbed in themselves, not by the view."[22] As the fashionable attire and disengaged attitude of the figures suggests, the stroll to Goat Island is no more perilous or challenging than a Sunday visit to a city park. These women have somehow crossed the footbridge to Goat Island in long heavy skirts while carrying a parasol and picnic basket.

Similarly, Hall and Mooney's 1844 lithograph of the *Ferry Landing on the American Side* (ill. 22), after a drawing by Bartlett, portrays another "improvement" at the falls that domesticated its primitive fury. The long stairway down the side of the American Falls, first constructed in 1818, made it possible to see Niagara from every angle and conveniently row across to the Canadian side for the dramatic view from Table Rock. The solidly built stairway and sturdy landing offered safe passage across the river, just as the footbridge allowed spectators to peep over the verge of the Horse-shoe. But what is most striking in this print is the focus on the stairway at the expense of the waterfall. Represented by the ethereal mists on the right side, the American Fall is dwarfed by the granite cliff on the left, while the cliff in its turn is subdued by softening vegetation and the ordered geometry of the stairway. The fall is undeniably majestic, but its power is confined to a narrow and controlled space. It barely disturbs the water around the landing, as the calm, mirror-like sheen of the pool on the right indicates. The tourists, like those in Bennett's engraving, remain untouched by the primal elements of water and rock, mist and spray, that comprise the very stuff of the iconic Niagara. They appear as concerned with the mechanics of tourism—climbing the stairway, crossing the river—as with the aesthetics of the sublime experience. Like visitors at a modern amusement park, these people have come for the ride, not the scenery. The stairway, and the implied attitude toward it, parallels other "improvements" at the falls, such as Terrapin Tower (1833) and the Niagara Railroad Suspension Bridge (1855), technological wonders that competed with the falls themselves for attention.[23]

Hawthorne's Niagara sketch combines the sublime iconography of Vanderlyn with the civilizing touches of the Bennett and Bartlett illustrations. One reason for this blend is historical: Hawthorne visited Niagara during that brief period when sufficient improvements had been made for convenient viewing, but before the most intrusive ones, such as Terrapin Tower, had been constructed. Another reason is temperamental: as already noted, the narrator arrives with sublime expectations, even though he is a self-conscious, sophisticated "pilgrim" taking the northern tour. He genuinely hopes to encounter primitive sublimity of the sort depicted by Vanderlyn, even while he knows he cannot achieve it without such artificial aids as footbridges, stairways, and ferries.

Almost by instinct—really, by careful acculturation—the tourist knows that he must free himself from the constraints of the present in order to experience sublimity fully. Thus, when he finally overcomes his apathy and heads toward the footbridge to Goat Island, he stops to purchase a twisted walking stick manufactured by a Tuscarora Indian, an object that literally puts him in touch with ancient culture and guides him away from the tawdry present of trifling souvenirs and daily newspapers. Almost as a consequence, the water below him on the bridge boils and foams like "a river of impetuous snow" imaging all the primal force of the great cascade. And when he sees the American Fall from Goat Island he is properly awestruck at "the vapor that never vanishes, and the Eternal Rainbow of Niagara" (see p. 57), twin icons of sublime infinity. Moving on to Horseshoe Falls, he walks out on the footbridge depicted in Bennett's engraving and minimizes its significance as a human "improvement." Instead of emphasizing its convenience and safety, he notes its fragility and tremulousness, and imagines it hanging "upon the rising mist, as if that were the foundation of the frail structure." Moving on to the stairway depicted in the lithograph after Bartlett, he continues to enforce a sublime reading on these icons of civilization: the stair winds "almost interminably" to the "base of the precipice . . . over slippery stones, and among great fragments of the cliff, to the edge of the cataract, where the wind at once enveloped me in spray." Both the language—"cataract," "precipice," "great fragments"—and the experience itself create a feeling of danger and place the narrator at the mercy of the very elements the tourists in the Bartlett lithograph sought to avoid. Finally, at Table Rock, the perspective from which the most sublime views of Niagara were painted, he feels fulfilled: "Never before," he says, "had my mind been in such perfect unison with the scene." And what has done this? Genuinely courting danger at last, he is sitting on the "utmost verge" with his legs dangling over the edge. The tourist, like a figure in a painting, has had to assume the conventional position of sublime awe before he can feel it.

The Niagara sketch has more complex tonalities and ironies than any other piece in the series. Sublimity is at hand, as the rapturous final description of the American cascade at sunset reveals; yet, as the souvenir stands, the stairways and bridges, and even the Tuscarora walking stick indicate, sublimity is rapidly becoming the handmaiden of commerce. The tourist's dilemma is something like that in George Catlin's *Table Rock from Below* (ill. 20). The falls are vast, rocky, looming, clearly sublime; but their innermost precincts, the dark space behind the great sheet of water itself, can be visited as readily as a park by any tourist who bothers to bring an umbrella. The popular excursion behind the falls necessarily violates their sanctity and diminishes their grandeur by an over-familiarity, a too-near proximity. Although Hawthorne personally took this sidetrip, his tourist avoids it, probably because it smacks too much of that very commercialism he criticizes. Instead of descending himself, the tourist observes from above "two adventurers" who undertake the mock-heroic journey behind the sure steps of their guide. The artifice is apparent even at this height:

The attempt to reach it [Termination Rock], appears both poetical and perilous, to a looker-on, but may be accomplished without much more difficulty or hazard, than in stemming a violent northeaster. In a few moments, forth came the children of the mist. Dripping and breathless, they crept along the base of the cliff, ascended to the guide's cottage, and received, I presume, a certificate of their achievement, with three verses of sublime poetry on the back.

The tourist's irony is unmistakable. Such "adventures" are mere tourist traps, ways to "certify" the experience of the sublime and profit from the exchange.

When Hawthorne revised this sketch in 1837, he added four paragraphs describing Goat Island and the ferry-house. As in the Bennett painting, Niagara Falls recedes into the background while the narrator busies himself sporting with "three lovely girls" in silk gowns on an island that "is no longer a tangled forest, but a grove of stately trees, with grassy intervals about their roots and woodland paths among their trunks." Flirtation replaces meditation in a passage that foreshadows Niagara as a paradise for honeymooners. The ferry-house paragraphs imply an even further loss of sublimity in a candid genre scene of Canadian fishermen bartering their catch for the half-drunk ferryman's whiskey. Like the merry boors in a Dutch tavern scene, they "were loquacious on trifling subjects, and merry at simple jests, with as little regard to the scenery as they could have shown to the flattest part of the Grand Canal." These additions demonstrate how far Niagara Falls had come from the sublime in a few short years, and how difficult it was for Hawthorne—or for anybody—to retain a sublime image in the face of increasing tourism and commercialism.[24]

*

The ruins of Ticonderoga offered the artist a rare opportunity: the chance to sketch a genuine American ruin. As Donald Ringe has noticed in his study of pictorialism in Bryant, Irving, and Cooper, ruins "had become by the early nineteenth century rather conventional elements in Romantic iconography," and all three of these early American writers were fascinated with the moral implications of decayed buildings and structures. But, as Ringe goes on to show, "they were handicapped in their treatment of the theme by the absence of such relics of past grandeur in the American landscape" and consequently employed, with mixed success, various technical stratagems designed to overcome this scenic flaw.[25] It was precisely the lack of ruins that caused many observers to condemn American scenery and prompted Thomas Cole's ingenious defense in his "Essay on American Scenery" (1836). Contrasting the Rhine and the Hudson, Cole concedes that the latter is "not besprinkled with venerated ruins, or the palaces of princes; but there are flourishing towns, and neat villas, and the hand of taste has already been at work. Without any great stretch of the imagination we may anticipate the time when the ample waters shall reflect temple, and tower, and dome, in every variety of picturesqueness and magnificence."[26] Like Cooper before him and N. P. Willis after, Cole encouraged Americans to look to the future, not the past, in their search for human embellishments to the natural landscape.

Had Cole looked back at his 1826 painting of Fort Ticonderoga, he might not have been quite so defensive. For here, early in his career, he had discovered an icon of the American past unrivalled for historic significance and scenic beauty (ill. 25). Just how deliberately Cole sought to heighten the sense of ruin and decay that hovered around the spot can be seen by contrasting his painting with one of the earliest depictions of the fort, Henry Reinagle's *View of the Ruins of Ticonderoga Forts on Lake Champlain* (ill. 23). Although the two views were taken within a span of eight years, they are remarkably different. Reinagle, rooted in a pastoral and topographical tradition, takes a panoramic view of the scene. As if ashamed to admit decay into his sketch, he stresses images of civilization: a rustic yet comfortable log cabin, busy fishermen launching their boat, a white sail in the distance, and, most dramatically, a smoking steamboat churning across the lake. Fort Ticonderoga is represented by a cluster of neat buildings on the distant shore, and only close inspection reveals that they are not villas or mansions but roofless and broken ruins. Cole, on the other hand, observes the fort up close, placing it in the center of his canvas and hallowing it with a stream of light etching its jagged ruin against a rugged landscape. Although the sheep in the foreground suggest a pastoral ambience, the turbulent sky and tangled undergrowth frame the fort above and below with images of wildness. There is no question that these are ruins, shattered, stark, and lonely, seemingly distant from civilization and its modern improvements. Like any good ruin, the old fort seems closer to nature than art as it reverts to the earth and stones from which it was made.

Sharply different though they may be, both illustrations are constructed visions, subject as much to the perceptual predispositions of their makers as to the realistic constraints of the actual scene. The two works reveal the shift toward romantic landscape values that occurred in the United States during the 1820s, and support Ringe's contention that the "ruins of time" theme was also gaining in popularity. But this shift was too modest to permeate the general consciousness at this time. When Theodore Dwight expanded the number of illustrations in the second edition of *The Northern Traveller* (1826), he chose a panoramic view of Ticonderoga to accompany his description (ill. 24). Here, the fort is placed even further in the distance than in the Reinagle sketch so that, in the duodecimo format of Dwight's guide, the old ruins appear as white dots against the distant hills far across the lake. Most visible are the two tourists in the foreground, and next is the predictable sailboat gliding across the middle distance. This engraving stayed in Dwight's guide until the final edition in 1841. A similar engraving by Peter Maverick, based on a sketch by William Guy Wall, appeared in the *Atlantic Souvenir* for 1828, although the obtrusive tourists were wisely removed from the scene. Thus, when Hawthorne visited the site in 1832, he was caught in the shift from topographical to romantic landscape values, a perceptual blend evident in his own description of Fort Ticonderoga.

The sketch opens with the narrator standing on the Vermont shore, the perspective from which the Reinagle, Dwight, and Wall sketches were all made. But the familiar panoramic view disappoints the romantic tourist, and he soon ventures across the lake to take the near view of the fort, the perspective used in Thomas Cole's painting. Although he must first free himself of the dispiritingly scientific guidance of the young West Point engineer, he eventually finds himself left alone to ramble among the old stones and revel in the "roofless barracks . . . now overgrown with grass, nettles, and thistles," the "bars of stanch old oak, which were blackened with fire," and especially the "verdant heap of vegetation" growing over the hearth on the second floor: "I felt that there was no other token of decay so impressive as that bed of weeds in the place of the back-log" (see p. 67). These icons stimulate the narrator to meditate upon the "ruins of time" theme that Ringe traced in Bryant, Irving, and Cooper, and carry his fancy back to the French and Indian War and the Revolution. As if transported from the Ticonderoga of Henry Reinagle to the Ticonderoga of Thomas Cole, the narrator is liberated from the disappointing tameness of the actual scene and can follow his imagination wherever it leads.

The historical reverie is only that, however, a dream, a fancy-work stimulated by solitude and selected images of ruin and decay. That other Ticonderoga, the place of commerce and agriculture, harshly reasserts itself when a bell rings and the tourist jumps up to find that "the steam-boat Franklin" is resuming its "progress northward, to reach Canada the next morning." This proud icon of industry, the steamboat, introduces a final rush of commercial images directly at odds with those within the fort: a sloop follows the steamboat, a skiff crosses the ferry, and a lumber scow spreads its "huge square sail." In a brief sentence that sums up the iconographic reality of Ticonderoga, the narrator observes, or perhaps laments, "The whole country was a cultivated farm." The pastoral imagery only hinted at in Cole's 1826 painting now dominates the scene. Although the narrator had "heard the tinkling of a cow-bell" while sitting within the ruined fort, its faintness symbolized the distance that ruin can place between the pastoral and the wild. Now fully awake to the busy reality around him, the tourist recognizes that Ticonderoga is more like Burlington, the busy "inland port" he had visited earlier, than a romantic English ruin.

The balanced iconography in "Old Ticonderoga," like the iconography in several of Hawthorne's travel sketches, again looks forward to the paintings of William Bartlett as engraved in *American Scenery* (ill. 26). Taking the same near view as Cole, Bartlett portrays just as much ruin and decay as his famous predecessor. He includes sheep grazing on the ruins and, as Hawthorne does, tufts of weeds and grass sprouting from the stones themselves. His treatment of the rocks and foreground is smoother than Cole's, however, and the sunny distant mountains look more like Hawthorne's "long and wooded ridge" than Cole's dark, storm-shrouded peaks. Most important, Bartlett, like Reinagle and Hawthorne, acknowledges the commercial developments on Lake Champlain. The lake is alive with sails, emblems of human activity, and one sloop in the center of the picture is literally framed by the ruins. As suggested earlier, Bartlett and Hawthorne share a similar sensibility when it comes to portraying American scenery, especially in their ability to blend romantic and topographical iconography in unified sketches of considerable power and interest. And once again, that interest shifts from the natural to the human, from the timeless past to the busy present that overwhelms self-absorbed meditation on a scene and compels personal interaction with it.

*

Studying Hawthorne's travel sketches in the context of the iconography of the period demonstrates several important qualities they have that we might otherwise miss. For one thing, it shows how closely the sketches parallel and even prefigure certain artistic trends of the time, as when they mirror the contrast between the landscapes of Thomas Cole and William Bartlett. This approach also demonstrates how fully Hawthorne was in touch with the visual norms of his era, especially those in travel guides and popular engravings. Like a John W. Hill, or a John Barber and Henry Howe,

Hawthorne was aware of the impact of technology upon the land-scape and understood that traditional ways of describing scenery were inadequate to register the changes taking place. In these two ways the travel sketches are important documents testifying to the shift away from the sublime toward more realistic modes of verbal and visual description.

Even more significantly, the iconographic approach reveals the place of the travel sketches in Hawthorne's literary development. In them, Hawthorne the tourist grapples with the problem he later made the theme of his greatest works, such as "Rappaccini's Daughter" and *The Scarlet Letter*: How can one deal with scenes or expe-riences that contradict one's preconceptions and training? Or, more largely, how can one resolve the dichotomy between subjective ex-pectations and apparent reality? Hawthorne's traveler on the north-ern tour came prepared for sublimity; but as the iconographic record shows, he seldom found it. He was too honest to create empty Byronic "rhapsodies" or inflated guidebook descriptions, yet like any tourist he desired and rightfully expected occasional mo-ments of true natural sublimity or beauty. Finding these only rarely, he had to create other means of organizing and recording his impressions. His varied strategies of persona, contrast, hyperbole, irony, and satire offered an imaginative solution to the dilemma. He could at once be a part of the scene and yet removed from it, not only a detached observer, but also a wry critic of observation itself.

Hawthorne realized that, by the 1830s, the sublime was more appropriate as a fictional device—as in "The Ambitious Guest"—than as a descriptive tool, and he either avoided it or undercut it in most of the travel sketches. Furthermore, by admitting icons of commercial, social, and technological progress into his descriptions, he almost entirely eliminated the nostalgia and sentimentality as-sociated with the sketches of his most important American prede-cessor in the genre, Washington Irving. With their candor, realism, and detail, Hawthorne's travel sketches imply greater possibilities for the genre and look forward to the travel books of Mark Twain and others who understood that traveling no more led to truth than did contemplation, and that both outward and inward visions were subject to the distortions and inaccuracies of all human endeavors to reproduce images of an elusive and ever-shifting reality.

HISTORY AND NATIONALISM IN
"OLD TICONDEROGA"
AND OTHER TRAVEL SKETCHES

Dennis Berthold

There seems no question that the primary impulse behind Hawthorne's 1832 tour was visual pleasure. Like the thousands of tourists who had preceded him on the northern tour and the millions who would follow, he wanted to view scenery and enjoy its lights and shades, its variety and immensity, its beauty and sublimity. The prefaces added by Hawthorne's editor, Park Benjamin, to the "Sketches from Memory" that appeared in the *New-England Magazine* in November and December 1835 stress the pictorial quality of the works they introduce and compare them to "the careless drawings of a master-hand, . . . that might be visibly embodied into life-like forms on the canvass" (see p. 35). These descriptions, intended to appeal to the eye, not the mind, are mere "loose sketches" from the portfolio of a casual and wayward youth.

Like the prefaces Hawthorne himself wrote for his later story collections and romances, however, Benjamin's brief paragraphs mislead as much as they introduce. For while the descriptive power and beauty of Hawthorne's travel sketches are undeniable, as in the set-piece "A Night Scene," they evince a subtle political theme that sounds below the shimmering surface and breaks through into overt commentary in "The Inland Port," "Rochester," "The Notch," and "Old Ticonderoga." These sketches demonstrate that no American of the time could view the sights of his native land without feeling pride in his country's past and hope for its future. The American tourist, in fact, was often as interested in defending his native country from the slurs of British travelers as he was in en-

joying and describing its visual beauty.[1] The collections of scenic
views that began appearing in the 1820s included such patriotic
sights as West Point, George Washington's tomb, and Bunker Hill.
In the earliest of these, Joshua Shaw's *Picturesque Views of American
Scenery* (1820), the picturesque traveler Shaw was struck by the combination of visual beauty and historical significance at West Point:

The deep and still water, the lofty cliffs, the black over-arching rocks from
which moss and wild flowers hang pendant like streamers, the white sail
gliding along the surface, and contrasting with the dark stream below it,
and the moral associations of the spot near which some of the most heroic
achievements of the revolutionary war were performed, give great interest
to the scenery of West-Point.[2]

Another early landscape book, William Guy Wall's *Hudson River
Portfolio* (1823–26), explains that the view of West Point from Fishkill "exhibits some of the finest scenery, of the Highlands, combining both beauty and sublimity," while the view from Fort Montgomery combines "historical interest with picturesque beauty."[3]
Wall mentions George Washington and gives the history of General
Henry Clinton, praising both as heroes of the Revolutionary War.
And in *American Scenery* (1840), a lavish tourbook published several
years after "Old Ticonderoga," even Nathaniel Parker Willis, whose
picturesque sensibility was as acute as anyone's, sometimes considered Revolutionary history more compelling than visual interest.
For instance, he found the view from Gowan's Heights, Brooklyn,
striking, but its associations with the Battle of Long Island even
more so, causing him to remark that here "the picturesque interest
of the spot yields to the historic."[4]

  This pattern of commentary suggests that, in the United States,
patriotism might have produced the picturesque tour, instead of
the other way around. Certainly, Americans' impulse to tour their
native country grew in proportion to nationalism, and Hawthorne
was no exception to this general rule. His first projected collection
of tales, after all, was "Seven Tales of My Native Land," a title
which, as Nina Baym has observed, "embodies his wish to write
identifiably American fiction."[5] The prefatory frame narrative of
"The Story Teller," the larger design Hawthorne had in mind for

his travel sketches, echoes this wish: "Thus my air-drawn pictures will be set in frames, perhaps more valuable than the pictures themselves, since they will be embossed with groups of characteristic figures, amid the lake and mountain scenery, the villages and fertile fields, of our native land" (CE, X, 408–9; see also discussion on pages 4–6).

Ostensibly, Hawthorne set out to do what every other popular American writer of the time was doing: develop a national literature.[6] More specifically, by turning to the American landscape, he was simply heeding the advice he had heard in the 1825 graduation address of his Bowdoin College classmate, Henry Wadsworth Longfellow: to aid in the "first beginning of a national literature: a literature associated and linked in with the grand and beautiful scenery of our country."[7] But for Hawthorne, even at this early stage in his career, straightforward patriotic moralizing would prove impossible. He was too sensitive to the ambiguity of human motives and too skeptical of material progress to accede unquestioningly to any popular movement. As is so characteristic of Hawthorne's work, a counter-movement develops in the sketches that implicitly questions emergent American chauvinism and optimism. Because the tourist seeks evidence of a specifically *American* history, he inevitably compares present scenes to past accomplishments and future probabilities. He tries to infer an American character from his current observations of people and landscape. And here the problem emerges. More often than he would prefer, the traveler finds the present unpromising and the past insubstantial. With so little to build on, the future necessarily seems clouded and uncertain. Such thoughts bode ill for the conventional theme of "the rising glory of America" and undermine the cultural aim of portraying the virtues of "our native land." Thus, even while they follow many of the prescribed patterns for evoking nationalistic sentiments, Hawthorne's travel sketches come to question the significance of the American past and the promise of the American present. As they balance criticism with celebration of "our native land," they suggest an ironic opposition between the beauties of the landscape and the realities of history and politics.

By making history and nationalism themes in his travel sketches,

Hawthorne was following the well-worn tracks of earlier picturesque travel writers. Nationalism was among the many reasons for
picturesque travel even in the supposedly purely aesthetic tours of
William Gilpin, the "High Priest of the Picturesque." Around 1760,
the time Gilpin began taking his local tours, most Englishmen still
considered the Grand Tour of Italy and Switzerland essential to
one's education. Young gentlemen and ladies conventionally toured
the distant Alps before they even considered traveling to Scotland
or Wales. Gilpin consciously sought to rectify this situation, a point
many later analysts of literary pictorialism such as Donald A. Ringe
and Blake Nevius have understated.[8] Insisting on the primacy of
sight to the picturesque, they fail to note that anyone reading one
of Gilpin's many *Tours* would learn a good deal about English history, local legends, and popular anecdotes. According to Gilpin's
biographer, William Templeman, early reviewers were as interested
in the "history," incidents, and poetry related in Gilpin's works as
in the landscape description.[9] And most often, Gilpin relates stories
and legends because of their peculiarly *English* quality, thus rein-
forcing visual beauty with patriotic associations. For example, of a
story of Cromwell defeating Basinghouse, Gilpin writes, "This
event, in a picturesque work, is a circumstance worth mentioning."
In giving the "biographical history" of particular trees in *Forest
Scenery,* he justifies felling great oaks for ship timber because "In
this fallen state alone, it is true, the tree becomes the basis of England's glory." And in New Forest on the Isle of Wight, he observes
that "A romantic place seldom wants a romantic story to adorn it."[10]

   In seeking to reconstruct national history, the English traveler
was fortunate in a way the American was not. The English countryside was dotted with provocative ruins, especially castles and abbeys, each one of which had its own story or legend. With rare
humor, Gilpin praises equally Cromwell and Henry the Eighth for
violently transforming medieval abbeys into picturesque ruins, and
stops to note virtually every ruin that crosses his path.[11] The picturesque traveler, for all his sophisticated pictorializing, is not im-
mune to the historical associations of places. Often, in fact, he may
visit a spot *because* it has historic value and enjoy its visual beauty

as a secondary reward. Ideally, the two go together, and satisfy the same taste for discovering moral and visual significance in scenery.

American tourists shared the same nationalistic impulses as Gilpin, as is evident in the many patriotic effusions in travel books of the period. Unfortunately, however, American landscapes offered few reminders of the young nation's brief history. As with American life and culture, the American landscape lacked a past. Even the keenest visual sensibilities required something more than surface interest. Writing in his journal in 1841, Thomas Cole remarked that, "although American scenery was often so fine, we feel the want of associations such as cling to scenes in the old world. Simple nature is not quite sufficient. We want human interest, incident, and action, to render the effect of landscape complete."[12] Irving, a generation earlier, in his preface to *The Sketch Book* (1819), defended the natural beauties of America but was ineluctably drawn to the historical richness of the old world: "No, never need an American look beyond his own country for the sublime and beautiful of natural scenery. But Europe held forth the charms of storied and poetical associations."[13] And as early as 1805 the ardent nationalist Charles Brockden Brown admitted that those accustomed to scenery accompanied by "the architectural monuments of ancient times" often find the face of uncultivated American nature, "which contains no vestige of other times, nothing to hint of battles, sieges, or murder . . . dreary, blank, and insipid."[14] Clearly, mere scene-sketching of the present American landscape, no matter how visually appealing it might be, was by itself insufficient to satisfy the nationalistic urges of the picturesque tourist. In addition to light and shade, roughness and variety, the ideal landscape had to contain some hint of the American past.

Hawthorne, of course, continued this tradition of complaint in the preface to *The Marble Faun* (1860): "No author, without a trial, can conceive of the difficulty of writing a Romance about a country where there is no shadow, no antiquity, no mystery, no picturesque and gloomy wrong. . . . Romance and poetry, like ivy, lichens, and wall-flowers, need Ruin to make them grow" (CE, IV, 3). In his conscious efforts to write about his country in the travel sketches

of 1832, Hawthorne first faced this problem and learned its true
dimensions. By employing various strategies to dramatize the people and scenes of "our native land," he devised that peculiar mix
of past and present characteristic of sketches such as "The Custom-
House," "The Old Manse," and "Main Street." And he may have
learned, through trial and error, the value of history as a resource
for fiction.

At the time of his travels, Hawthorne was searching for fictional
resources beyond those available in New England history. Behind
the 1832 tour itself lay his desire to grapple with and record American realities, to observe and understand the lively American present. Because of the powerful appeal of local values—the attractions
of "our native land"—descriptive sketches of real places had great
appeal, at least to the more patriotic reader.[15] Casual observations
accrue to confirm nationalistic values. This may be why the "Story
Teller" preface suggests that the "frames" to the tales might be
more valuable than the tales themselves. Certainly this descriptive
aim seems fulfilled in those sketches which depict the busy life of
the American boom towns, the "inland port" of Burlington on the
Vermont shore of Lake Champlain and the thriving city of Rochester on the Erie Canal. At Burlington the narrator describes "a
handsome and busy square" filled with the vitality of international
commerce and a stimulating variety of people: "There was a pleasant mixture of people in the square of Burlington, such as cannot
be seen elsewhere, at one view"—British officers, French Canadians, immigrants from Scotland and Ireland, Southern gentlemen,
Green Mountain Boys. The latter, with their aura of patriotism won
during the Revolutionary War, are "true Yankees in aspect, and
looking more superlatively so, by contrast with such a variety of
foreigners" (see p. 45). The variety the picturesque traveler seeks
demonstrates American superiority and reminds the reader of
America's successful revolution against British dominance. The unusual image that precedes this passage similarly reinforces a rather
narrow and unquestioning chauvinism: "British and American coin
are jumbled into the same pocket, the effigies of the king of England being made to kiss those of the goddess of liberty." Although

there is some slight meliorating effect in the sexual union of male and female effigies, the sentence is so constructed that the earthly "king" is forced to kiss the spiritual "goddess," implying the homage of monarchy to republicanism. This image adumbrates Americans' persistent belief that only they enjoy true freedom, while other political systems are necessarily oppressive. No wonder the hardworking and independent-minded Green Mountain Boys are here idealized as "true Yankees."

A similar scene occurs at Rochester, a classic American boom town that epitomizes the rapid pace of development characteristic of the United States:

The town had sprung up like a mushroom, but no presage of decay could be drawn from its hasty growth. Its edifices are of dusky brick, and of stone that will not be grayer in a hundred years than now; its churches are Gothic; it is impossible to look at its worn pavements, and conceive how lately the forest-leaves have been swept away. The most ancient town in Massachusetts appears quite like an affair of yesterday, compared with Rochester. Its attributes of youth are the activity and eager life with which it is redundant. (see p. 46)

Belying its hasty construction, it promises permanence and solidity, and with its "Gothic" church architecture even shares in the aesthetic traditions of Europe. It is as though Americans are creating instant traditions, rooting themselves in the newly turned soil more deeply than the forests they so recently had cleared.

These two scenes at Burlington and Rochester most fully portray the lively nationalism of the present, the bumptious, restless, progressive America that Hawthorne captured in Holgrave in *The House of the Seven Gables*. But as with Holgrave and other representatives of material progress in Hawthorne's fiction, the two city scenes have a darker side that undermines a facile chauvinism and suggests that the present may be less a sign of a proud past than a bleak future. The point is muted at Burlington by the structure of the sketch, where the description concludes with the positive image of the Green Mountain Boys. In the paragraph preceding, however, a long description of Irish immigrants suggests that the "charac-

teristic figures" of the American scene are changing, and not to the
good. The Irish at Burlington "swarm in huts and mean dwellings
near the lake, lounge about the wharves, and elbow the native citizens entirely out of competition in their own line." The chauvinistic
prejudice here is familiar. If immigrants are allowed to enter a
country unchecked, they will take over jobs held by natives. In this
case, the rude Irish will displace the "true Yankees." Furthermore,
as the tourist's syntactic opposition of "Irish" to "native citizens"
shows, only some residents in the United States share in the culture
and aspirations of "our native land."[16]

The skeptical note sounded at Burlington rings more loudly at
Rochester, where the final paragraph relates just how deep the inroads of immigrants into the American character have been. Every-
one at Rochester is energetically and productively occupied except
one group, "a party of drunken recruits for the western military
posts, principally Irish and Scotch, though they wore uncle Sam's
gray jacket and trowsers." The implication is clear. These louts do
not deserve to wear the garb of the United States military, and by
their behavior (and, probably, their ethnic origins) they dishonor
the uniform. In sharp contrast the narrator notices "one other idle
man. He carried a rifle on his shoulder and a powder-horn across
his breast, and appeared to stare about him with confused wonder,
as if, while he was listening to the wind among the forest boughs,
the hum and bustle of an instantaneous city had surrounded him."
Like the "true Yankees" who work hard and long, the stereotypical
American woodsman—a figure almost as pathetic as the Natty
Bumppo of James Fenimore Cooper's *The Pioneers* (1823)—is being
displaced by lesser men. The drunken recruits are headed west to
carry with them the dubious virtue of "instantaneous" cities, while
the woodsman, by staying in place, finds only confusion and isolation. The moving frontier has passed him by, and it seems unlikely
he will ever recapture it.

Hawthorne's tourist, in search of both the picturesque and the
nationalistic, faces a dilemma. Present realities undermine past accomplishments and deny future hopes. The American scene, just
as many British travelers have maintained, is a cultural wasteland

headed toward social and political chaos.[17] To some extent, the dilemma exists in the eye of the beholder, in the ugly strains of bigotry and elitism evident in the traveler's observations. As Hawthorne himself observed to Longfellow in an 1855 letter from England, "our country looks very disagreeable and uncomfortable, morally, socially, and climatically, from this side of the water, and I have many qualms at the idea of spending the residue of my days there. I *love* America, but do not *like* it" (CE, XVII, 406). In a more immediate and practical way, the traveler in these sketches shares this attitude. He wants to immerse himself in the life of the new country he loves, but much of that new life is unsavory and unpromising. He wants to celebrate the virtues of his "native land," but is uncertain about what is "native" and what is "foreign," and perhaps even about what constitutes "virtue." It is the same dilemma the traveler faced in "The Canal-Boat," when he discovered the high price of progress in the destruction of the forests and decided that an old-fashioned pedestrian tour to Syracuse might better suit him than a modern canal ride. Canal boat travelers are, compared to nature, "a vulgar and worldly throng" (see p. 42) and no more deserve to share in her secrets than the Irish or Scotch deserve to be in the United States Army.

One resolution to this dilemma is suggested at the end of "An Ontario Steam-Boat," the sketch most concerned with social divisions. Perhaps, the final paragraph states, "the stock of home-bred virtue is large enough to absorb and neutralize so much of foreign vice" that only the most depraved of immigrants will fail to "promote the welfare of the country that receives them to its bosom." But this sentiment hardly overrides the negative impression made by the forward passengers on the steamboat, described as "scum" morally damaged by the emigration journey itself. It is the thinnest of sops to American optimism, and fails utterly to outweigh the picture of poverty and hopelessness painted on the forward deck itself. Hawthorne may have included this facile moral precisely to show its ineffectuality, although whether he did or not is beside the point here. What matters is that the picturesque traveler in America has difficulty fulfilling the objective of nationalism. Steamboat travel on Lake Ontario, for example, does more to confuse than clarify the issue of national identity. The traveler considers himself "on the Canadian lakes," but the southern half of Lake Ontario, the likely location of a steamboat sailing from Ogdensburg to Rochester or any other American port, is well within the borders of the United States. The inherent indeterminacy of a water boundary makes the traveler uncertain of his political location and further sharpens his sense of national differences. Thus, when he observes a Canadian family on board, he feels both kinship and alienation:

There was good company, assuredly;—among others, a Canadian judge, with his two daughters, whose stately beauty and bright complexions made me proud to feel that they were my countrywomen; though I doubt whether these lovely girls would have acknowledged that their country was the same as mine. The inhabitants of the British provinces have not yet acquired the sentiment of brotherhood or sisterhood, towards their neighbours of the States.

National identity, so important to the traveler, here isolates him from the very people he would befriend. Observations such as these mitigate against the nationalism he seeks and make his task of praising his native land more difficult than if he had stayed at home.

If this was a personal struggle for Hawthorne in 1832, as it may have been, he was experimenting with ways to resolve it. He was learning both the necessity and difficulty of adding to the American scene that one ingredient it lacked: the past.[18] Other American writers had satisfied this need by exploiting Indian legends, and in "Our Evening Party among the Mountains" the narrator flirts with this popular solution by alluding to several Indian myths about the White Mountains, particularly the "poetical" legend of the "Great Carbuncle." Hearing these tales, however, only reveals their irrelevance to present-day Americans, those "pale-faces" (the narrator says somewhat mockingly) whose customs and beliefs are too different to sympathize with ancient Indian stories. There seems more than a hint of satire in Hawthorne's well-known abjuration of this conventional topic, "I do abhor an Indian story." Indian stories are too remote from present realities and sympathies. By romanticizing the past they distance it rather than bringing it closer, and thus counteract the traveler's—and the cultured American's—chief aim. Yet only by moving away from the present, with its morally ambiguous mix of material progress and social change, could the American writer discover unequivocal emblems of national pride and virtue. If both present realities and the popular conventions of Indian lore failed to provide adequate stimuli to patriotism, perhaps more recent deeds of a specifically American past would suffice.

The most visible emblems of national history were contained in the landscape itself. Longfellow's youthful advice to create American literature from American scenery echoed the larger cultural belief, expressed concisely in 1852 by E. L. Magoon, that "Grand natural scenery tends permanently to affect the character of those cradled in its bosom, is the nursery of patriotism the most firm and eloquence the most thrilling."[19] One of Hawthorne's fellow Brook Farm communitarians, Warren Burton, agreed in his 1844 textbook on the picturesque that "No scenery probably tends more to awaken and ennoble the sentiment of patriotism than mountains."[20] The example of Switzerland, where Alpine heights guaranteed spiritual and political freedom, justified this conventional link between mountains and liberty, a connection evident as recently as T. S. Eliot's *The Waste Land* (1922): "In the mountains, there you feel free."[21] Americans found their own version of Alpine sublimity in the White Mountains, the only really tall peaks east of the Mississippi. Travel writers such as Theodore Dwight noted the similarity between the Alps and the White Mountains, and over the years the area became known as "The Switzerland of the United States."[22] Thus, to visit the White Mountains was to visit a landscape symbolizing the American virtues of freedom and independence.

Significantly, it is at the Notch that Hawthorne's traveler makes his first overt appeal to nationalistic sentiments, when he praises the sublimity of Mount Washington in language that echoes popular formulations:

Let us forget the other names of American statesmen, that have been stamped upon these hills, but still call the loftiest—WASHINGTON. Mountains are Earth's undecaying monuments. They must stand while she endures, and never should be consecrated to the mere great men of their own age and country, but to the mighty ones alone, whose glory is universal, and whom all time will render illustrious. (see p. 29)

This sentiment, found in less inflated form in such travel books as Theodore Dwight's *Sketches of Scenery and Manners in the United States*, fuses history with landscape and provides a natural symbolism for nationalistic pride.[23] It comes closer to following the patriotic formulas of William Gilpin than anything in the travel sketches. Perhaps Warren Burton had Hawthorne's sketch in mind when he enthusiastically praised the view from the top of Mount Washington for its noble blend of "Patriotism and Piety in a momentary perfection."[24]

Unfortunately, the traveler finds few landscapes on the northern tour that inspire such nationalistic effusions. Once beyond the famous Presidential Range, profound historical associations diminish in the face of the absurdities of the present. The famous falls of the Genesee at Rochester bring on thoughts not of figures in American history, but of the antics of Sam Patch, the daredevil who won fame by leaping from waterfalls until he finally drowned at the Genesee Falls in 1829. While the narrator admits that the "legend" of Sam Patch constitutes his "chief interest" at the falls, he is obviously uncomfortable with this preference. He introduces his musings on Sam Patch as a confession, and concludes by praising him as the most successful among those mad fools "who throw away life, or misspend it in pursuit of empty fame." Sam Patch's fame is "invaluable," the narrator contends—except in comparison to those who quietly perform "virtuous and useful deeds." The irony behind such praise is confirmed when the traveler concludes his reverie with some self-analysis: "Thus musing, wise in theory, but practically as great a fool as Sam, I lifted my eyes and beheld the spires, warehouses, and dwellings of Rochester" (see p. 46).

The "legendary" Sam Patch is analogous to the Irish and Scotch recruits who now populate Uncle Sam's army. He is no more an adequate subject for legend than they are replacements for the hardy woodsman. Both signal a decline in native virtue and prowess, a decline sadly symbolized by the diminution of the Genesee Falls themselves. As the traveler notices at the beginning of the sketch, so much water has been used for canals and mill-dams that the falls may no longer be termed "grand." Commerce has displaced natural beauty as businessmen have "abstracted a part of the unprofitable sublimity of the cascade" and left the falls with a "diminished pomp." Even landscape has diminished under the hand of present realities, leaving an emotional vacuum that the legend-seeking traveler fills with the shallow deeds of a profit-seeking showman. Compared to the effusion over George Washington at the White Mountains, the historical reverie at Rochester signals a sense of national decline.

Perhaps the greatest disappointment is at Niagara Falls. Theoretically, it should be the perfect image of America—an "icon of the American sublime," as Elizabeth McKinsey has called it.[25] For Hawthorne's sensitive tourist, however, Niagara offers little food for nationalistic thought and, on reflection, like other landscapes does as much to undermine American nationalism as support it. For one thing, there is no memorable connection between Niagara Falls and American history. The most famous American military exploit in the vicinity—the battle of Lundy's Lane during the War of 1812— ended in a draw, hardly the stuff to inspire patriotic zeal.[26] Moreover, the battle took place in Canada, just across the Niagara River, and left no permanent scars to stimulate association. Even more damaging to national pride is the seldom-mentioned fact that the most scenic section of the falls, the famous "Horseshoe," is not even in the United States. Hawthorne's tourist follows the usual practice of the guidebooks and avoids mentioning this unpleasant reality or using the terms "Canadian Falls" or "British Falls," the alternate names for the Horseshoe. (Compare the English artist William Bennett's title for ill. 19.) And he patriotically frames his sketch with descriptions of the American cascade, the first and last part of the falls he observes. Nevertheless, geographical and political reality make it difficult to link American values with this most sublime of

American landscapes.[27] This problem is epitomized when the tourist observes another "native American" laboring to harmonize his view of the falls with the description in "captain Hall's tour." Such efforts frustrate the nationalistic aim of the northern tour. Instead of viewing them afresh, the Anglophiliac tourist forces Niagara Falls into the perceptual framework of the acerbic British critic of American society, Basil Hall.[28] Picturesque travel can lead to sentiments decidedly unflattering to native values and can even dull native capacity for independent perceptions and feelings. Predictably, the final lush description of the American Falls emphasizes pictorial qualities, while the nationalistic urge remains unsatisfied.

By the climax of the tour at Niagara, then, Hawthorne's tourist has failed to realize the nationalistic aims of the picturesque traveler. Neither the transient social scene nor the eternal landscape contain sufficient associations to stimulate nationalistic feeling and pride. Both, in fact, lead to sentiments opposed to nationalism, and thus frustrate the traveler's attempts to celebrate American character and scenery. But one scenic spot on the northern tour remains: Fort Ticonderoga. Here, if nowhere else, the American traveler should be able to connect himself with the American past and find materials for conveying that intimacy to a wider audience. This sketch offers both the greatest hope for a national literature and reveals most complexly the problems American writers faced.

"Old Ticonderoga" combines picturesque viewing with intellectual reminiscence to give historical and, specifically, nationalistic depth to the travel sketch. More than a commemorative name bestowed on a mountain, as at Mount Washington, Fort Ticonderoga fuses American energy and experience with the landscape itself. Popularly termed "the key to a continent," it was built by the French in 1755 to control the inland waterway from the St. Lawrence through Lake Champlain and Lake George to the Hudson.[29] Its importance was underscored when, almost as soon as it was completed in 1758, the British under General James Abercrombie launched a massive attack against it. Though repulsed by Montcalm, the British attacked again the following year and, under Lord Jeffrey Amherst, captured the fort for the crown. Ticonderoga's importance to the colonies was demonstrated in 1775 when Ethan Allen and his irregulars, the Green Mountain Boys—those "true Yankees" Hawthorne's tourist praised at Burlington—took the fort from the British in the first colonial offensive of the Revolutionary War. Recaptured by the British in 1777 and abandoned by them at the end of the war, the fort had over the years become that rarest of monuments, a genuine American ruin. At least as early as 1817, a traveler reporting his "Pedestrian Tour" in the *North-American Review* considered "Ticonderoga, where there are some remains of stone barracks and forts, quite picturesque," and articles on the fort, accompanied by Henry Reinagle's woodcut engraving (ill. 23), appeared in both the *Analectic* and the *Port Folio* for 1818.[30] In 1826, Theodore Dwight selected Ticonderoga for one of the nine illustrations in the second edition of *The Northern Traveller,* and in 1833 Gideon Miner Davison followed suit in the *Traveller's Guide.*[31] When Hawthorne made his journey, Ticonderoga was considered a standard stopover on the northern tour, for it combined natural beauty with historic interest in a way neither Genesee nor Niagara Falls could rival. Here, as nowhere else on the trip, one might supply "the want of associations" decried by Cole and find hints of the "battles, sieges, or murder" desired by Brown.

By focusing on Ticonderoga and making of it the most unified of his travel sketches, Hawthorne attempted to resolve the dilemma of landscape and nationalism in a fresh and realistic way. Other writers, notably James Fenimore Cooper, had tried to invest the American scene with ruins. Blake Nevius has pointed out Cooper's debt to this convention in *The Wept of Wish-Ton-Wish* (1829) and *The Deerslayer* (1841). Nevius finds such features as Mark Heathcote's blockhouse or Tom Hutter's "Muskrat Castle" "the native equivalent of those innumerable abbeys, castles, and ruined strongholds in Cooper's European romances, and they possess, in the later fiction, some of the associative value of their counterparts."[32] But neither the blockhouse nor Hutter's wooden castle satisfies the urge for an American past. Unlike European ruins, or the American ruin of Fort Ticonderoga, they are fictional. As such, they cannot evoke the actual past so important to the picturesque traveler, nor

can they contribute meaningfully to national pride. Cooper's picturesque imagery is more aesthetic than associational, and main-
tains that disjunction between spectator and object that blunts
emotional involvement and discourages psychological reverie. Nor
is Ticonderoga merely an American Tintern Abbey. Its associations
are not personal, but national. The reveries it inspires are, like the
place itself, public domain. Ticonderoga offers the sensitive American tourist much more than private visual pleasure. By connecting
him with his nation's past, it places his scenic aestheticism in the
service of national ideals and aspirations.

The initial motive for visiting the old fort, like the initial motive
for the whole tour, remains pictorial. The opening paragraphs indicate that Ticonderoga is in "a pleasant and lively spot" easily
accessible to travelers returning from Niagara. As at Burlington
and Rochester, the narrator "delighted in it, among other reasons,
on account of the continual succession of travellers, who spent an
idle quarter of an hour in waiting for the ferry-boat." Because of
its gently rolling topography, however, the natural scenery around
Ticonderoga fails to satisfy the tourist's discriminating vision. Most
notably, the "celebrated heights" of Mounts Defiance and Independence fall short of their lofty names—they are little more than tame
wooded ridges overlooking Lake Champlain. Yet the traveler's
knowledge of these hills and their reputations shows that his true
interest in the spot is historic. As he says, "the greatest attraction,
in this vicinity, is the famous old fortress of Ticonderoga; the remains of which are visible from the piazza of the tavern, on a swell
of land that shuts in the prospect of the lake." The ruins themselves,
not the "prospect," compel attention: "In truth, the whole scene,
except the interior of the fortress, disappointed me." At Ticonderoga, it seems, Willis's formula applies: "the picturesque interest of
the spot yields to the historic."

Even before he enters the fort, Hawthorne's tourist displays a fair
command of the fort's history. He knows that the earlier (and more
appropriate) name of Mount Defiance was Sugar Hill, and that the
height played a key role in the British recapture of the fort from
the Americans. Atop the hill the British forces under General John

Burgoyne placed cannons aimed straight at the fort's heart, forcing the Americans to evacuate under cover of darkness without a fight. The tourist wonders why the American commander, General Arthur St. Clair, failed to fortify Mount Defiance and concludes, rightly, that he simply lacked the manpower.[33] He also knows about the French origins of the fort and something about the military strategy behind its location, for he finds it "singular that the French never fortified this height, standing, as it does, in the quarter whence they must have looked for the advance of a British army." The traveler has arrived prepared with the historical knowledge necessary to appreciate fully one of the most scenic military sites in his young country.

When the tourist enters the ruins themselves, he gains another kind of knowledge under the "scientific guidance of a young lieutenant of engineers, recently from West Point." The predictable clash between the utilitarian and the romantic results, the kind of conflict Twain would use with such effect in *Innocents Abroad*. The young lieutenant's talk of "ravelins, counterscarps, angles, and covered ways" ignores the manifold historic associations of the spot, the "poetry that has clustered round its decay." Where the young lieutenant sees "straight lines and zigzags" and "oblong squares of masonry," the tourist sees confusion, disorder, and irregularity, as the picturesque eye confronts the engineering eye. The lieutenant, like the "wretches devoid of poetry" that the tourist observed at Niagara Falls, fails to see the "ancient strength" symbolized in the fallen walls and barracks that surround him. To him Ticonderoga is "an affair of brick and mortar and hewn stone, arranged on certain regular principles, having a good deal to do with mathematics but nothing at all with poetry."

A second visit frees the tourist's impulses for historical speculation by offering him solitude, a chief requirement of the picturesque traveler. Only when the tourist is free from the young lieutenant's geometric analyses of the site, when he is alone in one of the "roofless barracks," can the scene work its magic on his fertile fancy. He reminds himself that "these are old French structures," lending a foreign exoticism to his sentiments. He then notices the accoutrements of picturesque ruin: old oak beams "blackened with fire," "gray" stones, "peaked gables," and "roofless walls," all over-grown with weeds and flowers. The key image that shows how na-ture has reclaimed this American ruin is the "verdant heap of vegetation" that covers the hearth on the second floor, a hearth that had "often puffed the smoke over a circle of French and English soldiers. I felt," continues the narrator, "that there was no other token of decay so impressive as that bed of weeds in the place of the back-log."

Moved by this symbol of the past, the narrator shifts from visual to intellectual reflection, as though prompted by Theodore Dwight's observation that "the stillness which usually pervades the place, combined with the idea of seclusion and loneliness produced by the surrounding mountains, naturally disposes the mind to a kind of romantic musing, which awakens at once the excitement, and the ardour of battle."[34] The narrator launches into a reverie that chro-nologically recounts the history of the fort in a catalogue of striking American emblems. First, he imagines a "painted and feather-crested" Indian chief gliding over the lake in his birchbark canoe. Then he envisions the French in their "castle in the wilderness," complete with chevaliers, "merry soldiers," "swart savage maids," "a keg of the fire-water," and a Jesuit preaching "the faith of high cathedrals beneath a canopy of forest boughs." He hints at his na-tionalistic feelings by imagining that "a war-party of French and Indians were issuing from the gate to lay waste some village of New England." He imagines "Abercrombie's disastrous repulse, where thousands of lives were utterly thrown away," a remark that agrees with military historians' opinion of the first English assault on the fort. Next he paints a scene depicting Lord Jeffrey Amherst's cel-ebration after taking the fort for the British and imagines the "im-mense fire" blazing on the hearth, the vivid hues of "scarlet coats," and the thundering music that accompanies the festivities. Finally, he recounts Ethan Allen's bold victory and Burgoyne's futile re-capture of the fort. The narrator, seeking the picturesqueness of the past itself, takes American history back beyond the Revolution and endows it with a vitality few observers—certainly not the lieutenant of engineers, and probably few ordinary tourists—recognize.

With his historical reverie completed, the tourist hastens to continue his journey back to New England. But the old fort has altered his attitude toward the landscape. He now sees that the wider prospect is not just tame; it is, like Burlington and Rochester, commercialized. A lumber-boat and several small sailboats busily move across the lake, and William Pell's "neat villa" lies within musket-shot of the old ramparts, showing that the "spot for which France, England, and America have so often struggled" is now a wealthy businessman's pleasure-ground. The once wild site of bloody battles symbolizing "ancient strength" has been pastoralized into "a cultivated farm."

Many tourists might delight in such symbols of progress. This response was commonplace in the tourist guides, where authors conventionally rhapsodized over farms springing up in the very tracks of the Indian. But Hawthorne's tourist has seen too much of American progress at Burlington and Rochester. Too patriotic to condemn outright present-day commercialism, he nevertheless suggests his disappointment in the last three sentences of the sketch: "How forcibly the lapse of time and change of circumstances came home to my apprehension! Banner would never wave again, nor cannon roar, nor blood be shed, nor trumpet stir up a soldier's heart, in this old fort of Ticonderoga. Tall trees had grown upon its ramparts, since the last garrison marched out, to return no more, or only at some dreamer's summons, gliding from the twilight past to vanish among realities." Like the young lieutenant's mathematical analysis of the fort's structure, American progress obscures historical significance and relegates it to the status of dream. Past and present cannot coexist in this emergent native land. So great is American energy, so all-encompassing American materialism, mere historical thought and association must "vanish" before them, and the traveler, originally a sharp-eyed observer who aimed at recording "characteristic figures" of the American scene, now sees himself as a dreamer, a person out of touch with the present. The reverie at Ticonderoga has proved as insubstantial as other attempts at reaching the American past, and sure grounds for national pride remain distant.

Later events at Ticonderoga would support the traveler's sense that American history was slipping away before his eyes. William Pell, the owner of the ruins and much of the land around them, eventually lost interest in the site and in 1839 leased his summer-house as a hotel. The fort itself continued to crumble into non-existence. Fort Ticonderoga may have been one of the historic sites in Susan Cooper's mind when, twenty years later, she complained "there is no blending of the old and the new in this country; there is nothing old among us. If we were endowed with ruins we should not preserve them; they would be pulled down to make way for some novelty."[35] Not until 1909, when Pell's great-grandson Stephen Pell began restoration, was there any significant interest shown in preserving the site. By then, so little remained of the original structure that, as Susan Cooper had predicted, a "novelty" was erected: a facsimile of the original fort. Grateful as Americans should be for any monument memorializing the exploits of the Revolutionary War, a reproduction fails to blend the imagination of the present with the facts of the past. It is more a creature of progress than history, and erases historical truth even while seeking to commemorate it. The restored fortress of Ticonderoga reveals how much truth there is in Susan Cooper's observations and Hawthorne's unsettling conclusion. In America the past does indeed "vanish among realities."

Nevertheless, the American past could, with some imaginative effort, be recaptured. Even Thomas Cole, who emphasized the natural rather than the historical appeal of American scenery, admitted as much. In an essay published just one month before "Old Ticonderoga" in the same periodical, he concluded, "Yet American scenes are not destitute of historical and legendary associations—the great struggle for freedom has sanctified many a spot, and many a mountain, stream, and rock has its legend, worthy of a poet's pen or the painter's pencil."[36] As if in response, Hawthorne's sketch outlines a process of historical recollection and vivification that could be replicated by any dedicated and knowledgeable pic-

turesque tourist in search of his country's past. The first requirement is a knowledge of American history, including such details as
military strategy and memorable quotations. The second is a genuine historic locale with tokens of past human endeavor. A ruin, of
course, is perfect. The third requirement is solitude, which encourages meditation and quiet reflection. When combined with the
discerning eye of the picturesque traveler, mind and scene could
interact to produce the desired ideals—in this case, national history.

This is not to say that "Old Ticonderoga" is somehow more truth-
ful than the other sketches. On the contrary, the tourist omits all
mention of Benedict Arnold's role in capturing the fort from the
British, patriotically following the practice of other American com-
mentators on the event.[37] But as a sketch that overcomes present
realities to compel historical interest, "Old Ticonderoga" displays
considerable artistry and suggests that what the American landscape lacks—or what American progress is destroying—American
writers can supply. The literary artist, by turning to the past, can
endow his country with historical significance through the power
of his rhetoric and imagination. Properly used, tourism and travel
could provide American authors with a valuable resource for creating a vivid, striking, yet still historically significant national literature, even if that literature were less than enthusiastic about the
country's future. This is a process Hawthorne would undertake
again and again in his writing. As he wrote in the preface to *The
House of the Seven Gables,* an author, by connecting "a by-gone time
with the very Present that is flitting away from us," creates a "legendary mist" that can "float almost imperceptibly about the characters and events, for the sake of a picturesque effect" (CE, II, 2).
The process is mutual, like background music in a film, where
sound and sight corroborate each other and blend to create one
dominant mood. Visual beauty commands our initial attention, and
historical associations give lasting significance to our feelings.

Of course, America could never hope to have a past as rich as
Europe's. But too much historic interest, as Hawthorne discovered
during his six years in Europe, could suffocate the imagination.
The American scene, especially as Hawthorne saw it on his pictur-

esque tour in 1832, suggested the need for Americans to develop a sense of the past along with a proud sense of nationalism, without stifling either in a rigid adherence to historical patterns. It may be that this suggestion, early developed in "Old Ticonderoga," led Hawthorne to renew his interest in the rich vein of New England history he was to mine in the greatest works of his career.

HAWTHORNE'S IRONIC TRAVELER AND THE PICTURESQUE TOUR

Beth L. Lueck

Nathaniel Hawthorne's travel sketches from the 1832 tour of New England and western New York take his narrator on a trip that follows a typical route of the northern tour. In these sketches the many references to tourism and tourists, and the numerous allusions to tourist guides, attest to the author's knowledge of the customs and conventions of contemporary travel. Both from Hawthorne's description of his intended travels and from Park Benjamin's later editorial comments on the tour, it is clear that the format for the original trip was specifically modeled on the picturesque tour, a popular pastime of the period for travelers in America and abroad. In Hawthorne's 28 June 1832 letter to Franklin Pierce, he mentioned his plan for collecting materials during his travels for a proposed book, which would become the framed story-cycle called "The Story Teller" (CE, XV, 224). Later Park Benjamin, the editor to whom Hawthorne had submitted his work for publication, described the first published travel sketches, which appeared in the *New-England Magazine* in 1835, as sketches from the "portfolio of a friend, who traveled on foot in search of the picturesque over New-England and New-York" (see p. 27). Benjamin's comment astutely pinpoints both the motive behind the sketches and their format: the picturesque tour.

Yet allusions to tours and guidebooks in both these sketches and other works drawn from the author's travels in the summer of 1832 do not simply reinforce the idea that the picturesque tour was popular at this time and that tourists were frequently encountered at various stops on the northern tour. Rather, these references serve as an ironic counterpoint in the sketches—and in "The Story

Teller"—to the narrator's own increasing experience with the
world, its people, and their foibles. As the narrator moves from
innocence to experience, and as he changes from a naive and often
imitative tourist to an increasingly complex and ironic observer of
society, such references serve as more than the simple satires of
picturesque tourists and their excesses that they are in "The Notch
of the White Mountains" or even in "Our Evening Party among the
Mountains." Instead, in sketches such as "The Canal-Boat" and "My
Visit to Niagara," he develops an aesthetic distance from the su-
perficial responses to historical sites, natural landmarks, and technological innovations in the guidebooks of the day. While sometimes
such comments result in merely amusing commentary on the foibles
of human nature as evinced in the picturesque tourist, elsewhere
Hawthorne's judgment on this phenomenon is more pointed and
more meaningful for the work as a whole, as in the sketch on Niagara Falls. Here he effectively contrasts the narrator's experience
at the famous falls with the limited, imitative experiences of other
tourists. The narrator's increasing distance from the others suggests
not only his growing understanding of the meaning of the falls, but
also his increasing maturity, aesthetically and artistically. For in this
sketch he neatly presents and deftly solves both the problem of how
to "read" such a masterwork of the American sublime in a fresh,
original way and how to arrange his perceptions into a form com-
prehensible by the reader. Herein lie both the beauty and the value
of the sketch, and its extraordinary complexity.

Transforming the experience of his tour into literature, however,
called on Hawthorne's familiarity with the conventions of the picturesque tour, a popular type of travel that dated back to the 1790s.
The picturesque tour, which had become enormously popular in
the United States by the 1820s and 1830s, originated in England.
As formulated by William Gilpin, an English clergyman, traveler,
and writer, it was a tour in search of picturesque beauty, or that
kind of landscape beauty which would be suitable in a picture.
Picturesque travelers searched for landscapes that featured contrasts in light and shadow; rough textures; compositional unity; and
historical, legendary, or other associations. The pleasures of the

tour centered on the anticipation and discovery of picturesque beauty, and the later recollection of the scenery by sketching or writing about it. Travel books often combined observations about scenery with reflections about its effect on the writer.[1] In addition, published tours such as Gilpin's often included historical anecdotes, local legends, and accounts of colorful personalities encountered on the tour, all of which contributed to the associations that were necessary for true picturesque beauty in a landscape.[2] By the second decade of the nineteenth century this mode of travel and the picturesque perspective on landscape were both familiar to and popular with educated men and women, whether middle class or upper class, in Great Britain and America.[3] The trend took hold more slowly in the United States, for a nation had to be built, leisure time had to become available, and transportation innovations had to take place before picturesque travel could become a fashionable pastime.

Hawthorne put his knowledge of the picturesque tour and its unique perspective on landscape to work in several of his sketches drawn from the 1832 tour. "The Notch of the White Mountains" and "Our Evening Party among the Mountains" serve as a conventional opening for a picturesque tour, with the traveling storyteller responding like any other tourist to landscapes and only occasionally indulging in satirical reflections on other travelers. In "The Notch" he describes himself "loitering towards the heart of the White Mountains," an appropriate pose for the fashionable picturesque tourist, albeit a self-conscious one. Adopting the same sauntering, casual pace that Geoffrey Crayon assumed in Washington Irving's *Sketch Book*, he takes time to discover and enjoy the kind of picturesque landscapes advocated by Gilpin and sought by countless tourists thereafter. For Hawthorne's narrator, though, the White Mountains hold a special attraction: the "mysterious brilliancy" of these "old crystal hills," he writes, "had gleamed upon our distant wanderings before we thought of visiting them" (ill. 2).

For their aesthetic value alone, the White Mountains of New Hampshire appealed to any tourist weaned on the scenic attractions of the Old World, whether on a personal Grand Tour or through armchair travel of the sort Hawthorne indulged in during his formative years in the 1820s and 1830s. For example, charge-books from the Salem Athenaeum reveal that either Hawthorne himself or Mary Manning (who checked out books for her nephew) read omnivorously in travel literature during this time, ranging from travels in Great Britain, Germany, Turkey, and Africa to those in his native land, including Bartram's *Travels,* and to his compatriot Washington Irving's *Tales of a Traveller.*[4] The White Mountains may have attracted Hawthorne as the closest available territory for a tour through the kind of picturesque and sublime landscapes he had only read of before this, and the popular travel guides he used in planning his tours touted the attractions of "the Switzerland of the United States," as this area came to be called.[5] Theodore Dwight's popular tourist guide, *The Northern Traveller* (1825), highly recommends the scenic beauty of the White Mountains:

> Too much cannot be said to the traveller in favour of this delightful region, if he be a man of taste, as all that he especially loves in the varying face of nature is here presented to view, by a country abounding with the most sublime and interesting objects and scenes to be found in the whole circuit of New England, scenes which, while present to the eye, communicate the highest pleasure, and at parting leave a deep and permanent impression on the mind which can never be forgotten.[6]

Hawthorne's travels in the White Mountains impressed him deeply enough for him to use not only the landscape, but also the people and legends encountered there as material for several travel sketches and tales: "The Ambitious Guest" (1835), "The Great Carbuncle" (1837), and "The Great Stone Face" (1850), for example. Translating his own experiences into the autobiographical fiction of the travel sketch, he adopts a persona similar to what he himself must have been like in his late twenties and describes the narrator doing things he must have done: appreciating landscape beauty, observing the various types of humanity encountered during a tour, and collecting local legends from the natives.

From what is known of his 1832 tour, both the setting and movement of the narrator in "The Notch of the White Mountains" reflect

Hawthorne's own experiences, though some of the incidents and characters may be exaggerated or altered for greater effect. In the opening lines of the sketch, Hawthorne deftly sets the scene with a few phrases, establishing the time as September, the place as the Saco River valley in New Hampshire, and his narrator as traveling north from Bartlett and heading toward the tourist attraction of the Notch. The traveling storyteller describes his gradual penetration into "the heart of the White Mountains," revealing his increasing knowledge of both the geographical and legendary history of the place. At the same time, he invites the reader to share his growing sense of awe at the secrets to be discovered there. Describing himself in the midst of the mountains, he sketches the following scene from his journey: "Height after height had risen and towered one above another, till the clouds began to hang below the peaks. . . . We had mountains behind us and mountains on each side, and a group of mightier ones ahead. Still our road went up along the Saco, right towards the centre of that group" (see p. 28). Since one of the charges against the American landscape was its lack of history—a charge that even Washington Irving had echoed, though he acknowledged the "youthful promise" of his native land[7]—Hawthorne is careful to note the traces of history present in the landscape: the pathways of the slides, avalanches of past and near-present times now nearly "effaced by the vegetation of ages" (ill. 3), and the traces of old Indian paths through the mountains, one of which had become the trail taken by the narrator on his tour. Both of these vestiges of the past suggest possible associations with the landscape, a necessary ingredient of the picturesque. The slides recall the recent (1826) disaster of the Willey family, which he would develop later into "The Ambitious Guest." The evidence of Indians suggests the native legends Hawthorne will exploit later in this sketch.

The narrator's musings on the legendary or mythological past of the mountains not only become the source of the associations requisite for the picturesque landscape, they also lead him to consider the presence of the divine in the landscape. Introductory remarks prepare the reader for both kinds of associations by noting that the road running through the valley of the Saco River appears "to climb above the clouds, in its passage to the farther region," as if it leads to the dwelling place of the gods, like some New World Olympus.[8] The narrator allows his fancy to consider the origin of the Notch itself and of the old Indian paths that, leading down through the mountains, created the "wondrous path" he now treads. He imagines a demon or Titan

travelling up the valley, elbowing the heights carelessly aside as he passed, till at length a great mountain took its stand directly across his intended road. He tarries not for such an obstacle, but rending it asunder, a thousand feet from peak to base, discloses its treasures of hidden minerals, its sunless waters, all the secrets of the mountain's inmost heart, with a mighty fracture of rugged precipices on each side.

Edwin Fussell comments on this remarkable image, suggesting that it "involves Hawthorne's sense of his creative self at the deepest and most primitive level, identified with the gods, the processes of insemination and birth, the concupiscences and traumas of the New World," an image almost sexual in nature.[9] Yet though the tone of the passage is wonder at such an imagined feat, the narrator apparently feels at least some ambivalence if not outright horror at such a violent rending of the earth. Like Roger Chillingworth, who is criticized for probing the secrets of the human heart, the Titan here exposes "the secrets of the mountain's inmost heart," laying its hidden treasures open to the traveler's or explorer's eye—and, later, but more humorously, to the mineralogist's hammer.

Just after this passage the narrator suddenly shifts in mood and berates himself for such thinking: "Shame on me," he writes, "that I have attempted to describe [the Notch] by so mean an image." Even if Hawthorne were unaware of what Fussell calls the "obstetric, not to say vaginal" nature of the image,[10] his narrator's mixed feelings about the fanciful demon's actions are evident here. The passage closes with a return to the sublime imagery the author had originally intended: the Notch, he states, is "one of those symbolic scenes, which lead the mind to the sentiment, though not to the conception, of Omnipotence." In truth, other than the cloud-topped peaks of the opening section of the sketch and the magical way the road appears to lead on to a mysterious "farther region" beyond the horizon, like the distance in a Claude painting, there is not a great deal of the conventional Burkean sublime in the description of the White Mountains or the Notch.[11] One looks in vain for the references to the mountains' grandeur and the traveler's awed response to them that fill other accounts of the White Mountains. The emphasis is instead on the tourist's entering into the landscape itself by the very act of traveling through it and on his discovery and revelation of its secrets—secret treasures, as in Hawthorne's tale "The Great Carbuncle," or secret legends, as in the Indian tales that follow in the next sketch.

The second part of "The Notch of the White Mountains" alternates between the sublime setting and the ridiculous characters who enter the scene at this point. Once again the scene is dramatically staged: the narrator enters a narrow passage that almost seems to have been cut into the mountain by superhuman, rather than natural forces. As he enters the "romantic defile" known as the Notch,[12] whose high granite walls and narrow path suggest the sublimity associated with it, a party of tourists appears out of nowhere. Piled into a rumbling stagecoach, the travelers provide a lively contrast to the narrator, whose search for picturesque beauty has brought him thus far. The description of the party is surely ironic: "To my mind, there was a sort of poetry in such an incident," the narrator states, likening the entrance of stagecoach and tourists to "the painted array of an Indian war-party, gliding forth from the same wild chasm." Hawthorne is well aware that while the latter would be truly picturesque, not to say exciting or even sublime in the frisson it would engender in the traveler, the former is just faintly ridiculous, especially in view of his comments on the tourists and their various activities: a mineralogist, "a scientific, green-spectacled figure in black," wielding a hammer, "did great damage to the precipices," while a foppish young man carrying a gold-trimmed opera-glass in lieu, no doubt, of a quizzing glass, "seemed to be making a quotation from some of Byron's rhapsodies." Other characters from the stagecoach include a trader, a fat lady, and the ubiquitous "fair young girl" of Hawthorne's fiction. The traveling storyteller includes these characters both to enliven the sketch, with its emphasis on landscape description, and to introduce those who will play a role in the following work, "Our Evening Party among the Mountains."

The balance of the sketch features the kind of commentary on landscape scenery that was typical of guidebooks of the day, though with Hawthorne's own twist. In his popular *Traveller's Guide*, for example, Gideon Miner Davison effused over the White Mountains, whose magnificence "strikes the traveller with awe and astonishment." According to this guidebook, the emotions aroused by the "grand and majestic scenery" that surrounds Mount Washington are "utterly beyond the power of description."[13] Similarly, the narrator in "The Notch of the White Mountains" stops at dusk at a natural amphitheater and comments on the surrounding group of mountains, "They are majestic, and even awful, when contemplated in a proper mood," a state of mind easily achieved in such circumstances by the man of taste whose eye and mind have been trained to read sublimity into every towering mountain range. Mount Washington, in particular, elicits the most comments both from travel guides and the narrator: like Melville describing Mount Greylock in northwestern Massachusetts in "The Piazza" in the 1850s, Hawthorne's tourist personifies the mountain as an old man "as white as snow" who "had caught the only cloud that was sailing through the atmosphere, to veil his head." He moralizes on the symbolic value of mountains, comments on the brisk air, and ends the sketch by imagining himself before a cozy fire with good company at Ethan Crawford's mountain inn, the subject of the next sketch.

The second part of "Sketches from Memory," "Our Evening Party among the Mountains," is set at Ethan Crawford's inn, a popular stopover for travelers on the northern tour. Here the narrator spends two nights, as Hawthorne himself did in 1832 (CE, XV, 226). Noting the "picturesque group" of local woodcutters, traders, and travelers, the narrator describes the inn as "at once the pleasure-house of fashionable tourists, and the homely inn of country travellers" (ill. 5). Although he does not comment on his own motives for travel here, the storyteller might consider himself somewhere in between these two groups since he is no mere "fashionable tourist," yet he travels with a higher aesthetic purpose in mind than the typical country traveler or trader.

The balance of this sketch satirizes various guests at the inn and describes the numerous local legends the storyteller collected on his tour. Ethan Crawford, the proprietor of this famous inn, is a colorful character who mixes well with the fictional group described elsewhere in the sketch. As the travelers arrive at the inn, Crawford blows a long tin trumpet whose echo among the hills gives the author an opportunity to embroider fancifully on its sound, in which he imagines "an airy band" playing a "dreamlike symphony of melodious instruments." Their imaginary presence here provides yet another possible legend for these mountains.

The second half of the sketch is dominated by the past, whether in Ethan Crawford's reminiscences about life in the White Mountains a half-century earlier or in the legends of the earliest inhabitants of the mountains, the Indians. Although the narrator's comment—"I do abhor an Indian story"—near the end of "Our Evening Party" has become famous, his supposed attitude toward Indian legends is belied by the straightforward tone of his recitation of such tales earlier in the sketch. Indeed, the narrator himself characterizes the general conversation as "animated and sincere." The first legend mentioned here reminds the reader of the Biblical story of the flood. Native tribes of the White Mountains believed, writes Hawthorne,

that the father and mother of their race were saved from a deluge by ascending the peak of Mount Washington. The children of that pair have been overwhelmed, and found no such refuge. In the mythology of the savage, these mountains were afterwards considered sacred and inaccessible, full of unearthly wonders, illuminated at lofty heights by the blaze of precious stones, and inhabited by deities, who sometimes shrouded themselves in the snowstorm, and came down on the lower world.

What is significant here is not only that the narrator recounts an Indian legend, but also that he relates it to the present in such a

way as to add immeasurably to the romantic associations of the
mountains for his contemporaries. Although the parents of the Indian race were themselves saved, and the mountains ever after believed to be occupied by their deities, the descendants of that
mythical pair "have been overwhelmed, and found no such refuge."
As told here, the legend reads as a brief but dark commentary on
the status of Indians in Hawthorne's own time. By the 1830s most
native inhabitants of the White Mountains were long gone, pushed
west by white settlers and by governmental policy. In a few words
Hawthorne has not only given the mountains the requisite associations for them to be truly picturesque or "romantic," in the language of the period; more significantly, he has also implied that
the remaining traces of native tribes are, essentially, the ruins otherwise missing from the landscape. Hawthorne links himself with
other writers of his time in portraying, if not lamenting, the gradual
disappearance of Native Americans from the landscape. Only a few
years earlier, for example, James Fenimore Cooper's *The Last of the
Mohicans* (1826), *The Prairie* (1827), and *The Wept of Wish-ton-Wish*
(1829) had appeared, all of which comment upon the effects of
white encroachment on native tribes in the East.

Both the narrator and his audience remain uncertain of the Indians' place in American fiction. The tourist notices that the "habits
and sentiments" of Indians and whites are too distinct to admit of
any "real sympathy," and he regrets his own "inability to see any
romance, or poetry, or grandeur, or beauty in the Indian character,
at least, till such traits were pointed out by others." Yet, simply by
retelling some legends, Hawthorne ironically suggests that Indian
tales do have a place in American literature. The White Mountains
have become a "haunted region" partly due to Hawthorne's efforts
here and in later tales based on Indian legends such as "The Great
Carbuncle."

Unlike the two preceding sketches, in which the tone remains
fairly straightforward except when the narrator satirizes other tourists, in "The Canal-Boat" the tone is more complex. It changes from
paragraph to paragraph and creates a sophisticated sketch that
ranges from realistic description to high comedy and low humor,

and from pointed satire to dark irony. Once again the picturesque tour is the narrative framework for the story. In this sketch the youthful protagonist travels in search of the picturesque in western New York, poking fun at his fellow tourists and taking aim at the inflated rhetoric about the Grand Canal itself. The sketch becomes more complex by the end, as it culminates in the narrator's dark vision of a landscape made accessible by technology but also destroyed by it, and concludes with a midnight search for meaning that offers little hope for the future.

In "The Canal-Boat" the wandering storyteller's picturesque tour continues via packet boat on the Erie Canal, by 1832 a standard part of the northern tour. Spafford's popular *Pocket Guide for the Tourist and Traveller*, for example, focused almost exclusively on the Erie Canal, with brief mentions of scenic attractions along the canal route.[14] Dwight's *Northern Traveller* recommended nearby historic sites from the Revolutionary War and the War of 1812, and landscape scenery, particularly cascades, as well as interesting "manufactories" in the vicinity of the canal.[15] Davison's *Traveller's Guide* gave a detailed description of the canal route, including various landscapes worth viewing on the trip west and the historical attractions of the towns through which the canal passed, though more space was devoted to mills and factories than to historical sites.[16] Indeed, Davison's comments on the attractions of the canal for the tourist reflect the very considerations Gilpin emphasizes in his essay "On Picturesque Travel" for the picturesque tourist, whose "love of novelty" requires the stimulation of "new scenes continually opening, and arising to his view."[17] Thus Gilpin celebrated the River Wye, in England, whose "gentle, uninterrupted stream . . . adorns, through its various reaches a succession of the most picturesque scenes."[18] Had he lived another half-century and traveled to America, Gilpin might have equally celebrated western New York's varied views as seen from the deck of a canal boat (ill. 8). In a section entitled "Canal Passage," for example, Davison writes: "Of the sources of gratification to the tourist, during the canal passage, that of novelty is perhaps the greatest." He admits, however, that canal scenery may be "too little diversified with incident" for the "man of pleasure" to repeat the canal trip, though the "man of business" would not be bothered by such considerations.[19] The tourist's taste for picturesque beauty along the canal route was whetted by such guidebook commentary.

In "The Canal-Boat" Hawthorne opens the sketch with the narrator recalling his inflated romantic attitude toward a proposed trip on the Erie Canal. "I was inclined to be poetical about the Grand Canal," he states dramatically in the opening line. He imagines De Witt Clinton, principal sponsor of the canal, as a kind of magician who created an enchanted "watery highway" linking two worlds with one another. More important, he writes, "This simple and mighty conception had conferred inestimable value on spots which Nature seemed to have thrown carelessly into the great body of the earth, without foreseeing that they could ever attain importance" (see p. 35). The narrator rhapsodizes about the canal itself not only because it is a major feat of the imagination and of technology, but also because it serves to open up new landscapes for the tourist, the discovery of which was one of the most important goals for the picturesque traveler. In "The Canal-Boat" the narrator is, in fact, so enchanted with the canal initially that as he sets forth on his trip he promises himself a second voyage that same summer on the artificial waterway. Of course, since the love of novelty in particular is what draws the picturesque traveler, the tone here is most likely ironic, particularly since he may be satirizing Spafford, who recommends "the constantly varying scenery" along the canal and reveals that he traveled the entire canal route two times in one season to gather the information necessary for his *Pocket Guide*.[20]

The opening of "The Canal-Boat" not only describes the narrator's expectations about the proposed tour, but also raises the reader's own expectations. But such highly inflated rhetoric almost begs to be deflated, and this is exactly what happens in later passages. In the descriptive section that follows, the narrator introduces a mythological allusion that is undercut almost immediately: "Behold us, then, fairly afloat, with three horses harnessed to our vessel, like the steeds of Neptune to a huge scallop-shell, in mythological pictures. Bound to a distant port, we had neither charter nor compass, nor cared about the wind, nor felt the heaving of a billow, nor dreaded shipwreck, however fierce the tempest, in our adventurous navigation of an interminable mud-puddle." As for the narrator's— and the reader's—expectations of the picturesque landscapes recommended by Spafford and others, these too are deflated: the Erie Canal, he writes, meanders "through all the dismal swamps and unimpressive scenery, that could be found between the great lakes and the sea-coast."

To be fair, Hawthorne and his peevish narrator almost deserve their ennui: the narrator had, in fact, begun his trip just east of Utica, which is past the sections of the canal generally accounted to be most picturesque, such as the Mohawk Valley. The part he focuses on in "The Canal-Boat" was widely acknowledged at the time to be the most tedious.[21] Robert J. Vandewater stated: "There is nothing of much interest on the canal for the first sixty miles west of Utica. It is perfectly level and marshy country, without a lock in the whole distance."[22] That Hawthorne's narrator chooses the most boring section of the canal for his sketch suggests that he plans to put this very tediousness to good use, as indeed he does. For although the narrator acknowledges that "there is variety enough, both on the surface of the canal and along its banks, to amuse the traveller," mostly he emphasizes the "overpowering tedium" that would "deaden [the] perceptions" of even the most eager tourist.

By this point no one should expect to see any picturesque landscapes, but Hawthorne continues to tease the reader trained by the conventions of picturesque travel to expect scenic beauty. Beginning a section describing scenes along the canal route, the narrator recalls: "Had I been on my feet at the time, instead of sailing slowly along in a dirty canal-boat, I should often have paused to contemplate the diversified panorama along the banks of the canal." Yet what is the panorama that would have repaid such leisurely contemplation? Dark, dense forests unrelieved by sunlight and gutted tracts of land covered with "dismal black stumps." And although some of the scenes depicting the urban picturesque—thriving villages and busy cities—may contain the variety essential to a picturesque scene (ill. 12), the lengthy portrait of a poor woman, "lean and aguish," living along the canal, who appears as "Poverty personified," dominates the various views and suggests that the canal has brought at least as much poverty as prosperity to western New York. The narrator peevishly complains that these scenes were "tiresome in reality" and recalls the childish amusements he and his fellow passengers stooped to for entertainment on the canal boat: pelting ducks with apples, shooting at squirrels from the deck, and mocking an unlucky passenger who accidentally fell into the muddy canal waters. Once again Hawthorne stresses the contrast between the narrator's inflated expectations and the tedious reality of a tour by canal boat.

One way in which the narrator relieves the tedium of his tour is by satirizing his fellow travelers. Observing an Englishman who is "taking notes in a memorandum-book," he indulges his "ill-humor" by imagining the comments on Americans made by the foreigner: the pedantic Virginia schoolmaster, the Puritanical yeoman farmer of Massachusetts, the Detroit merchant who worships Mammon, and the unnaturally modest "western lady" who shrinks from the observer's roving eye. While other critics have noted Hawthorne's use of the Englishman and his stereotyped Americans,[23] this character's central role in the satire has gone largely unrecognized. In the midst of his comments on his fellow travelers the narrator notes: "I went all through the cabin, hitting everybody as hard a lash as I could, and *laying the whole blame on the infernal Englishman*" (emphasis added). The narrator explicitly avoids responsibility for satirizing his compatriots, placing it instead on the much-maligned English traveler, as if Hawthorne dare not admit his own culpability here, though he hints at it in the underscored phrase. The irony of this passage deepens when the narrator catches a glimpse of his own image in a mirror and realizes that the Englishman's eyes are, in turn, focused on him. In the mirror's reflection, a favorite device of Hawthorne's, the narrator has been caught at what he has accused the Englishman of doing—satirizing fellow travelers—and ironically it is the American, not the Englishman, who later exploits the scene for its literary value by writing this travel sketch.

After an unsuccessful attempt to sleep on the narrow, shelf-like berths of the canal boat, the narrator dramatically falls out of bed, setting off a chain of events that will lead him straight to the symbolic conclusion of the sketch. That the protagonist compares his narrow berth to a coffin does not seem accidental, for the reference introduces a whole series of images of death and darkness. Going on deck at night, the narrator discovers a "darkness so intense, that there seemed to be no world" except the canal boat (ill. 13). "Yet," he remarks, "it was an impressive scene"—indeed an otherworldly scene, one in which references to death, ruin, and destruction occur frequently:

There can hardly be a more dismal tract of country. The forest which covers it . . . is now decayed and death-struck, by the partial draining of the swamp into the great ditch of the canal. Sometimes, indeed, our lights were reflected from pools of stagnant water, which stretched far in among the trunks of the trees, beneath dense masses of dark foliage. . . . Often, we beheld the prostrate form of some old sylvan giant, which had fallen, and crushed down smaller trees under its immense ruin. In spots, where destruction had been riotous, the lanterns showed perhaps a hundred trunks, erect, half overthrown, extended along the ground, resting on their shattered limbs, or tossing them desperately into the darkness, but all of one ashy-white, all naked together, in desolate confusion.

Unlike the picturesque ruins of the Old World, created by wars or by the ravages of time, these New World ruins were wrought by technology and offer little of aesthetic value other than their symbolic value for the writer. Hawthorne suggests this in the narrator's analysis that follows the lengthy death-in-life description just cited: "My fancy had found another emblem," he states. "The wild Nature of America had been driven to this desert-place by the encroachments of civilized man." Building the canal in this area had meant draining the adjacent land, thereby destroying the forests that had previously thrived there. The narrator and his fellow travelers are intruders on this desolate scene, and his final comment on it ironically summarizes the contrast between Old and New World ruins: "In other lands, Decay sits among fallen palaces; but here, her home is in the forests." Had he ended his sketch here, Hawthorne's em-

blem would have spoken clearly enough about the destructive power
of technology, exemplified by the canal's destruction of the wilderness in western New York. But the author extends and reinforces
his symbolism, widening the meaning and significance of his brief
sketch by developing it further in the conclusion.

When the canal boat's towrope becomes tangled and causes a
brief delay, the narrator decides "to examine the phosphoric light
of an old tree" in the decaying forest that borders the canal. "It was
not," he notes dryly, "the first delusive radiance that I had followed." The fallen tree, "converted into a mass of diseased splendor," throws a "ghastliness" into the atmosphere. "Full of conceits
that night," as the narrator describes himself, he calls it variously
a "frigid fire" and a "funeral light, illumining decay and death."
The fallen, phosphorescent tree is, he says, "an emblem of fame,
that gleams around the dead man without warming him; or of
genius, when it owes its brilliancy to moral rottenness." These images suggest death and despair. More than this, they remind the
reader that this phosphorescent "flame" burns without consuming,
yet without warming either. The source of this light, Hawthorne
suggests, is the "moral rottenness" at the core—a physical rottenness for the tree, but a spiritual rottenness for mankind. Is this,
then, the "moral rottenness" at the heart of American civilization
that, in blind pursuit of material wealth, would wantonly destroy
Nature by technological feats such as the Erie Canal? Hawthorne
may have been hinting at this earlier when the narrator prostrates
himself at the cry "bridge! bridge! . . . like a pagan before his idol."

At the end of the sketch the narrator, who has been abandoned
by the captain of the canal boat, seizes a phosphorescent flambeau
from the decaying old tree and sets out on a "midnight tour" of
the dying wilderness. The flambeau, he writes, burns but "con-
sumes not." Like an *ignis fatuus* or a jack-o'-lantern, to use Hawthorne's simile, this flickering, delusive light is an appropriate
symbol for the chastened narrator, whose dreams of the picturesque
tour by canal boat have fallen victim to reality. The wandering
storyteller's midnight tour seems, indeed, strangely appropriate for
the Gothic nether world Hawthorne describes in the sketch.

Reading the conclusion of "The Canal-Boat" on another level, one might interpret the narrator's midnight search for his journey's end as a symbolic search for truth, a common enough metaphor in Hawthorne's writings. In this instance darkness obscures reality, and the narrator's path is lit only by the deceptive light of the decaying, phosphorescent trees that suggest the "moral rottenness" of the writer's world. Another sketch based on Hawthorne's 1832 tour portrays the traveling protagonist in pursuit of a different goal, metaphorically speaking. In "My Visit to Niagara" the narrator's aim in the story, to comprehend the meaning of the falls for himself alone, becomes a metaphor for understanding the relationship between perception and point of view, between the reflections of others' experiences and the hard-won, original response to experience.

"My Visit to Niagara" is the climactic sketch in Hawthorne's series of travel sketches from his 1832 tour, and it may well have originally been intended as the climactic piece of the framework of "The Story Teller," just as Niagara Falls often served as the climax of the northern tour for nineteenth-century tourists. As one recent critic notes, by traveling north on the Hudson River and then west on the Erie Canal, the tourist views scenery that seems designed by nature to demonstrate various kinds of landscape—the beautiful, the picturesque, and the sublime—with the trip culminating in that glorious "icon of the American sublime," Niagara Falls.[24] Whether one is taking the northern tour or reading about it in a group of sketches such as these, "My Visit to Niagara" reflects the great expectations felt by the traveler-reader in approaching the falls. The phenomenon of the picturesque tour itself both calls for and reinforces this sense of expectation. Since William Gilpin, the picturesque tourist par excellence, had decreed that the main object of picturesque travel was the discovery of new scenes, a traveler's explorations of scenery as much celebrated in literature and painting as Niagara Falls would be bound to evoke a certain measure of disappointment, as Elizabeth McKinsey demonstrates in her recent work on the falls as cultural icon. Once the falls had been written and rewritten by countless travelers in the eighteenth and early nineteenth centuries, some travelers found they had to account for their disappointment in viewing something they had read so much about or, in other cases, to revile their contemporaries for ruining one of the wonders of the New World with inns, souvenir shops, and mills.[25] This is the context in which Hawthorne writes in "My Visit to Niagara" and, quite likely, also the personal experience behind his characterization of the narrator's deeply felt disappointment on his first view of the famous falls.[26]

From the very beginning of exploration and travel in America, Niagara Falls served not only as a symbol of the sublime, but also, more importantly, in its enormity, overwhelming power, and grandeur, as the dominant symbol of the New World's potential. No wonder, then, that it was an essential part of the northern tour and that viewing the falls became a goal for every American and European tourist. Added to this, every traveler who scribbled his or her thoughts on the American landscape and its people included a section on Niagara Falls, usually one that hauled in every aesthetic cliche, however redundant, celebrating its sublimity, grandeur, awfulness, and majesty. Hawthorne portrays the narrator of the Niagara sketch as one whose expectations about the falls had been shaped by previous reading and who approached Niagara with the awe and high expectations of a pilgrim who travels to worship at a celebrated and revered shrine. In the opening lines of the sketch, he writes:

> Never did a pilgrim approach Niagara with deeper enthusiasm, than mine. I had lingered away from it, and wandered to other scenes, because my treasury of anticipated enjoyments, comprising all the wonders of the world, had nothing else so magnificent, and I was loth to exchange the pleasures of hope for those of memory so soon. (see p. 55)

The narrator's use of the pilgrim motif in this opening passage serves the sketch that follows in three important ways. First, it recognizes Niagara Falls as the ultimate in scenic wonders of the American tour and acknowledges the worshipful attitude on the part of the countless travelers who made a pilgrimage to this holy land. Second, the exaggerated tone and diction suggest the dual point of view that adds complexity to the Niagara Falls sketch: though the narrator makes his bow to those who have come before him in admiring the falls, his reference to them as "pilgrims" lends a note of irony in its equation of a natural phenomenon with a religious shrine. For Hawthorne, applying the word "pilgrim" to the picturesque traveler had additional significance. As an avowed admirer of James Kirke Paulding, whom he later was to describe in a letter as "the admired and familiar friend of every reader in the land" (CE, XV, 468) the author would have known Paulding's *The New Mirror for Travellers* (1828). He was probably equally familiar with the nickname wags had given Paulding's book, a name that distinguished it from serious guidebooks of the day and established it as satire: *The New Pilgrim's Progress*. The nickname alludes, of course, to Bunyan's famous allegory, Hawthorne's old favorite and one he would later use for an extended allusion in "The Celestial Railroad." Hence his use of the word "pilgrim" to describe a tourist whose object of devotion was Niagara Falls may carry a meaning beyond that of the usual term, and in this case, it foreshadows the satirical tone he adopts frequently in the sketch since Paulding's attitude toward picturesque travel and tourists in *The New Pilgrim's Progress* is largely satirical.

Third, this passage introduces the attitude of anticipation or expectancy on the part of the tourist that had been essential to picturesque travel at least since Gilpin's time. Here, too, exaggeration paves the way for later developments in the sketch. The hyperbole evident in Hawthorne's description of the narrator's "treasury of anticipated enjoyments" and the reference to his future exploration of "all the wonders of the world" ironically prepare the reader for the narrator's disappointment. His statement that he was "loth to exchange the pleasures of hope for those of memory so soon" foreshadows the disappointment ahead and introduces his almost comical efforts to put off the moment when he must confront the object of his longstanding devotion.

The balance of the opening section of "My Visit to Niagara" reinforces the reader's sense that the sketch not only satirizes the stereotypical views of others about the falls but also presents the narrator ironically. Paradoxically, the narrator simultaneously mocks some tourists' approaches to the falls and mimics their ridiculous attempts to discover an original approach to Niagara: hence the mention of the English tourist who traveled thousands of miles to view the falls and then "turned back from the point where he first heard the thunder of Niagara," without having actually seen it.

The narrator's response to the falls is unusual but not wholly unexpected, given the mixed feelings with which he has approached Niagara, for he neither rushes to view the falls nor turns back from his journey unfulfilled. Instead, a strange sort of apathy overtakes him, and he writes: "[M]y mind had grown strangely benumbed, and my spirits apathetic, with a slight depression, not decided enough to be termed sadness. My enthusiasm was in a deathlike slumber." Further on, he explains this unusual response: "Such has often been my apathy, when objects, long sought, and earnestly desired, were placed within my reach." Elizabeth McKinsey calls this passage "a strange drama of delayed gratification,"[27] yet the narrator's attitude is consonant with his feelings described earlier in the sketch; he is simply "loth to exchange the pleasures of hope for those of memory" regarding the falls. He would prefer to look forward to Niagara and even to continue his journey with the falls unseen rather than risk possible disappointment. He contrasts his own point of view with that of the "French gentleman" traveling on the stagecoach with him who leans forward to gain his first glimpse of the falls from the window and loudly admires the view: "I was glad to think," he writes, "that for me the whole burst of Niagara was yet in futurity."

The structure of "My Visit to Niagara" suggests that Hawthorne's narrator must deal with his own preconceptions and others' views of the falls before he can discover or create his own view. The title, significantly, is not "A Visit to Niagara" but rather "*My* Visit to Niagara," implying the importance of the writer's view as distinct from those of other tourists, writers, and painters. Thus he spends a large portion of the sketch describing and often satirizing the various ways other travelers respond to Niagara rather than establishing his own viewpoint right from the beginning—other than to suggest, as noted above, that his attitude is not going to be the expected one. The balance of the sketch is then taken up with the narrator's many attempts to comprehend Niagara and its meaning for him personally.

The narrator's first view of the falls, with his concomitant attempt to comprehend its meaning, occurs just after the opening of the sketch. First, however, he purchases a walking stick made by a Tuscarora Indian. The "twisted stick" is "curiously convoluted, and adorned with the carved images of a snake and a fish." This "pilgrim's staff," as he describes it, reminds the reader once again that the narrator is on a pilgrimage to the holy land of the American sublime, though his linking himself with the countless "pilgrims" who have gone before him is as ironic as it is self-conscious.[28]

The narrator's immense disappointment at his initial view of the falls, then, is foreshadowed not only by the hints of impending disillusionment early in the sketch but also by the suggestion here of the meaning of the experience in the symbolic walking stick. Nor are readers themselves disappointed. In spite of the "glorious sunshine" and a glimpse of the "Eternal Rainbow of Niagara," the narrator resists the scene and its conventional impact on the observer. Like the dark rock, unaffected by the churning water, in the midst of the "river of impetuous snow," the narrator "resist[s] all the physical fury" before him. And although he wants desperately to respond to the falls and to comprehend its meaning, he fears that he, too, is a "cold spirit" whose resistance prevents him from responding to "the moral influence of the scene."

After a series of initial impressions of the falls, the narrator concludes: "Still, I had not half seen Niagara." What follows is a record of his attempt, instead, to see it *whole*.[29] Moving from one observation point to another, and always descending from a higher viewpoint to a lower one, until he is in direct contact with wind and spray, he tries unsuccessfully to capture the meaning of the falls. At one point the narrator even attempts a panoramic view that, predictably, also fails: "Casting my eyes across the river, and every side, I took in the whole scene at a glance, and tried to comprehend it in one vast idea." Still the sublime scene resists comprehension. In the essay "On Sketching Landscape" Gilpin had considered the very problem facing Hawthorne and his narrator in this sketch. He suggests that the picturesque tourist find "the best point of view" to sketch a landscape, a perspective Hawthorne's narrator cannot settle on, and he warns would-be artists of the problem of reducing the scale of a landscape, particularly an extensive one, to the smaller scale of the paper.[30]

The narrator's initial reaction comes as no surprise to the perceptive reader:

Oh, that I had never heard of Niagara till I beheld it! Blessed were the wanderers of old, who heard its deep roar, sounding through the woods, as the summons to an unknown wonder, and approached its awful brink, in all the freshness of native feeling. Had its own mysterious voice been the first to warn me of its existence, then, indeed, I might have knelt down and worshipped. But I had come thither, haunted with a vision of foam and fury, and dizzy cliffs, and an ocean tumbling down out of the sky—a scene, in short, which Nature had too much good taste and calm simplicity to realize. My mind had struggled to adapt these false conceptions to the reality, and finding the effort vain, a wretched sense of disappointment weighed me down. I climbed the precipice, and threw myself on the earth—feeling that I was unworthy to look at the Great Falls, and careless about beholding them again.[31]

Between this initial response to the falls and his second attempt to comprehend the meaning of Niagara, the narrator lies awake night after night, listening to the "dread sound" of the falls, a sound heard, significantly, "for ages past and to come."[32] This is the narrator's first hint that he might sometime take his place among the "wanderers of old" who could respond instinctively and immediately, without a screen of received ideas coming between him and the falls. It becomes necessary for him to cast away all secondhand conceptions and respond to Niagara Falls directly and intimately, as he states explicitly:

Gradually, and after much contemplation, I came to know, by my own feelings, that Niagara is indeed a wonder of the world, and not the less wonderful, because time and thought must be employed in comprehending it. Casting aside all pre-conceived notions, and preparation to be direstruck or delighted, the beholder must stand beside it in the simplicity of his heart, suffering the mighty scene to work its own impression.

For the man of taste "time and thought must be employed" to comprehend fully the impact of Niagara. Only the simple soul (the young farmer, for example, whose instinctive response to the sublimity of the falls is admired by the narrator later in the sketch) can respond immediately and freshly to Niagara. Although it is not known how many days Hawthorne spent at the falls, his narrator appears to spend at least several days there,[33] until his visit finally culminates on the last day.

The narrator's final impressions of Niagara Falls appear at the end of his sketch and are interrupted, once more, by other visitors, whose various responses to Niagara he satirizes. Yet in spite of the repeated interruptions, the narrator achieves his long-sought comprehensive impression of the falls: "Never before had my mind been in such perfect unison with the scene," he writes, describing the rare harmony that can result between the receptive observer and his surroundings, which was the ideal of Gilpin's tourist whose eye was trained in the picturesque and the sublime.

Hawthorne's narrator assumes the position most often recommended by the guidebooks for the picturesque tourist to observe the falls. Taking a seat on Table Rock, which had once projected fifty feet out over the falls but now was truncated from an earlier collapse,[34] he "felt as if suspended in the open air" (ill. 21). He recalls, "There were intervals, when I was conscious of nothing but the great river, rolling calmly into the abyss." The narrator communes directly and intensely with the river and falls, and his comments suggest that he transcends this particular moment in time to participate in the eternal time in which Niagara dwells.[35] He compares its "unhurried motion" to "the march of Destiny," suggesting something fateful about the river's course and fall into the abyss, and emphasizes the permanence of its flow rather than its transience: the "eternal storm" of Niagara. Given its existence in a framework of eternal time rather than earthly time, the narrator disagrees with observers who comment on its tumultuous qualities and emphasizes instead its calmness: "It soothes, while it awes the mind." Paradoxically, instead of arousing wild emotions in the observer, Niagara calms him.

At last the reader expects to hear the narrator's long-sought view of the falls, but Hawthorne frustrates the reader once more—as he himself must have often been frustrated—by the parade of tourists who periodically block his view of Niagara. Except for the absence of cameras clanking around their necks, these early nineteenth-century tourists could easily be mistaken for their modern-day counterparts. They interrupt the narrator's "contemplations" of the scene, and the reader shares his impatience at their presence and enjoys his satirizing them. With their untrained eyes and clumsy attempts at appreciating nature's sublimity, these tourists offer various limited, naive, and sometimes downright foolish means of viewing the falls that Hawthorne contrasts effectively with his own hard-won perspective at the end. First the narrator watches as two "adventurers" descend into the "lower regions" and, accompanied by a guide, disappear behind the falls to attempt to reach Termination Rock, surrounded by mist and spray (ill. 20). Despite the hazardous appearance of the venture, the narrator notes that the passage is actually safer than it seems. Satirizing the adventures of these "children of the mist," he concludes by mentioning the "certificate of their achievement, with three verses of sublime poetry on the back" received by the tourists. Ironically, Hawthorne had received such a certificate himself when he visited the falls in September 1832, the only proof extant of his stop there.[36]

Then a series of tourists appears, each skewered in turn by the narrator's satirical pen. First John Bull arrives in the person of a "short, ruddy, middle-aged gentleman" and his "robust" spouse. His "broad grin" at the falls, the sort of aesthetically crude response one might expect from an untutored Englishman (particularly when the observer is a patriotic American), contrasts humorously with that of his wife, whose "sweet example of maternal solicitude" concerning her child's safety prevents her from so much as glancing at the phenomenon she crossed the ocean to view. Another traveler, whom Hawthorne characterizes as "a native American, and no rare character among us" pulls out a copy of Captain Basil Hall's famous travel book and "labor[s] earnestly to adjust Niagara to the captain's description, departing, at last, without one new idea or sensation of his own." Once again Hawthorne satirizes the most typical of the American tourists—those dependent on the guidebook and stigmatized, as Paulding had characterized the species, for their slavish devotion to others' perceptions and interpretations of landscape scenery.[37] "My Visit to Niagara" might even be read as a response to Hall's statement that because the scale of the falls "baffles every attempt of the imagination to paint" Niagara, "it were ridiculous, therefore, to think of describing it."[38] A different tourist pulls out his sketching pad and tries to capture the falls on paper, following Gilpin's dictum that the picturesque tourist must sketch his ideas while still fresh, preferably on the scene. Gilpin's influence is evident in the narrator's conversation with the sketcher: the would-be artist's suggestion that the position of Goat Island is somehow defective and ought, ideally, to be moved "so as to widen the American falls" recalls the English writer's advice that a scene may be altered by the artist when nature fails to provide exactly the right balance in the composition of a landscape.[39]

Two Michigan tradesmen, like countless other businessmen before them, offer the expected commercial viewpoint on Niagara Falls by wanting to harness its power for industry. Their preference for the manmade wonders of the Grand Canal is also the sort of attitude one might expect in businessmen as observed—and stereotyped—by the aesthetically superior narrator. These economically motivated tourists contrast effectively with the young traveler "in a home-spun cotton dress" who succeeds them in Hawthorne's sketch of this little band of tourists. His naive, untutored eye lacks the vulgar qualities of the English visitors, the pseudo-artistic sensibility of the sketcher, and the utilitarian perspective of the Michigan traders. The young man's response to the sublimity of the falls is immediate and fresh: "His whole soul seemed to go forth and be transported thither" as he gazed at Horseshoe Falls. As McKinsey states, he "has the natural naive capacity for the sublime . . . that the storyteller has had to recover after he arrived."[40]

The narrator achieves his final views of Niagara as he descends
from his position above the falls on Table Rock and follows a winding road away from the scene.[41] Here the varying perspectives offered by his changing position are significant, recalling, once again,
Gilpin's advice on finding the right point of view from which to
view a scene to the best advantage. The narrator writes: "The indirectness of my downward road continually changed the point of
view, and shewed me, in rich and repeated succession" the various
pictures presented by his changing perspective. Significantly, Hawthorne describes these views in artistic terms: the familiar lights
and shadows of his verbal sketching technique characterize the rapids; "the lovelier *picture*" of Goat Island underscores the artistic
quality of the description; and "the long vista of the river" presents
an "unrivalled scene." As in a Claude painting, "golden sunshine"
colors the whole composition: it "*tinged* the sheet of the American
cascade, and *painted* on its heaving spray the broken semicircle of
a rainbow" (emphasis added). The sketch suggests a metaphorical
reading of this climactic scene in its description of the rainbow, the
reminder of God's covenant with mankind, as "Heaven's own
beauty crowning earth's sublimity."[42]

As the narrator slowly departs from the scene of his triumphant
reclamation of Niagara's sublimity, he "lingers and pauses" as one
"who discerns a brighter and brightening excellence in what he
must soon behold no more." Since the time of day is sunset, the
brightening here could refer not only to the brilliance of the setting
sun, but also to the intense clarity of the experience and its newly
understood meaning in the narrator's mind. The storyteller has
finally captured the meaning of the falls not just for his own time,
but within the framework of eternal time in which "the wanderers
of old" first stood awestruck at the glory of Niagara: "The solitude
of the old wilderness now reigned" over the scene. He concludes:
"My enjoyment became the more rapturous, because no poet
shared it—nor wretch, devoid of poetry, profaned it: but the spot,
so famous through the world, was all my own!" Significantly, like
Emerson before him and Thoreau later, the narrator needs solitude

for his ultimate experience of the sublime in nature. In the end, undistracted by other travelers, the narrator of Hawthorne's sketch lays personal claim to Niagara Falls. The purpose of "My Visit to Niagara," then, becomes fulfilled, and the picturesque tourist as storyteller can move on to other stops on the American Grand Tour, making them equally his own.

In "My Visit to Niagara" the sketch serves as much more than a vehicle for Hawthorne to satirize tourists and the popular pastime of picturesque touring, and certainly as more than a means to celebrate the sublime wonders of Niagara Falls, both of which countless other writers had done before him, with varying degrees of success. In contrast, "The Notch of the White Mountains" is a more straightforward celebration of the American landscape, though both this sketch and "The Canal-Boat" satirize the absurdities of the picturesque tourist as effectively as the Niagara sketch. Yet like the Erie Canal sketch, "My Visit to Niagara" develops into a sophisticated study that is more than a social satire. "The Canal-Boat" criticizes American technology and its wanton destruction of the landscape in favor of economic progress. The protagonist's midnight travels along the canal offer little light—or hope—in the darkened, morally unsound world he explores. On the other hand, the Niagara sketch is not half so dark in its themes, offering instead of a pessimistic view of contemporary America an exploration of the artist's quest for understanding and a study of the problem of conveying his conclusions to his readers. Here the choice of a hackneyed symbol of the American sublime is brilliant, since it allows Hawthorne to address the problem of achieving an original view of a much described and interpreted site. Only by presenting and then rejecting the most common views of Niagara Falls can the narrator clear his mental slate and begin to come to terms with it on his own. After this lengthy process of sifting through others' interpretations of the falls he can approach Niagara directly and intimately, capturing its meaning for himself and conveying it to his readers. At last the wandering storyteller can state that this place, "so famous through the world," is his own. In the end Hawthorne's ironic tourist is overcome by the overwhelming sublimity of Niagara Falls, and he abandons satire for his wholehearted embrace of the falls. This cultural and natural icon has brought him a new understanding about himself as tourist and, more importantly, as an artist and writer.

NOTES

ABBREVIATIONS

CE   The Centenary Edition of the Works of Nathaniel Hawthorne. Edited by William Charvat et al. 20 vols. Columbus: Ohio State University Press, 1962–.

SLE   The Standard Library Edition of *The Works of Nathaniel Hawthorne*. Edited by George Parsons Lathrop. 15 vols. Boston: Houghton, Mifflin and Company, 1891. Its first twelve volumes provide almost the same text as The Riverside Edition of *The Complete Works of Nathaniel Hawthorne*. Edited by George Parsons Lathrop. 13 vols. Boston: Houghton, Mifflin and Company, 1882.

HAWTHORNE'S TOUR OF 1832 THROUGH NEW ENGLAND AND UPSTATE NEW YORK

1. Arlin Turner, *Nathaniel Hawthorne*, vi. Randall Stewart, *Nathaniel Hawthorne*, 44, adds: "By his travels over New England, he was recreating his mind, enlarging his knowledge of human nature, and gathering impressions which could be used in his writings (was making himself indeed the chief literary authority in New England life and manners)."

2. Julian Hawthorne, *Nathaniel Hawthorne and His Wife* in SLE, XIV, 96–97.

3. Marion L. Kesselring, *Hawthorne's Reading, 1828–1850*, 9, comments on this reading pattern:

Was it the memory of a skipper father who had traveled in distant places . . . that was responsible for Hawthorne's absorption in travel books? Even when he was busy in the workaday world upon his return to Salem, travel books did not lose their fascination for him. There seemed no limit to the horizons he reached through reading, nor was there a favorite spot that lured him back. South America, Europe, Turkey, India, Africa, New Zealand, Iceland and the American Rockies: he visited them all on vicarious trips from his attic room.

She goes on to quote a passage from the "Fragments from the Journal of a Solitary Man" (CE, XI, 315).

4. See Nelson F. Adkins, "The Early Projected Works of Nathaniel Hawthorne," 139–40; Randall Stewart, *Nathaniel Hawthorne*, 41–43; David William Pancost, "Washington Irving's *Sketch Book*," 202–66; James R. Mellow,

Nathaniel Hawthorne in His Times, 51–57; and Turner, *Nathaniel Hawthorne*, 71–72.

5. The letter continues:

I still hope that the pestilence will disappear, so that it may be safe to go in a month or two. If my route brings me into the vicinity of Hillsboro' [obviously New Hampshire], I shall certainly visit you. As to the Cholera, if it comes, I believe I shall face it here. By the by, I have been afflicted for two days past with one of the symptoms of it (viz. a diarrhoea) which has weakened me considerably, and makes me write rather a tremulous hand. I keep it secret, however, for fear of being sent to the Hospital. (CE, XV, 224)

Obviously Hawthorne was familiar with the symptoms of the cholera from the many publications that had sprung up right after the epidemic had struck the southeast of Canada in early June, and he, no doubt, observed its progress through the northeast of the United States.

6. This was still a good time for travel according to Gideon Miner Davison's *Traveller's Guide* (1833), 193: "Heretofore, the months of July and August have been selected for an excursion to the west; but exp[e]rience has abundantly proved, that the early part of September is far preferable. The heat of summer having then in a measure subsided, the air is more salubrious, and the pleasure of a journey less interrupted by dust, perplexity and fatigue. Added to this, it is the season of peaches."

7. Quoted by James R. Mellow, *Hawthorne in His Times*, 51.

8. For a detailed discussion of the "Seven Tales" and "Provincial Tales," see Alfred Weber, *Die Entwicklung der Rahmenerzählungen Nathaniel Hawthornes*, 30–50 and 61–100. See also Turner, *Nathaniel Hawthorne*, 49–51; Nina Baym, *The Shape of Hawthorne's Career*, 23–29, 30–34; Neal Frank Doubleday, *Hawthorne's Early Tales*, 26–29. For an analysis of "The Story Teller," see Weber, "The Outlines of 'The Story Teller,'" *passim*.

9. A few scholars have tried to reconstruct the work. Nelson F. Adkins, in his 1945 article on "The Early Projected Works," was the first. His bibliographical study has become obsolete now, but it was a pioneer work and initiated all the following studies of Hawthorne's early career. See the contributions of Richard P. Adams and Seymour L. Gross listed in the bibliography. Later studies which deal with "The Story Teller" are Turner, *Nathaniel Hawthorne*, 69–79; Baym, *The Shape of Hawthorne's Career*, 39–50; Doubleday, *Hawthorne's Early Tales*, 71–73; J. Donald Crowley's "Historical Commentary" in the editions of Hawthorne's tales in CE, IX and XI; and Pancost, "Washington Irving's *Sketch Book*," 208, 212.

10. These first two installments of "The Story Teller" were taken apart in the later book publications of Hawthorne's: "Mr. Higginbotham's Catastrophe" was published separately in the 1837 edition of *Twice-told Tales* (CE, IX, 106–20), and the rest appeared only very much later, in the 1854 edition of *Mosses from an Old Manse* (CE, X, 405–21) under the title "Passages from a Relinquished Work." See the editorial comments in CE, X, 523–26, 579–80, 647–48, and the critical notes in Lea Newman, *A Reader's Guide to the Short Stories of Nathaniel Hawthorne*, 243–45.

11. "Fragments from the Journal of a Solitary Man" (CE, XI, 312–28) was never included in Hawthorne's collections of short fiction during his lifetime, only later by Lathrop in 1883 in the Riverside Edition (see SLE, XII, 23–41). In *Die Entwicklung der Rahmenerzählungen*, 344–49, Weber offers a close analysis of the text and proves that the article as it stands must have been put together by Park Benjamin out of remaining fragments of the frame of "The Story Teller." This view is essentially corroborated by David William Pancost, "Evidence of Editorial Additions to Hawthorne's 'Fragments from the Journal of a Solitary Man,'" 210–13. The problems of textual criticism raised by "Fragments" are not dealt with in CE. See page 62 of this book. See also Newman, *A Reader's Guide to the Short Stories*, 125–27.

12. Weber, *Die Entwicklung der Rahmenerzählungen*, 142–307, analyzes Hawthorne's early phase from 1825 to 1835 and his development of various devices of the frame narrative. Based on all available biographical and bibliographical facts and a newly developed method of a structural analysis of frame narratives, this study arrives at a new view of Hawthorne's early literary development and a hypothetical reconstruction of "The Story Teller."

A total of more than thirty-two tales, sketches, and essays have been connected with "The Story Teller" by Hawthorne scholars. After a thorough bibliographical and critical study, Weber regards *with certainty* only the sketches and stories marked with two asterisks as having been part of the work. There is a *high probability* that those marked with one asterisk belonged to "The Story Teller." The attribution of the other texts as parts of the framed story cycle is *possible* but there is no clear evidence either pro or con. A close analytical reading of all the texts involved leads to the following hypothetical arrangement of the tales and sketches in "The Story Teller":

Opening Frame: Departure and first adventures of the wandering storyteller

At Home** .... CE, X, 405–9
A Flight in the Fog** .... CE, X, 409–11
A Fellow-Traveller** .... CE, X, 411–17
The Village Theatre [A]** .... CE, X, 417–20
Mr. Higginbotham's Catastrophe** .... CE, IX, 104–20
The Village Theatre [B]** .... CE, X, 420–21

In the White Mountains of New Hampshire

The Notch [A]** .... CE, X, 422–23
The Ambitious Guest* .... CE, IX, 324–33
The Notch [B]** .... CE, X, 423–25
Our Evening Party Among the Mountains** .... CE, X, 425–29
The Great Carbuncle .... CE, IX, 149–65

Along the shores of Lake Champlain

The Inland Port** .... CE, XI, 298–301
Old Ticonderoga* .... CE, XI, 186–91

On the Erie Canal

The Canal-Boat [A]** .... CE, X, 429–33
A Rill from the Town Pump * .... CE, IX, 141–48
The Canal-Boat [B]** .... CE, X, 433–35
Wakefield* .... CE, IX, 130–40
The Canal-Boat [C]** .... CE, X, 435–38

En route to Niagara

An Ontario Steam-Boat ..... Turner, *Hawthorne as Editor,* 58–64
Rochester [A]** .... CE, XI, 301–2
The Old Maid in the Winding-Sheet (The White Old
    Maid)* .... CE, IX, 370–82
Rochester [B]** .... CE, XI, 302–4
My Visit to Niagara [A]* .... CE, XI, 281–84
Fragments from the Journal [fragment 4]** .... CE, XI, 320–22
The Vision of the Fountain* .... CE, IX, 213–19
My Visit to Niagara [B]** .... CE, XI, 284–88
Fragments from the Journal [fragment 3]** .... CE, XI, 319–20

The last stages and the return home

A Night Scene** .... CE, XI, 304–5
Young Goodman Brown* .... CE, X, 74–90
The Canterbury Pilgrims .... CE, XI, 120–31
My Home Return** .... CE, XI, 322–27

The lonely years in the native village

Alice Doane's Appeal .... CE, XI, 266–80
Little Annie's Ramble .... CE, IX, 121–29
Night Sketches: Beneath an Umbrella .... CE, IX, 426–32
The Mermaid (The Village Uncle) .... CE, IX, 310–23
The Haunted Mind .... CE, IX, 304–9
Graves and Goblins* .... CE, XI, 289–97

Closing Frame: The death of the storyteller and the obituary of his friend

The Devil in Manuscript* .... CE, XI, 170–78
Fragments from the Journal [editorial report]* .. CE, XI, 312–14
Fragments from the Journal [fragment 1]** .... CE, XI, 314–17

Fragments from the Journal [editorial report]* .... CE, XI, 317
Fragments from the Journal [fragment 2]** .... CE, XI, 317–18
Fragments from the Journal [editorial report]* .. CE, XI, 318–19
Fragments from the Journal [editorial report]* .... CE, XI, 322
Fragments from the Journal [fragment 6] ** ... CE, XI, 327–28

There are a number of tales attributed by various scholars to "The Story Teller" which cannot be placed in the context of this work:

The Gray Champion .... CE, IX, 9–18
The Wedding Knell .... CE, IX, 27–36
The Maypole of Merry Mount .... CE, IX, 54–67
The Minister's Black Veil .... CE, IX, 37–53
The Threefold Destiny .... CE, IX, 472–82

13. Roger Haydon, ed., *Upstate Travels*, 10.

14. Robyn Asleson and Barbara Moore, *Dialogue with Nature*, 4.

15. Washington Irving, "The Author's Account of Himself," *The Sketch Book*, 8.

16. Kesselring, *Hawthorne's Reading, 1828–1850*, 32, 54.

17. Hawthorne had certainly read Hall's book which was notorious for its author's sharp criticism of America and Americans. He may also have read, after his return and one year before the publication of "The Story Teller," an anonymous article on "Recent Travellers in America," a critical review of a travel book by two Scotsmen, Mr. Stuart and Colonel Hamilton, which appeared in the *New-England Magazine*, 5 (November 1833): [361]–68.

18. See the references to these events in "The Ambitious Guest" (CE, IX, 324–33) and "Rochester."

19. See the bibliographical list of all the tourist guides published around 1832 and consulted for the essays in this book.

20. *The Traveller's Guide, or, a few weeks tour in the New-England States* (1823), 3.

21. Davison, *The Traveller's Guide* (1834), 17.

22. This was the title of the first edition of 1825. It was slightly changed and expanded in the later editions.

23. The fourth route leads from Quebec east, along the St. Lawrence River, through Montreal, over Lakes Ontario and Erie, to Buffalo and Detroit. Those who had enough money, time, and courage left, could embark in Detroit on the "Grand Tour": over Lakes Huron and Michigan to Fort Mackinaw and Chicago—down the Illinois and Mississippi Rivers through St. Louis and New Orleans—and from there back to New York via ship. To take a canal boat and steamboat was the most convenient way of traveling at this time, and it is astonishing to read that this Grand Tour, even if it was begun in New York, could be performed with only 108 miles of land carriage. See John Melish, *The Traveller's Directory* (1822), 176.

24. This was at the time a widely popular tourist route described also in other tourist guides and travel books. There is no evidence that Haw-

thorne had read Vandewater's *Tourist* but it seems very likely that he had access to this book because of his uncle Richard Manning's involvement in the stagecoach business.

25. Charles E. Rosenberg, in his detailed study *The Cholera Years*, 2–3, gives the following description of the disease:

The symptoms of cholera are spectacular; they could not be ignored or romanticised as were the physical manifestations of malaria or tuberculosis. . . . The onset of cholera is marked by diarrhea, acute spasmodic vomiting, and painful cramps. Consequent dehydration gives to the sufferer a characteristic and disquieting appearance: his face blue and feet drawn and puckered. "One often," recalled a New York physician, "thought of Laocoön, but looked in vain for the serpent." Death may intervene within a day, sometimes within a few hours of the appearance of the first symptoms. And these first symptoms appear with little or no warning.

26. The most important sources are these: *The Cholera Record* (1832); Dudley Atkins, ed., *Reports of hospital physicians, and other documents* (1832); C.B. Coventry, *Epidemic Cholera* (1849); John E. Doyle, "The Epidemic Cholera in Springfield, 1832 and 1849"; M. C. Hand, *From a Forest to a City: Personal Reminiscences of Syracuse* (1889); James R. Manley, "Essay on Cholera" (1835); David Meredith Reese, *A plain and practical treatise on the epidemic cholera, as it prevailed in the city of New York, in the summer of 1832* (1833); Donald E. Shaw, *Erie Water West* (1966); Augustus Walker, "Early days on the Lakes, with an account of the cholera visitation of 1832"; E. T. Winter, *The Asiatic Cholera* (1849).

27. In *The Northern Traveller* of 1830, 329–30, Dwight describes the "Routes from Boston" and says:

Coaches go in so many directions, that a choice may be made between a great many, all of them pleasant. . . . In the first place, the noble scenery of the *White Hills* may be taken in the way to Lake Champlain, Canada, the Springs, or Niagara. . . . Those who can first pass through the Notch in the White Mountains, will find its beauties greatly enhanced by the contrast [with the route along the Connecticut River]. Since the devastation caused by the flood in 1826, the road has been so much repaired as to be very good; and great improvements have been made at E. A. Crawford's, in the ascent of Mount Washington and in accomodations.

The route to Lake Champlain through the Notch, by way of Crawford's Inn and Mount Washington is exactly the one Hawthorne took.

28. Cole and Pratt's route went from Concord to Lake Winnipesaukee and Conway, through the Notch to E. A. Crawford's, to the Franconia Notch and its "Old Man of the Mountain" to Plymouth, N. H. See Catherine H. Campbell, "Two's Company," *passim*.

On his way to the White Mountains, Oberon in "The Story Teller" meets a young theologian from Andover (see "The Fellow-Traveller," CE, X, 411–17). Dwight in *The Northern Traveller* (1830), 334, mentions a route to Concord through Andover, "a small village, situated on high ground, 20 miles from Boston, remarkable for the *Philips Academy and Theological Seminary*." According to Darby and Dwight's *New Gazetteer* (1832), 24–25, it is "the oldest in the U.S." This route, according to Dwight, *The Northern Traveller*,

337–67, leads from Concord on to Lake Winnipesaukee, Conway, Lovel's Pond, The Willey House, and The Notch, to the Camp at the Ammonoosuc River, from where travelers ascend to the peak of Mount Washington. It leads on to Littleton, N. H., and Burlington, Vt. In the year 1725 there was a bloody battle at Lovel's Pond between the Pickwacket Indians and a company of troops from Massachusetts. It is possible that Hawthorne visited the place of "Roger Malvin's Burial" (CE, X, 337–60), one of his earlier "Provincial Tales."

29. Dwight, *The Northern Traveller* (1830), 341.

30. This is the way described in "The Notch."

31. Kenneth Walter Cameron in *The Genesis of Hawthorne's "The Ambitious Guest"* published a great number of newspaper clippings showing how widely the Willey disaster had caught the public attention at the time.

32. Davison, *The Traveller's Guide* (1834), 350–52. Davison also refers to the geological interests of the time which Hawthorne alludes to in "The Notch" by mentioning a mineralogist traveling through the White Mountains. Davison points out that the

effects produced by the flood . . . will offer many new objects interesting to an intelligent traveller. It will afford him a very desirable opportunity to observe, in some places, the structure of the mountains, where their interior has been laid bare by the falling of vast quantities of earth and rocks; and in others, exemplifications to confirm the modern geognostical theories, to explain the phenomena observable in valleys, plains, and the courses of rivers. Geologists and mineralogists, too, may expect to meet with curious and valuable specimens, among the enormous wrecks they will observe on either hand. (351)

33. Dwight, *The Northern Traveller* (1830), 355–56. Dwight describes it in detail thus:

A road was first made through the Notch in 1785. It was 50 or 60 feet higher than the present turnpike, and so steep that it was necessary to draw horses and wagons up with ropes. The assessment for the turnpike was made in 1806.

Two rocks stand at the sides of this remarkable passage, one 20, and the other about 30 feet, in perpendicular height. . . . The part which appears to have been cut through is about 120 feet long. The Notch meadow opens beyond; and after a ride of 4½ miles, the traveller reaches another comfortable house, kept by Mr. E. A. Crawford, where also he will be received and entertained.

Compare the description of "the romantic defile of the Notch" in Hawthorne's sketch.

34. The road through the Notch was not only taken by tourists but used both ways also by commercial traffic, and Crawford's Inn was also a favorable spot for teamsters from, or on their way to, the Connecticut valley and Burlington. See R. Stuart Wallace, "A Social History of the White Mountains," in Donald D. Keyes, *The White Mountains*, 26–27.

35. Dwight, *The Northern Traveller* (1830), 357–59.

36. Dwight in *The Northern Traveller* (1830), 357, describes in detail the ascent to Mount Washington: Ethan A. Crawford

also will act as a guide, and is qualified for the office, both by his intimate acquaintance with the way, and the various kind attentions and amusing anecdotes with which he knows how to relieve the tediousness of the ascent. The best arrangement is to set out in the afternoon, spend the night at the wigwam or 'Camp,' ascend the mountain early in the morning, to have the benefit of the view by sunrise, and return to the inn before the ensuing evening. It is 6 or 7 miles to the 'Camp,' 3 of which are passable in a carriage and the rest on horseback, though much impeded by the devastations of the great storm.

"The Great Carbuncle" (CE, IX, 149–65) is certainly based on Hawthorne's own ascent of Mount Washington.

37. R. Stuart Wallace, "A Social History," in Donald D. Keyes, *The White Mountains,* 26.

38. Donald D. Keyes, "Perceptions of the White Mountains," in Donald D. Keyes, *The White Mountains,* 41.

39. Thomas Cole, "Essay on American Scenery," *The American Monthly Magazine* n.s. 1 (January 1836); reprinted in John Conron, *The American Landscape,* 572.

40. See the sketch of Burlington in "The Inland Port." In their *New Gazetteer* (1833), 77, Darby and Dwight give a short description of this "large and flourishing" village of 3,525 inhabitants:

The [village] is on a slope of 1 m. to a fine harbor. On the top of the hill is the college, and many of the private houses are in beautiful taste, with large gardens &c. It has the county buildings, an academy, bank, ($150,000 capital) &c. Many of the vessels on the lake belong to this village. . . . First settled just before the revolution. . . . Very good stage coaches travel by day light to Boston. . . . Two steam boats which ply between Whitehall, and St. John's Canada, touch here, and another runs to Plattsburgh, 25 ms.

Horatio Gates Spafford in his *Pocket Guide* (1825), 26, gives the steamboat distances and fares on Lake Champlain and mentions a connection that Hawthorne might have used by stagecoach and packet boat to Montreal. The anonymous *Traveller's Pocket Directory* (1831), 48, lists a mail stage three days a week between Whitehall and Montreal via Ticonderoga and Plattsburgh.

41. [Gideon Miner Davison,] *The Fashionable Tour* (1828), 211. John Disturnell in *A Gazetteer of the State of New-York* (1843) comments on the "scenery of the most picturesque description; the headlands which are seen to great advantage, and the vast ranges of mountains on either side, [which are] truly grand and romantic."

42. Peru is situated ten miles southwest of Plattsburgh on the Little Au Sable River. It has a convenient landing on the west side of Lake Champlain. See Disturnell, *A Gazetteer of the State of New-York* (1843), 321.

43. Hawthorne had the alternative of going north to Montreal, or south to Ticonderoga, Lake George, and the Erie Canal. Since the narrator of the sketches mentions Montreal a couple of times and says that he had crossed the lake in the morning from the New York shore and reached Burlington in a little skiff from Peru, N.Y., it is possible that Hawthorne, after having written to his mother from Burlington, made a short excursion

to southern Canada before taking a steamboat from Burlington to the southern part of Lake Champlain. Davison, in *The Fashionable Tour* (1828), 122, says that the passage in a Champlain steamboat to Plattsburgh "is generally in the night." The excursion could have taken Hawthorne about two days. Whether or not he took this brief excursion cannot be finally settled. I believe that Hawthorne turned south from Burlington to Ticonderoga, Lake George, Saratoga Springs, and the Erie Canal. Davison describes this as one of the main routes of tourism:

At present the most usual arrangements of the tourist are, after visiting Lake George and Ticonderoga, to return to the Springs, from thence to take passage in the regular stage to Utica, by way of Johnstown; or proceed to Schenectady, where he can meet, any day in the week, except Sundays, the line of Post Coaches or Canal Boats, from Albany to Niagara. (122)

44. This is the original opening paragraph omitted in later reprintings. It may have been added by Benjamin, like the introductory notes to "Sketches from Memory." Orwell lies forty-seven miles south of Burlington on the Vermont shore of Lake Champlain, opposite Ticonderoga. The place on the shore mentioned in the sketch is called Shoreham, as Elizabeth E. McCaughlin, curator of the Hancock House, Ticonderoga Historical Society, pointed out in a letter of 15 November 1980. She quotes from the *History of the Town of Shoreham, Vermont* by Josiah F. Goodhue (Ticonderoga, N.Y., 1861): 37–38: "The place was then known as Rowley's Point. The late John S. Larabee, then a young man, bought out Rowley in 1787, kept a tavern and established the ferry. He . . . made it a prosperous and popular establishment. This house was burned about 1838."

45. John Disturnell in his *Gazetteer of the State of New-York* (1843), 172, gives a short description of the history of this important military fortification on the west side of Lake Champlain, at the entrance of the outlet of Lake George, and says, that after the close of the Revolutionary War, the fortress

has been suffered to go to decay, and now presents one of the most interesting ruins of the kind in this country, and is annually visited by a great number of travellers. Near by, on the lake shore, is situated a well kept hotel for the accomodation of visit[o]rs, where steamboats, during the season of navigation, daily land and received passengers.

46. *Ibid.*, 182. It is very probable that Hawthorne passed Lake George, because it was on the route from Burlington and Ticonderoga south to the Erie Canal, and because Lake George is described in "Monsieur du Miroir" (1837), a later sketch. Darby and Dwight in their *New Gazetteer* (1833), 247, give the following description:

This lake is surrounded by high mountains, and is surpassed in the romantic by no lake scenery in the world. Water deep and clear, abounding with the finest of fish. The lake abounds with small isl[e]s. It is a fashionable place of resort in summer. In consequence of the extraordinary purity of the waters of this lake, the French formerly procured it for sacramental purposes; on which account they denominated it Lac Sacrament.

Robert J. Vandewater, *The Tourist* (1834), 86, describes it thus:

There are few places where a greater variety of inducements attract the stranger than at Lake George. Besides the interest which is excited from an association of many important historic events, this place is rendered peculiarly interesting from the unrivalled exhibition of the beautiful and romantic scenery presented by the lake and its environs.

47. John Disturnell, *A Gazetteer of the State of New-York* (1843), 360.
48. Davison, *The Fashionable Tour* (1828), 124. The distance to Little Falls is sixty-five miles. For Dwight, *The Northern Traveller* (1830), 59, it is "the most romantic scene on the course of the Erie canal." Vandewater, *The Tourist* (1834), 51–52, describes Little Falls in more detail:

These are rapids rather than falls. On each side the mountains are very high, leaving but a narrow space for the river, canal, and road to pass through. For about 2 miles the canal is formed by throwing up a wall into the river from 20 to 30 feet high, then excavating into the mountain and filling it up. This was one of the most difficult and expensive parts of the canal, as it was necessary to blast the rock with gunpowder to form the bed of the canal, for nearly the whole distance. A beautiful *marble aqueduct* crosses the river at this place, and leads into a basin opposite, where boats discharge and receive lading. . . . [The aqueduct] is elevated about 25 feet above the surface of the river, 'a foaming torrent, dashing over the bare rocks in a fearful and sublime style.' . . . There are a number of fine buildings in the village on the opposite side of the river, principally of stone. Passengers disposed to pedestrianism generally leave the boat at the second lock, and walk until they reach the last. They are six in number, by which the boat is so much detained that a person may walk quite leisurely through the most wild and romantic scenery that can easily be imagined. . . . After leaving Little Falls, you pass through a most delightful plain, called *German Flats.*

Finally, after twenty-two miles, you reach "the beautiful and flourishing city of Utica."

49. Andrist, *The Erie Canal*, 76.
50. Patricia Anderson, *The Course of Empire*, 17.
51. Dwight, *The Northern Traveller* (1830), 47–48.
52. Dwight, *Sketches of Scenery and Manners*, 151.
53. Vandewater, *The Tourist* (1830), 39–40, calls Syracuse "the most important place between Utica and Rochester." He says it "contains about four hundred buildings; among which are a church, two very extensive Hotels, one on each side of the Canal, which is lined with lofty warehouses, giving it the appearance of New-York in miniature."
54. Vandewater, *The Tourist* (1834), 56, gives an outline of a possible route up the Oswego Canal, which commenced at Salina, a mile and a half north of Syracuse:

Parties visiting *Niagara* frequently take the canal from this place [Syracuse] to Oswego, 38 miles northward: proceed by steamboat on Lake Ontario to Lewiston, whence a stage ride of seven miles takes them to the *Falls.*

There is a line of fine packet-boats on this route [to Oswego]. The scenery is very interesting; and during the last season it received a great portion of the fashionable northern and western travel.

Instead of going from Oswego directly to Rochester, Lewiston and Niagara, Hawthorne may have made a detour via Ogdensburg, New York, by steamboat and by stage. Horatio Spafford's *Pocket Guide* (1825), 27–28, lists a steamboat connection on Lake Ontario between Ogdensburg, Sacket's Harbor, Genesee River [Rochester], Lewiston and Niagara. This is confirmed by Davison, *The Traveller's Guide* (1833), 249, and Disturnell, *The Traveller's Guide* (1836), 50. This seems the probable itinerary also in view of the statement of the narrator of "An Ontario Steam-Boat" that he had "embarked at Ogdensburgh, and was voyaging westward, to the other extremity of Lake Ontario." That he could have made a detour is also suggested by a passage in the sketch "My Visit to Niagara" where the narrator comments on his trip to Niagara: "I had lingered away from it, and wandered to other scenes, because my treasury of anticipated enjoyments, comprising all the wonders of the world, had nothing else so magnificent."

55. Vandewater, *The Tourist* (1830), 44.

56. Spafford, *Pocket Guide* (1825), 64–65.

57. Disturnell in *The Traveller's Guide* (1836), 54, adds the following details:

LEWISTON, 7 miles below the Falls of Niagara, and 8 miles from lake Ontario . . . is at the head of navigation on the Niagara River. . . . The route from Lewiston to Niagara Falls on the American side, ascends somewhat precipitous for about two miles, when the ascent is gained, it affords an imposing prospect of the expanse below. Three and a half miles from Lewiston towards the falls, you pass the *Devil's Hole*, a most terrific gulf, formed by a chasm in the eastern bank of the Niagara, about 200 feet deep.

MANCHESTER, three and a half miles further, is near the Niagara Falls, on the American side, where are a number of well kept hotels, for the accommodation of visitors.

Spafford, *A Pocket Guide* (1825), 67, makes the following recommendation: "To see the Falls to the best advantage, go from Lewiston to Whitney's; and after going on to the islands, cross the river immediately below the Falls, ferriage 25 cents, descending and ascending the stairways. In my opinion the best *single view* is from Forsyth's piazza, on the Canada side." Forsyth's is mentioned in Hawthorne's sketch of Niagara Falls.

58. Patricia Anderson, *The Course of Empire*, 19.

59. Vandewater, *The Tourist* (1834), 69–79. He describes the approach to the Falls from the American side:

The Falls on the American side (divided from the British Falls by Goat Island, which stands on the very verge of the precipice) are truly magnificent, though of less magnitude than the other. Here the admirer is presented with a variety of charming views and an effective arrangement of the picturesque. . . . Goat Island, sometimes called Iris, is laid out in delightful walks, which are shaded by a great variety of the lofty trees of the American forest. It derived its name from the fact of an aged and venerable goat having resided, and held undisputed right there, for several years prior to its being trodden by human feet. There are many fine views of the rapids above, and on the grand fall on the Canada side, from several points on the island. (70–71)

He also describes the way to the British side:

for a single view [of the Falls], in which you would gaze on sublimity itself, take your stand on Table Rock. A flight of stairs has been erected a few rods below the falls descending to the ferry, where a boat with good oarsmen is always ready to convey passengers to the opposite shore. Many are of opinion that the view from the boat, whirling about in the eddies, is more interesting than any other: we advise all to cross and judge for themselves. (70)

In a preceding passage, he also describes the attractions on the British side:

Table Rock, which projects about 50 feet, is generally considered the most eligible place for viewing the falls on the Canada side. The descent from the rock is by circular steps, which are enclosed; at the foot of these stairs commences the passage under the great sheet of water, where visitants are supplied with dresses and a guide. The farthest approachable distance is *Termination Rock,* 153 feet from Table Rock. (68)

60. Vandewater, *The Tourist* (1834), 67, states: "Steamboats leave twice each day, morning and evening, for *Detroit,* via. *Erie,* Grand River, Cleveland, and Sandusky; distance 305 miles." Dwight, *The Northern Traveller* (1830), 111–12, says: "At Buffalo opens a very extensive route, for those who are disposed to travel still farther westward. . . . Michigan is a territory fast rising in population, wealth, and importance. A large branch of the tide of emigration from the eastern states and New-York has been turned in that direction, and still further west."

61. William Williams, in *The stage, canal, and steamboat register* (1830?), 5, lists a stagecoach line from Buffalo to Albany via Utica, with a steamboat connection to New York, taking four days. Between Albany and Boston there is also a stage line connection by various routes, over a distance of 165 to 170 miles. See *The Traveller's Pocket Directory* (1831), 46. A number of travel guides also describe a route from Niagara to Montreal, mainly by steamboat, taking about two days.

62. Haydon, *Upstate Travels,* x.

63. Herman Melville, "Hawthorne and His Mosses," *Writings,* IX, 249.

A LITERARY AND PICTORIAL ICONOGRAPHY
OF HAWTHORNE'S TOUR

1. E. H. Gombrich, *Art and Illusion: A Study in the Psychology of Pictorial Presentation,* especially ch. 2, "Truth and Stereotype," 55–73.

2. Jean Normand, *Nathaniel Hawthorne: An Approach to an Analysis of Artistic Creation,* 39.

3. Robert L. McGrath, "The Real and the Ideal: Popular Images of the White Mountains," in Donald D. Keyes, *The White Mountains*, 59.

4. *Ibid.*, 58–59, ills. 69 and 70.

5. Donald D. Keyes, "Perceptions of the White Mountains: A General Survey," in Keyes, *The White Mountains*, 42.

6. John F. Sears, "Hawthorne's 'The Ambitious Guest' and the Significance of the Willey Disaster," *American Literature* 54, 354–67, traces the popularity of the Willey tragedy in New England newspapers, sermons, and magazines in the years preceding Hawthorne's visit to the locale, and argues that both the author and his audiences were "thoroughly familiar with [the Willey story] from the numerous accounts that had already been written and from prints showing the scene of the disaster" (356).

7. R. Stuart Wallace, "A Social History of the White Mountains," in Keyes, *The White Mountains*, 26.

8. Nathaniel Parker Willis, *American Scenery* (1840; reprinted 1971), 194.

9. Alexander M. Ross, *William Henry Bartlett: Artist, Author, Traveller*, 38.

10. R. Stuart Wallace, "A Social History of the White Mountains," in Keyes, *The White Mountains*, 27.

11. Keyes, "Perceptions of the White Mountains: A General Survey," in Keyes, *The White Mountains*, 43.

12. Joshua Shaw, *Picturesque Views of American Scenery*, n.p.

13. According to Roger Haydon in *Upstate Travels*, 185, for many British visitors Canandaigua "seemed a lovely place transported by inexplicable circumstance to the wilderness," an elegant and beautiful village that offered the "quiet promise of civilized life."

14. See for example Patrick Brydone's classic description in the frequently reprinted *A Tour Through Sicily and Malta in a Series of Letters to William Beckford* (1776), 14.

15. William Cullen Bryant, ed., *Picturesque America; or, The Land we Live in* (1876), 2:369.

16. Anderson, *The Course of Empire*, 27.

17. Gideon Miner Davison, *The Traveller's Guide* (1833), 199–200.

18. N. P. Willis, *American Scenery*, 265, 227. Of the four engravings of the Erie Canal included in *American Scenery*, three are of Little Falls. For similar iconography, see also two watercolors of Little Falls sketched in 1852 and 1853 by William Rickarby Miller in Anderson's *The Course of Empire*, 72–73.

19. Elizabeth McKinsey, *Niagara Falls*, 7–17.

20. *Ibid.*, 65.

21. See discussion *ibid.*, 293n.

22. *Ibid.*, 144.

23. *Ibid.*, 253–65, for the record of these developments.

24. McKinsey records the "Fall of Niagara" in her book's final section, "The Icon Shattered," *ibid.*, 249–82.

25. Donald A. Ringe, *The Pictorial Mode*, 123–64. The quotations are on 129 and 133.

26. Thomas Cole, "Essay on American Scenery," *The American Monthly Magazine* n.s. 1 (January 1836); reprinted in John Conron, *The American Landscape*, 575.

HISTORY AND NATIONALISM IN "OLD TICONDEROGA" AND OTHER TRAVEL SKETCHES

1. See Hans Huth, *Nature and the American*, 38. For the specifically literary dimensions of this rivalry see also Christopher Mulvey, *Anglo-American Landscapes*, *passim*.

2. Joshua Shaw, *Picturesque Views*, no page, letterpress accompanying the plate "View on the North River."

3. William Guy Wall, *Hudson River Portfolio*, no page, letterpress accompanying plates 15 and 18.

4. Nathaniel Parker Willis, *American Scenery*, 323.

5. Nina Baym, *The Shape of Hawthorne's Career*, 27. See also Arlin Turner, *Nathaniel Hawthorne*, 49–51. The most thorough study of Hawthorne's early projected story collections is Alfred Weber, *Die Entwicklung der Rahmenerzählungen Nathaniel Hawthornes*, especially 30–50, and 61–100.

6. This well-known trend is summarized extensively in Benjamin Townley Spencer, *The Quest for Nationality*.

7. In Richard D. Ruland, ed., *The Native Muse*, 1:237. Longfellow, of course, was repeating the ideas set forth during the preceding decade by William Tudor and others in the *North American Review*. These articles are also reprinted in Ruland.

8. Donald A. Ringe, *The Pictorial Mode: Space and Time in the Art of Bryant, Irving and Cooper*, and Blake Nevius, *Cooper's Landscapes: An Essay on the Picturesque Vision*.

9. William Templeman, *The Life and Work of William Gilpin (1724–1804)*, 260–64.

10. William Gilpin, *Observations on the River Wye*, 356; *Remarks on Forest Scenery*, 117; *Observations on the Mountains and Lakes of Cumberland and Westmoreland*, 1:187.

11. Gilpin, *Cumberland and Westmoreland*, 2:122–23.

12. Quoted in Louis Legrand Noble, *The Life and Works of Thomas Cole*, 219.

13. Washington Irving, *The Sketch Book*, 8–9.

14. Charles Brockden Brown, "American Prospects," 93.

15. Robert E. Streeter, "Association Psychology and Literary Nationalism in the *North American Review*, 1815–1825," shows how the theories in Archibald Alison's *Essay on Taste* (Boston, 1815) validated the aesthetic and moral significance of local scenery.

16. For a full discussion of Hawthorne's attitude toward the Irish and other groups of immigrants he encountered on his 1832 tour, see Beth L. Lueck, "'Meditating on the Varied Congregation of Human Life': Immigrants in Hawthorne's Travel Sketches," *The Nathaniel Hawthorne Review* 14 (Fall 1988): 1–7.

17. Jane Louise Mesick, *The English Traveller in America, 1785–1835*, surveys the negative attitudes of early British travel writers, 270–98.

18. Nina Baym, commenting in *The Shape of Hawthorne's Career* on the early biographical sketches "Mrs. Hutchinson," "Sir William Phips," "Sir William Pepperell," and "Dr. Bullivant," believes that the young Hawthorne "saw history and fiction as two different genres because fiction is invented and history is not" (35) and that "at this point in his career Hawthorne had not yet found a fictional use for actual historical event" (37).

19. E. L. Magoon, "Scenery and Mind," in *The Home Book of the Picturesque* (1852), 25.

20. Warren Burton, *The Scenery-Shower*, 77.

21. T. S. Eliot, *The Waste Land*, 29, l. 17.

22. Theodore Dwight, *Sketches of Scenery and Manners in the United States*, 77; Theodore Dwight, *The Northern Traveller* (1825), 173.

23. Dwight, *Sketches of Scenery*, 153–54.

24. Burton, *The Scenery-Shower*, 83.

25. Elizabeth McKinsey, *Niagara Falls: Icon of the American Sublime*.

26. A Canadian study, Ralph Greenhill and Thomas D. Mahoney, *Niagara*, 32, interprets the battle of Lundy's Lane as a British victory that "led to a Canadian tradition of a victory against overwhelming odds." Certainly, the Americans were frustrated in their bid to annex lower Canada.

27. For a discussion of the historical and geographical problems associated with Niagara Falls, see McKinsey, *Niagara Falls*, 51–52 and 105–7.

28. Mesick, *The English Traveller in America*, 287, considers Hall's *Travels in North America in the Years 1827 and 1828* (1830) along with Francis Trollope's *Domestic Manners of the Americans* (1831) as the two British travel books most notoriously hostile toward American culture.

29. These and the following facts about Fort Ticonderoga are based on Robert B. Roberts, *New York's Forts in the Revolution*, 149–86.

30. "Pedestrian Tour," *North-American Review* 4 (January 1817): 178; "Art. IV: View of Ticonderoga," *Analectic* 11 (April 1818): 272; "Fort Ticonderoga on Lake Champlain. (with an Engraving.)," *Port Folio* [5th Series] 6 (September 1818): 222.

31. Dwight, *The Northern Traveller* (1826); Gideon Miner Davison, *The Traveller's Guide* (1833).

32. Nevius, *Cooper's Landscapes*, 16.

33. Roberts, *New York's Forts*, 177, adds that St. Clair subordinated his views on defending the fort to those of his commander, Major General Horatio Gates, who saw no need for fortifying the heights.

34. Dwight, *The Northern Traveller* (1825), 127.

35. Susan Cooper, "A Dissolving View," in *The Home Book of the Picturesque*, 89.

36. Thomas Cole, "Essay on American Scenery," *The American Monthly Magazine* n. s. 1 (January 1836); reprinted in John Conron, *The American Landscape*, 577.

37. For a discussion of Arnold's role at Ticonderoga and its deliberate lapse into obscurity, see Edward Hamilton, *Fort Ticonderoga*, 112–14.

HAWTHORNE'S IRONIC TRAVELER AND THE
PICTURESQUE TOUR

1. Charles L. Batten, Jr., *Pleasurable Instruction: Form and Convention in Eighteenth-Century Travel Literature*, 112–13. He devotes an entire chapter to "Descriptive Conventions in Eighteenth-Century Travel Literature" (82–115).

2. See William Gilpin, "On Picturesque Travel," in *Three Essays*, 41–58. For a typical example of one of Gilpin's highly influential tours, see his *Observations on the River Wye*.

3. Christopher Mulvey, *Anglo-American Landscapes*, 253.

4. Marion L. Kesselring, *Hawthorne's Reading*, entries 30, 62, 94, 192, 235, and 366.

5. Theodore Dwight, *The Northern Traveller* (1825), 173.

6. *Ibid.*

7. Washington Irving, *The Sketch Book*, 9.

8. William Cullen Bryant uses a similar conceit in "Monument Mountain" (1824). According to this poem, native tribes of this region believed in the Great Spirit inhabiting the mountaintops. They believed, Bryant wrote, "Like worshippers of the elder time, that God / Doth walk on the high places and affect / The earth-o'er-looking mountains" (ll. 100–102). The poem is collected in Bryant's *Life and Works*, ed. Parke Godwin, 3:253.

9. Edwin Fussell, *Frontier: American Literature and the American West*, 81.

10. *Ibid.*

11. Kesselring, *Hawthorne's Reading*, lists Burke's *Works*, notably *[A Philosophical Enquiry into the Origins of our Ideas of]* the *Sublime and the Beautiful*, as among the books borrowed from the Salem Athenaeum by Mary Manning and, presumably, read by Hawthorne in November 1828 (entry 66).

12. Hawthorne's comment here—"This is the entrance, or, in the direction we were going, the extremity of the romantic defile of the Notch"—is one of several that suggests he used one or more travel guides both in planning and, perhaps, in writing about this tour. According to Gideon Miner Davison's *The Fashionable Tour* (1830), for example, most travelers would be moving in a southerly direction here rather than the northerly direction Hawthorne followed on his tour. Thus the entrance, for him, was the extreme end of the Notch for the typical tourist. His first view of the White Mountains, described at the beginning of the sketch, is also similar to that of Davison's *Fashionable Tour*, 334–41, though not close enough to suggest a borrowing or paraphrase.

13. Davison, *Fashionable Tour*, 334.

14. Horatio Gates Spafford, *Pocket Guide for the Tourist and Traveller* (1824), 17–50.

15. Dwight, *The Northern Traveller* (1830), 47–78.

16. Davison, *Fashionable Tour* (1830), 233–57.

17. Gilpin, "On Picturesque Travel," in *Three Essays*, 47–48.

18. Gilpin, *Observations on the River Wye*, 7.

19. Davison, *Fashionable Tour* (1830), 236.

20. Spafford, *Pocket Guide for the Tourist and Traveller* (1824), 18.

21. Roger Evan Carp, "The Erie Canal and the Liberal Challenge to Classical Republicanism, 1785–1850," 713.

22. Robert J. Vandewater, *The Tourist* (1834), 55. See also Spafford, *Pocket Guide for the Tourist and Traveller*, 36, where little of interest to the picturesque traveler is noted between Utica and Syracuse. Vandewater advises tourists to avoid this section of the canal by taking the stage instead (55–56).

23. Leo B. Levy, "Hawthorne's 'The Canal Boat': An Experiment in Landscape," 213–14; Alfred Weber, *Die Entwicklung der Rahmenerzählungen Nathaniel Hawthornes*, 225.

24. See Roger Haydon, *Upstate Travels*, 10, and Elizabeth McKinsey, *Niagara Falls: Icon of the American Sublime*. My understanding of the cultural context of "My Visit to Niagara" was deepened by McKinsey's study of Niagara Falls, and I wish to acknowledge that debt here.

25. McKinsey, *Niagara Falls*, 189—90 ff.

26. McKinsey, *ibid.*, 198, points out that Hawthorne's oblique references in *The Italian Notebooks* to his experience at Niagara Falls suggest that he found "the same disappointment and recovery of the sublime" as his narrator in "My Visit to Niagara."

27. *Ibid.*, 192.

28. Commenting on the symbolism of the walking stick, McKinsey finds the "motif suggestive of a knowledge of good and evil." She argues that the staff "might facilitate a fall from the innocence of anticipation into experience and knowledge," interpreting the narrator's disappointment in Niagara as a kind of fall from his initial anticipation and his growing understanding of the Falls as his coming to terms with the experience's real meaning for him, rather than simply the stereotypical and rather limited views of other tourists. *Ibid.*, 192–93.

29. Hawthorne appears to have taken the advice of Dwight's *The Northern Traveller* (1830), 85, on viewing the falls: "It may be recommended to the traveller to visit this place as often as he can, and to view it from every neighbouring point; as every change of light exhibits it under a different and interesting aspect. The rainbows are to be seen from this [the British] side only in the afternoon; but at that time the clouds of mist, which are continually rising from the gulf below, often present them in the utmost beauty." Note that the narrator in Hawthorne's sketch is indeed viewing the falls in the afternoon—in fact, he has put off his first visit until then— and that he moves from place to place, following Dwight's advice to see the falls "from every neighbouring point" for the best effects. It is interesting that in the Library of Congress an 1830 edition originally owned by Daniel Ricketson of New Bedford, Massachusetts, bears the following note on the passage quoted above: "This must be a mistake, for there was a beautiful rainbow there at 9½ o'clock A.M. May 19, 1833. D. R." (handwritten on 85).

30. Gilpin, "On Sketching Landscape," in *Three Essays*, 63.

31. McKinsey, *Niagara Falls*, 193, states that "the reader expects an affirmative answer" to the rhetorical questions about whether the narrator's hopes had been fulfilled, but I think a careful reader ought to have picked up enough clues by this point in the sketch to be prepared for the "devastating" response that follows.

32. McKinsey, *ibid.*, notes that "the turning point comes at night when he [the narrator] is caught unaware, in a completely passive state of unselfconscious receptivity, no longer haunted by dead conventions and exaggerated expectations."

33. "Night after night," he writes, "I dreamed of it," suggesting anywhere from a few days to a week spent at the falls.

34. Dwight, for example, recommends the view from Table Rock in *The Northern Traveller* (1830), 79 and 84, and gives an account of its fall on page 87.

35. Emphasizing the spatial structure of the scene, McKinsey, *Niagara Falls*, 194, notes that Hawthorne's position here is above the falls, where he "has *risen* to a feeling of perfect unison with the scene." The narrator, she points out, "looks down (literally and figuratively) on others who have not achieved a similar transcendence."

36. James R. Mellow, *Nathaniel Hawthorne in His Times*, 51.

37. James Kirke Paulding, *The New Mirror for Travellers* (1828), 90.

38. Basil Hall, *Travels in North America in the Years 1827 and 1828*, 1:109.

39. Gilpin, "On Sketching Landscape," in *Three Essays*, 66–70.

40. McKinsey, *Niagara Falls*, 194.

41. Hawthorne may have followed the route described in Dwight's *Northern Traveller* (1830), 83, which notes the various views seen along the Niagara River and suggests that a "leisurely walk" there "may please the admirer of nature."

42. McKinsey, *Niagara Falls*, 195, argues that "If his experience on first approaching Niagara was a 'fall,' then it was certainly a fortunate fall," with the rainbow serving as "a sign that he has indeed recovered an authentic experience of the Falls' sublimity."

BIBLIOGRAPHY

I: WORKS CITED

Adams, Richard P. "Hawthorne: A Study of his Literary Development."
Ph.D. Diss., Columbia University, 1951.
———. "Hawthorne's *Provincial Tales.*" *New England Quarterly* 30 (1957):
39–57.
Adkins, Nelson F. "The Early Projected Works of Nathaniel Hawthorne."
The Papers of the Bibliographical Society of America 39 (1945): 119–55.
Anderson, Patricia. *The Course of Empire. The Erie Canal and the New York
Landscape. 1825–1875.* Exhibition and Catalogue by Patricia Anderson.
Memorial Art Gallery of the University of Rochester, Rochester, N.Y.,
16 June–12 August 1984.
Andrist, Ralph K. *The Erie Canal.* 3d ed. New York: American Heritage
Pub. Co., 1946.
"Art. IV: View of Ticonderoga." *Analectic* 11 (April 1818), 323–25.
Asleson, Robyn, and Barbara Moore. *Dialogue with Nature: Landscape and
Literature in Nineteenth-Century America.* Washington, D.C.: The Corcoran
Gallery of Art, 1985.
Atkins, Dudley, ed. *Reports of hospital physicians, and other documents in relation
to the epidemic cholera of 1832.* Published by order of the Board of Health.
New York, 1832.
Barber, John W., and Henry Howe. *Historical collections of the state of New
York: containing a general collection of the most interesting facts, traditions,
biographical sketches, anecdotes, &c. relating to its history and antiquities, with
geographical descriptions of every township in the state. Illustrated by 230 en-
gravings.* New York: S. Tuttle, 1842.
Batten, Charles L., Jr. *Pleasurable Instruction: Form and Convention in Eigh-
teenth-Century Travel Literature.* Berkeley: University of California Press,
1978.
Baym, Nina. *The Shape of Hawthorne's Career.* Ithaca: Cornell University
Press, 1976.
Brown, Charles Brockden. "American Prospects." *The Literary Magazine and
American Register* 3 (February 1805): 93.
Bryant, William Cullen. *The Life and Works of William Cullen Bryant.* Edited
by Parke Godwin. Vol. 3. New York: D. Appleton and Company, 1883.
———, ed. *Picturesque America; or, The Land we Live in.* 2 vols., 1876. Reprint
Secaucus, N.J.: Lyle Stuart, Inc., 1974.

Brydone, Patrick. *A Tour Through Sicily and Malta in a Series of Letters to William Beckford.* London: W. Strahan, 1776.

Burton, Warren. *The Scenery-Shower, With Word-Paintings of the Beautiful, the Picturesque, and the Grand in Nature.* Boston: William D. Ticknor & Co., 1844.

Cameron, Kenneth Walter. *The Genesis of Hawthorne's "The Ambitious Guest."* Hartford: Transcendental Books, 1955.

Campbell, Catherine H. "Two's Company: The Diaries of Thomas Cole and Henry Cheever Pratt on Their Walk through Crawford Notch, 1828." *Historical New Hampshire* 33 (Winter 1978): 309–33.

Carp, Roger Evan. "The Erie Canal and the Liberal Challenge to Classical Republicanism, 1785–1850." Ph.D. Diss., University of North Carolina at Chapel Hill, 1986.

The Cholera Record, containing a list . . . of those who died of cholera in the city of Albany, together with tables exhibiting a daily progress and decline of the disease, in Quebec, Montreal, Rochester [etc.]. Albany: n.p., 1832.

Cole, Thomas. "Essay on American Scenery." *The American Monthly Magazine* n.s. 1 (January 1836). Reprinted in John Conron. *The American Landscape: A Critical Anthology of Prose and Poetry.* New York: Oxford University Press, 1973, 568–78.

Coventry, Charles Brodhead. *Epidemic Cholera: Its History, Causes, Pathology, and Treatment.* Buffalo: Geo. H. Derby & Co., 1849.

Crowley, J. Donald. "Historical Commentary" to his edition of *Twice-told Tales.* CE IX, 485–533.

———. "The Uncollected Tales," part of the "Historical Commentary" to his edition of *The Snow-Image and Uncollected Tales.* CE XI, 395–409.

Darby, William. *A Tour from the City of New York, to Detroit in the Michigan Territory, Made Between the 2nd of May and the 22nd of September, 1818.* 1819: Facsimile ed., Chicago: Quadrangle Books, 1962.

Doubleday, Neal Frank. *Hawthorne's Early Tales, a Critical Study.* Durham, N.C.: Duke University Press, 1972.

Doyle, John E. "The Epidemic Cholera in Springfield, 1832 and 1849." *Historical Journal of Western Massachusetts* 3, no. 2 (Fall 1974): 1–14.

[Dwight, Theodore]. *Sketches of Scenery and Manners in the United States.* New York: A. T. Goodrich, 1829.

———. *Things as They Are: or, Notes of a Traveller through Some of the Middle and Northern States.* New York: Harper & Bros., 1834.

Eliot, T. S. *The Waste Land and Other Poems.* New York: Harcourt, Brace, and World, Inc., 1962.

"Fort Ticonderoga on Lake Champlain. (with an Engraving.)." *Port Folio* [5th Series] 6 (September 1818), 222.

Fussell, Edwin. *Frontier: American Literature and the American West.* Princeton, N.J.: Princeton University Press, 1965.

Gilpin, William. *Observations on the Mountains and Lakes of Cumberland and Westmoreland.* 2 vols. 1786. Reprint edited by Sutherland Lyall. Richmond, U.K.: The Richmond Publishing Co., 1973.

————. *Observations on the River Wye, and several parts of South Wales, &c. relative chiefly to picturesque beauty; made in the summer of the Year 1770.* 1782. Reprint edited by Sutherland Lyall. Richmond, U. K.: The Richmond Publishing Co., 1973.

————. *Observations on the Western Parts of England.* 1798. Reprint edited by Sutherland Lyall. Richmond, U. K.: Richmond Publishing, 1973.

————. *Remarks on Forest Scenery, and Other Woodland Views (Relative Chiefly to Picturesque Beauty).* 1791. Reprint edited by Sutherland Lyall. Richmond, U.K.: The Richmond Publishing Co., 1973.

————. *Three Essays: On Picturesque Beauty; On Picturesque Travel; and On Sketching Landscape: to which is added a poem, on Landscape Painting.* 2d ed. London: R. Blamire, 1794. Reprint Westmead, U.K.: Gregg International, 1972.

Gombrich, E. H. *Art and Illusion: A Study in the Psychology of Pictorial Presentation.* 5th ed. London: Phaidon Press, 1977.

Greenhill, Ralph, and Thomas D. Mahoney. *Niagara.* Toronto: University of Toronto Press, 1969.

Gross, Seymour L. "Four Possible Additions to Hawthorne's 'Story Teller.'" *Papers of the Bibliographical Society of America* 51 (1957): 90–95.

————. "The Technique of Hawthorne's Short Stories." Ph.D. Diss., University of Illinois, 1954.

————. "Hawthorne's 'Vision of the Fountain' as a Parody." *American Literature* 27 (1955): 101–5.

Gross, Seymour L., and Alfred J. Levy. "Some Remarks on the Extant Manuscripts of Hawthorne's Short Stories." *Studies in Bibliography: Papers of the Bibliographical Society of the University of Virginia* 14 (1961): 254–57.

Hall, Basil. *Travels in North America in the Years 1827 and 1828.* 2 vols. Philadelphia: Carey, Lea & Carey, 1829.

Hamilton, Edward. *Fort Ticonderoga: Key to a Continent.* Boston: Little, Brown and Company, 1964.

Hand, Marcus Christian. *From a Forest to a City: Personal Reminiscences of Syracuse, N.Y.* Syracuse: Masters & Stone, 1889.

Hawthorne, Julian. *Nathaniel Hawthorne and His Wife.* In *The Works of Nathaniel Hawthorne.* Edited by George Parsons Lathrop. Vol. 14. Boston: Houghton, Mifflin and Company, 1882.

Hawthorne, Nathaniel. *The American Notebooks.* Edited by Claude M. Simpson et al. The Centenary Edition of the Works of Nathaniel Hawthorne. Vol. 8. Columbus: Ohio State University Press, 1972.

————. "Fragments From the Journal of a Solitary Man. [Two Extracts]." *American Monthly Magazine* n. s. 4 (July 1837): 45–56.

————. *The House of the Seven Gables.* Edited by William Charvat et al. The Centenary Edition of the Works of Nathaniel Hawthorne. Vol. 2. Columbus: Ohio State University Press, 1971.

————. *The Letters, 1813–1843.* Edited by Thomas Woodson et al. The Centenary Edition of the Works of Nathaniel Hawthorne. Vol. 15. Columbus: Ohio State University Press, 1984.

―――. *The Letters, 1853–1856.* Edited by Thomas Woodson et al. The Centenary Edition of the Works of Nathaniel Hawthorne. Vol. 17. Columbus: Ohio State University Press, 1987.

―――. *The Marble Faun: Or, The Romance of Monte Beni.* Edited by William Charvat et al. The Centenary Edition of the Works of Nathaniel Hawthorne. Vol. 4. Columbus: Ohio State University Press, 1968.

―――. *Mosses from an Old Manse.* Edited by William Charvat et al. The Centenary Edition of the Works of Nathaniel Hawthorne. Vol. 10. Columbus: Ohio State University Press, 1974.

―――. "My Visit to Niagara." *New-England Magazine* 8 (February 1835): 91–96.

―――. "Old Ticonderoga. A Picture of the Past." *American Monthly Magazine* n. s. 1 (February 1836): 138–42.

―――. "An Ontario Steam-Boat." *American Magazine of Useful and Entertaining Knowledge* 2 (March 1836): 270–72.

―――. "Sketches from Memory. By a Pedestrian. No. 1." *New-England Magazine* 9 (November 1835): 321–26.

―――. "Sketches from Memory. By a Pedestrian. No. II." *New-England Magazine* 9 (December 1835): 398–409.

―――. *Tales and Sketches.* Edited by Roy Harvey Pearce. New York: The Library of America, 1982.

―――. *Twice-told Tales.* Edited by William Charvat et al. The Centenary Edition of the Works of Nathaniel Hawthorne. Vol. 9. Columbus: Ohio State University Press, 1974.

―――. *The Snow-Image and Uncollected Tales.* Edited by William Charvat et al. The Centenary Edition of the Works of Nathaniel Hawthorne. Vol. 11. Columbus: Ohio State University Press, 1974.

Haydon, Roger, ed. *Upstate Travels: British Views of Nineteenth-Century New York.* Syracuse: Syracuse University Press, 1982.

The Home Book of the Picturesque: or American Scenery, Art, and Literature. 1852. Reprint edited by Motley F. Deakin. Gainesville, Fla.: Scholars' Facsimiles and Reprints, 1967.

Huth, Hans. *Nature and the American: Three Centuries of Changing Attitudes.* Berkeley: University of California Press, 1957.

Irving, Washington. *The Complete Works of Washington Irving.* Edited by Richard Dilworth Rust. Vol. 8, *The Sketch Book of Geoffrey Crayon, Gent.* Edited by Haskell Springer. Boston: Twayne Publishers, 1978.

Kesselring, Marion L. *Hawthorne's Reading, 1828–1850: A Transcription and Identification of Titles Recorded in the Charge-Books of the Salem Athenaeum.* 1949. Reprint n.p.: Norwood Editions, 1976.

Keyes, Donald D., ed. *The White Mountains: Place and Perceptions.* Hanover, N. H.: The University Press of New England, 1980.

Levy, Leo B. "Hawthorne's 'The Canal Boat': An Experiment in Landscape." *American Quarterly* 16 (1964): 211–15.

Lueck, Beth L. "'Meditating on the Varied Congregation of Human Life': Immigrants in Hawthorne's Travel Sketches." *The Nathaniel Hawthorne Review* 14 (Fall 1988): 1–7.

Manley, James R. "Essay on Cholera." *Transactions of the Medical Society of the State of New York*. Albany, 1835.

McKinsey, Elizabeth. *Niagara Falls: Icon of the American Sublime*. Cambridge: Cambridge University Press, 1985.

McNulty, J. Bard. *The Correspondence of Thomas Cole and Daniel Wadsworth*. Hartford: The Connecticut Historical Society, 1983.

Mellow, James R. *Nathaniel Hawthorne in His Times*. Boston: Houghton Mifflin, 1980.

Melville, Herman. "Hawthorne and His Mosses." In *The Writings of Herman Melville*, Vol. 9, 239–53. Chicago: Northwestern University Press and the Newberry Library, 1987.

Mesick, Jane Louise. *The English Traveller in America, 1785–1835*. New York: Columbia University Press, 1922.

Mulvey, Christopher. *Anglo-American Landscapes: A Study of Nineteenth-Century Anglo-American Travel Literature*. Cambridge: Cambridge University Press, 1983.

Nevius, Blake. *Cooper's Landscapes: An Essay on the Picturesque Vision*. Berkeley: University of California Press, 1976.

Newman, Lea Bertani Vozar. *A Reader's Guide to the Short Stories of Nathaniel Hawthorne*. Boston: G. K. Hall, 1979.

Noble, Louis Legrand. *The Life and Works of Thomas Cole*. 1853. Reprint edited by Elliott S. Vesell. Cambridge, Mass.: Harvard University Press, 1964.

Normand, Jean. *Nathaniel Hawthorne: An Approach to an Analysis of Artistic Creation*. Translated by Derek Coltman. Cleveland: The Press of Case Western Reserve University, 1970.

Pancost, David William. "Evidence of Editorial Additions to Hawthorne's 'Fragments From the Journal of a Solitary Man.'" In *The Nathaniel Hawthorne Journal 1975*, 210–26. Edited by C. E. Frazer Clark, Jr. Englewood, Colorado: Microcard Editions Books, 1975.

———. "Washington Irving's *Sketch Book* and American Literature to the Rise of Realism: Framed Narrative, the Pictorial Mode, and Irony in the Fiction of Irving, Longfellow, Kennedy, Poe, Hawthorne, Melville, Howells, Twain, James & Others." Ph.D. Diss., Duke University, 1977. Pancost devotes a whole chapter to "Nathaniel Hawthorne and the Irvingesque Framed Narrative," 202–66.

Paulding, James Kirke. *The New Mirror for Travellers; and Guide to the Springs*. New York: G. & C. Carvill, 1828.

"Pedestrian Tour." *North-American Review and Miscellaneous Journal* 4 (January 1817): 175–86.

"Recent Travellers in America." *New-England Magazine* 5 (November 1833): [361]-68.

Reese, David Meredith. *A plain and practical treatise on the epidemic cholera, as it prevailed in the city of New York, in the summer of 1832. . . .* New York: Conner & Cooke, 1833.

Ringe, Donald A. *The Pictorial Mode: Space and Time in the Art of Bryant, Irving and Cooper*. Lexington, Ky.: University Press of Kentucky, 1971.

Roberts, Robert B. *New York's Forts in the Revolution.* Rutherford, N. J.: Fairleigh Dickinson University Press, 1980.

Rosenberg, Charles E. *The Cholera Years: The United States in 1832, 1849, and 1866.* Chicago: University of Chicago Press, 1962.

Ross, Alexander M. *William Henry Bartlett: Artist, Author, Traveller.* Toronto: University of Toronto Press, 1973.

Ruland, Richard D., ed. *The Native Muse: Theories of American Literature from Bradford to Whitman.* 2 vols. New York: E. P. Dutton & Co., Inc., 1976.

Sears, John F. "Hawthorne's 'The Ambitious Guest' and the Significance of the Willey Disaster." *American Literature* 54 (October 1982): 354–67.

Settlement in the West: Sketches of Rochester: with incidental notices of western New-York. Arranged by Henry O'Reilly. Rochester: William Alling, 1838.

Shaw, Donald E. *Erie Water West: A History of the Erie Canal.* Lexington, Ky.: University Press of Kentucky, 1966.

Shaw, Joshua. *Picturesque Views of American Scenery.* Philadelphia: M. Carey & Son, 1820.

Spencer, Benjamin Townley. *The Quest for Nationality: An American Literary Campaign.* Syracuse, N. Y.: Syracuse University Press, 1957.

Steele, Oliver Gray. *Steele's Niagara falls port-folio, containing eight new views of Niagara falls taken from the most striking points. Also, a fac simile of a view taken by Father Hennepin in 1678. Lithographed by Hall and Mooney.* [3d ed.] Buffalo: Steele's press, 1844.

Stewart, Randall. *Nathaniel Hawthorne: A Biography.* New Haven: Yale University Press, 1948.

Streeter, Robert E. "Association Psychology and Literary Nationalism in the *North American Review,* 1815–1825." *American Literature* 17 (1945): 242–54.

Templeman, William. *The Life and Work of William Gilpin (1724–1804), Master of the Picturesque and Vicar of Boldre.* Urbana: The University of Illinois Press, 1939.

Turner, Arlin. *Hawthorne as Editor: Selections from his Writings in "The American Magazine of Useful and Entertaining Knowledge."* Baton Rouge: Louisiana State University Press, 1941.

———. *Nathaniel Hawthorne: A Biography.* New York: Oxford University Press, 1980.

Walker, Augustus. "Early days on the Lakes, with an account of the cholera visitation of 1832. From manuscript records of Captain Augustus Walker." *Publications of the Buffalo Historical Society* 5 (1902): 287–318.

Wall, William Guy. *Hudson River Portfolio.* N. p.: H. I. Megarey & G. & C. & H. Carvill, 1823–26.

Weber, Alfred. *Die Entwicklung der Rahmenerzählungen Nathaniel Hawthornes: "The Story Teller" und andere frühe Werke (1825–1835).* Berlin: Erich Schmidt Verlag, 1972.

———. "The Outlines of 'The Story Teller,' the Major Work of Hawthorne's Early Years." *The Nathaniel Hawthorne Review* 15 (Spring 1989): 14–19.

Willis, N. P., Esq. *American Scenery. With 121 Steelplate Engravings from drawings by W. H. Bartlett.* 1840. Reprint Barre, Mass.: Imprint Society, 1971.
Willis, Nathaniel Parker. *American Scenery; or, Land, Lake, and River. Illustrations of Transatlantic Nature.* 2 vols. London: George Virtue, 1840.
Winter, E. T. *The Asiatic cholera! Its symptoms, cure, and preventives. . . . Also, a brief history of the disease and its present threatening aspect.* New York: n.p., 1849.

II: TOURIST GUIDES AND GAZETTEERS CITED AND CONSULTED

Darby, William, and Theodore Dwight. *A New Gazetteer of the United States of America; containing a copious description of the states, territories, counties, parishes, districts, cities and towns—mountains, lakes, rivers and canals—commerce, manufactures, agriculture, and the arts generally of the United States; including other interesting and valuable geographical, historical, political, and statistical information; with the population of 1830.* Hartford: Edward Hopkins, 1833. A fifth edition appeared in 1837.
[Davison, Gideon Miner.] *The Fashionable Tour: or, A Trip to the Springs, Niagara, Quebec, and Boston, in the Summer of 1821.* Saratoga Springs: G. M. Davison, 1822.
———. *The Fashionable Tour, in 1825. An Excursion to the Springs, Niagara, Quebec and Boston.* 2d ed. Saratoga Springs: G. M. Davison, 1825.
———. *The Fashionable Tour; an excursion to the Springs, Niagara, Quebec, and through the New England States: interspersed with geographical and historical sketches.* 3d ed. Saratoga Springs: G. M. Davison, 1828.
———. *The Fashionable Tour: A Guide to Travellers Visiting the Middle and Northern States, and the Provinces of Canada.* 4th ed. Saratoga Springs: G. M. Davison, 1830.
———. *The Traveller's Guide: through the middle and northern states, and the provinces of Canada.* 5th ed. Saratoga Springs: G. M. Davison, 1833. Sixth and seventh editions with this title appeared in 1834 and 1837.
Disturnell, John. *The Traveller's Guide through the State of New-York, Canada, &c. Embracing a General Description of the City of New-York; the Hudson River Guide, and the Fashionable Tour to the Springs and Niagara Falls; with Steam-Boat, Rail-Road, and State Routes, accompanied by current maps.* New York: J. Disturnell, 1836.
Disturnell, John. *A Gazetteer of the State of New-York: comprising its topography, geology, mineralogical resources, civil divisions, canals, railroads and public institutions; together with general statistics: the whole alphabetically arranged. Also, statistical tables, including the census of 1840; and tables of distances.* 2d. ed., with additions and corrections. Albany: C. van Benthuysen & Co., 1843.
[Dwight, Theodore.] *The Northern Traveller; containing the routes to Niagara, Quebec, and the Springs; with descriptions of the principal scenes, and useful hints to strangers.* New York: Wilder & Campbell, 1825.

———. *The Northern Traveller; containing the routes to Niagara, Quebec, and the Springs, with the tour of New England, and the route to the coal mines of Pennsylvania.* 2d. ed. New York: A. T. Goodrich, 1826.

———. 3d. ed., 1828.

———. *The Northern Traveller, and Northern Tour; with the routes to the springs, Niagara, and Quebec, and the coal mines of Pennsylvania; also, the tour of New-England. Embellished with 32 copperplate engravings.* 4th ed. New York: J. & J. Harper, 1830.

———. 5th ed., 1834

———.*The Northern Traveller; containing the routes to the Springs, Niagara, Quebec and the coal mines; with the tour of New-England, and a brief guide to the Virginia Springs, and southern and western routes, with eighteen maps, and nine landscapes.* 6th ed. New York: J. P. Haven, 1841.

[Gilpin, Henry Dilworth.] *A Northern Tour: being a guide to Saratoga, Lake George, Niagara, Canada, Boston, &c., &c., through the States of Pennsylvania, New-Jersey, New-York, Vermont, New-Hampshire, Massachusetts, Rhode-Island, and Connecticut; embracing an account of the canals, colleges, public institutions, natural curiosities and interesting objects therein.* Philadelphia: H. C. Carey & I. Lea, 1825.

Melish, John. *The Traveller's Directory through the United States, consisting of a geographical description of the United States, with topographical tables of the countries, towns, population, &c, and a description of the roads [including tables and maps], compiled from the most authentic materials.* Philadelphia: n.p., 1818. The first edition appeared in 1814.

———. *The Traveller's Directory through the United States of America; being a complete list of the direct and cross roads, together with the conveyance by water throughout the different states and territories: including the connecting roads and distances, in measured miles, from New York, Philadelphia, Baltimore, and Washington, to Pittsburgh, New Orleans, and St. Louis [including maps and tables]. Compiled from the most authentic materials.* Philadelphia: Printed for J. Melish & S. Harrison, 1819.

———. *The Traveller's Directory through the United States containing a description of all the principal roads through the United States, with copious remarks on the rivers, and other objects. To which is added, an appendix containing post office regulations, land-offices, military posts, census of the United States.* Philadelphia: n.p., 1822.

Spafford, Horatio Gates. *A Pocket Guide, for the Tourist and Traveller, along the line of the canals, and the interior commerce of the State of New-York.* New York: T. and J. Swords, 1824. Dwight recommended this work to his readers in the *Northern Traveller* (1825), 6.

———. *Pocket Guide for the Tourist and Traveller, Along the Line of the Canals, and the Interior commerce of the State of New-York.* 2d. ed. Troy: n.p., 1825.

Tanner, Henry Schenck. *The traveller's guide; map of the roads, canals, and steam boat routes of the United States.* Philadelphia: n.p., 1825.

The traveller's guide, a table of distances of the principal roads, steam-boat and canal routes. Boston: T. F. Adams, 1833. One sheet.

The Traveller's Guide, or, a few weeks tour in the New-England States. New York: A. T. Goodrich, 1823.

The Traveller's Pocket Directory and Stranger's Guide; exhibiting distances on the principal canal and stage routes in the State of New York. Schenectady: S. Wilson, 1831. There was another edition published in 1832.

[Vandewater, Robert J.] *The Tourist, or Pocket Manual for Travellers on the Hudson River, the Western Canal and Stage Road; comprising also the Routes to Lebanon, Ballston, and Saratoga Springs.* New York: J. & J. Harper, 1830.

————. *The Tourist, or Pocket Manual for Travellers on the Hudson River, the Western Canal and Stage Road to Niagara Falls down Lake Ontario and the St. Lawrence to Montreal and Quebec. Comprising also the Routes to Lebanon, Ballston, and Saratoga Springs.* 3d. ed. New York, 1834. A 4th ed., enlarged and improved, appeared in 1835.

Western Traveller's Pocket Directory and Stranger's Guide; exhibiting distances on the principal canal and stage routes in the states of New-York and Ohio, in the territory of Michigan, and in the province of Lower Canada, &c., containing also descriptions of the rail roads now building and in contemplation in this state: with a list of broken banks—rates of tolls on the canals for 1834—and a variety of other matter, highly valuable to the traveling community. Schenectady: S. S. Riggs, 1834.

[Williams, William.] *The stage, canal, and steamboat register, etc. etc., for 1830.* Utica: n.p., [1830?]. At the end: "The Tourist's Map of the State of New York, compiled from the latest authorities in the Surveyor General's office."

INDEX

Abercrombie, General James, 66, 68, 144, 148
Albany, N.Y., 2, 3, 10, 21
Allen, Ethan, 66, 69, 96, 145, 148
American Magazine of Useful and Entertaining Knowledge, 49
American Monthly Magazine, 5, 25, 35, 62, 64, 99
American Scenery, 103, 116
Amherst, Lord Jeffrey, 66, 68, 144, 148
Ammonoosuc River, 74 (ill.), 79 (ill.)
Analectic, 145
Anderson, Patricia, 17, 19, 82, 114
Andrist, Ralph K., 17
Arnold, Benedict, 151
Atlantic Souvenir, 125

Ballston, N.Y., 16
Baltimore, Md., 108
Barber, John W., and Henry Howe, 108; *Central Part of Buffalo Street, Rochester, N.Y.*, 88 (ill.), 111; *View of Ogdensburg*, 87 (ill.), 112; *Western View in the Central Part of Syracuse*, 86 (ill.), 112
Bartlett, N.H., 13, 27, 157
Bartlett, William H., 105, 127; *Ferry Landing on the American Side*, 94 (ill.), 120; *Mount Jefferson (from Mount Washington)*, 78 (ill.), 106; *Mount Washington and the White Hills*, 79 (ill.), 107; *Notch House*, 77 (ill.), 105, 106; *Utica*, 84 (ill.), 113; *View of the Ruins of Fort Ticonderoga*, 98 (ill.), 127; *Village of Little Falls*, 81 (ill.), 116–117; *Willey House*, 76 (ill.), 107
Baym, Nina, 132
Benjamin, Park, 5, 6, 25, 27, 34, 62, 99, 131, 153
Bennett, William James, 143; *View of the British Fall Taken from Goat Island*, 91 (ill.), 120

Boston, Mass., 3, 10, 11, 21
Bowdoin College (Brunswick, Maine), 133
Bretton Woods, N.H., 74
Brook Farm, 141
Brown, Charles Brockden, 135, 145
Brown, George Loring, 35, 99
Bryant, William Cullen, 7, 21, 124
Buffalo, N.Y., 19, 20
Bufford, J. H.: *The Upper Falls of the Genesee*, 89 (ill.), 110
Bunker Hill, 132
Burgoyne, General John, 69, 146, 148
Burke, Edmund, 101
Burlington, Vt., 2, 3, 10, 15, 30, 43, 109, 127, 136
Burton, Warren, 141, 142
Byron, George Gordon, Lord, 29, 105, 128, 159

Canada, 2, 3, 7, 12
Canadians, 45, 50, 54, 62, 63, 123, 136, 140
Canandaigua, N.Y., 109
Canterbury, N.H., 2
Carrigain, Philip, 101
Catlin, George: *View of Niagara, No. 6: Table Rock from Below*, 92 (ill.), 122
Champlain canal, 10, 15
Champlain, Lake, 10, 15, 16, 65, 127, 146; description, 43
Cholera, 2, 3, 11, 21, 22; pattern of spread, 11
Claude Lorraine. *See* Lorraine, Claude
Clinton, De Witt, 35, 164
Clinton, Henry, 132
Cole, Thomas, 7, 12, 21, 77, 127; "Essay on American Scenery," 15, 20, 124, 145, 150; journal, 135; *Ruins of Fort Ticonderoga, New York*, 97 (ill.), 124; *View of the White Mountains*, 74 (ill.), 101, 107
Concord, N.H., 2, 12

209

Conway, N.H., 30
Cooper, James Fenimore, 7, 124; *The Prairie*, 162; *The Deerslayer*, 145; *The Last of the Mohicans*, 162; *The Pioneers*, 138; *The Wept of Wish-Ton-Wish*, 145, 162
Cooper, Susan, 150
Coos, N.H., 31
Crawford House (also called the Notch House), 3, 14, 15, 77 (ill.), 160, 161
Crawford, Ethan, 3, 14, 30, 31, 103, 106, 161
Crown Point, N.Y., 15, 69
Currier & Ives, 77, 105

Darby, William, and Theodore Dwight: *A New Gazetteer of the United States of America*, 17
Davison, Gideon Miner: *The Fashionable Tour*, 13, 15; *The Traveller's Guide*, 9, 81, 115, 145, 160, 163
Detroit, Mich., 20, 48
Dettingen, Battle of (1743), 69
Disturnell, John: *A Gazetteer of the State of New-York*, 16
Doughty, Thomas, 35, 99
Drake, Joseph Rodman: "The Culprit Fay," 106
Durand, Asher B., 7, 21
Dwight, Theodore, 18, 141, 148; *A New Gazetteer of the United States of America*, 17; *The Northern Traveller*, 9, 12, 14, 17, 73 (ill.), 96, 117, 125, 145, 156, 163; *Sketches of Scenery and Manners in the United States*, 8, 142; *Things As They Are*, 75, 104

Eliot, T. S.: *The Waste Land*, 141
Erie Canal, 10, 16, 17, 18, 22, 80–83 (ills.), 85 (ill.), 109, 112, 113, 114, 163, 165; long level, 41, 43, 165
Erie, Lake, 10, 19, 20, 48

Fenn, Harry, 111
Fields, James T., 25, 26, 27, 34
Fishkill, N.Y., 132
Flying Dutchman, 42
Fontenoy, Battle of (1745), 69
Forsyth's Hotel, 60
Frame narrative, 4, 5, 6, 22, 25, 132, 136, 169

French and Indian War (1754–63), 15, 126
Fussell, Edwin, 158

Galway, N.Y., 16
Genesee Falls, 8, 19, 22, 89–90 (ills.), 110, 111, 142, 143, 145; description, 45
George, Lake, 10, 16
Gilpin, William, 134, 142, 154, 155, 169, 171, 175, 177, 178; *Forest Scenery*, 134; *On Picturesque Travel*, 163; *On Sketching Landscape*, 173
Goat Island, 56, 60, 61, 63, 91 (ill.), 93 (ill.), 119, 120, 121, 123, 177
Gombrich, E. H., 99
Goodrich, Samuel G., 5
Gothic architecture, 137
Gowan's Heights, Brooklyn, 132
Green Mountain Boys, 45, 136, 137, 145
Green Mountains, Vt., 15, 30, 43, 109

Hall and Mooney: *Ferry Landing on the American Side*, 120
Hall, Basil, 60, 144, 177; *Travels in North America*, 8
Hawthorne, Nathaniel: cholera epidemic, 12, 15; itinerary of travel, 10, 12, 15, 17–20, 22, 160, 175; letters, 2, 6, 10, 11, 25, 62, 100, 139, 153, 171; reading, 2, 8, 156
Hawthorne, Works: "The Ambitious Guest," 14, 75, 102, 108, 128, 156, 157; *American Magazine of Useful and Entertaining Knowledge*, 100; *American Notebooks*, 100; "An Afternoon Scene," 34, 35, 47; "An Ontario Steam-Boat," 25, 49, 87, 113, 139; "The Canal-Boat," 16, 17, 26, 34, 113, 139, 162, 179; "The Celestial Rail-road," 171; "The Custom-House," 136; *Fanshawe*, 4; "Fragments from the Journal of a Solitary Man," 6, 35; "Fragments from the Journal of a Solitary Man [Two Extracts]," 55, 62; "The Gray Champion," 55; "The Great Carbuncle," 74, 156, 159, 162; "The Great Stone Face," 156; *The House of the Seven Gables*, 137, 151; "The Inland Port," 15, 34, 43, 109, 131, 136; "Main

Street," 136; *The Marble Faun*, 22, 135; *Mosses from an Old Manse*, 25, 26, 27, 34; "Mr. Higginbotham's Catastrophe," 26; "My Home Return," 34; "My Visit to Niagara," 19, 20, 55, 121, 143, 169; [Niagara Fragments], 123; "A Night Scene," 20, 34, 35, 48, 131; "The Notch of the White Mountains" (later title for "The Notch"), 26, 27, 155, 156, 179; "The Old Manse," 136; "Old Ticonderoga," 16, 64, 126, 131, 144; "Our Evening Party Among the Mountains," 26, 27, 106, 140, 155, 160; *Our Old Home*, 22; "Passages From a Relinquished Work," 26; "Provincial Tales," 4; "Rappaccini's Daughter," 128; "Rochester," 34, 45, 89, 110, 131, 137, 142; *The Scarlet Letter*, 128, 158; "Seven Tales of My Native Land," 4, 132; "Sketches from Memory," 6, 25, 26, 27, 34, 99, 131; "Sketches From Memory. [Second Series]," 34; "The Story Teller," 4, 5, 6, 8, 21, 22, 25, 26, 49, 55, 62, 132, 136, 153, 154, 169; *Twice-told Tales*, 26

Haydon, Roger, 7, 21
Hennepin, Father Louis, 20, 119
Hill, John William, 114; *Erie Canal, 1831*, 82 (ill.), 116, 117; [*Scene of Night-Time Traffic on the Erie Canal*], 85 (ill.), 118; *View of the Erie Canal*, 83 (ill.), 114
Howe, Henry. *See* Barber, John W.
Hudson River, 7, 10, 15, 21, 124

Immigrants, 7, 17, 37, 44, 49, 51, 53, 55, 110, 136, 137, 138, 139
Immigration, 22
Indians, 28, 29, 36, 56, 63, 66, 68, 69, 94, 119, 121, 140, 148, 149, 157–58, 159; legends, 32, 140, 161–162; Tuscarora, 56, 173
Inman, Henry: *Travelling on the Erie Canal*, 80 (ill.), 117
Irish, 44, 45, 47, 48–49, 51, 110, 137–38, 139, 142
Irving, Washington, 6, 7, 21, 124, 128, 157; *The Sketch Book*, 7, 8, 99, 135, 155; *Tales of a Traveller*, 8, 156

Johnston, N.Y., 16

Kensett, John, 77
Keyes, Donald D., 101, 108

Lathrop, George Parsons, 34, 49, 55, 62
Lewiston, N.Y., 19, 55
Little Falls, N.Y., 16, 81–82 (ills.), 115, 116, 117
Lockport, N.Y., 60
Longfellow, Henry Wadsworth, 133, 139, 141
Lorraine, Claude, 35, 99, 116, 159, 178
Lundy's Lane, Battle of (1814), 143

Magoon, E. L., 141
Manchester, N.Y., 19, 55, 56
Manning, Mary, 156
Manning, Samuel, 2
Marlborough, John Churchill, Duke of, 69
Maverick, Peter, 125; *Travelling on the Erie Canal*, 117
McGrath, Robert L., 101
McKinsey, Elizabeth, 119, 120, 143, 169, 172, 177
Melish, John: *The Traveller's Directory through the United States*, 8
Melville, Herman: *Hawthorne and His Mosses*, 22; *The Confidence-Man*, 113; "The Piazza," 160
Merrimack River, 12
Mohawk River, 16, 80–81 (ills.), 115
Mohawk Valley, 165
Montcalm, Marquis de, 144
Montgomery, Fort, N.Y., 132
Montreal, Quebec, 2, 10, 15, 44

Naples, Bay of, 109
Nationalism, 7, 21, 131; difficulty attaining, 138, 142–44
Nevius, Blake, 134, 145
New-England Magazine, 5, 25, 26, 34, 55, 131, 153
New Haven, Conn., 2
New York City, N.Y., 10, 11, 12, 21
Niagara Falls, 2, 3, 7, 10, 16, 19, 20, 22, 91–94 (ills.), 101, 119, 143, 145, 169–70; as Canadian Falls, 143; Goat Island. *See* separate entry; Niagara Railroad Suspension Bridge, 121; Table Rock. *See* separate entry;

Niagara Falls (*continued*)
  Termination Rock, 176; Terrapin
  Tower, 121
Normand, Jean, 100
North-American Review, 145

Oberon, 5, 62
Ogdensburg, N.Y., 18, 49, 87 (ill.),
  108, 112
Ontario, Lake, 10, 18, 49, 53, 113, 140
Orwell, Vt., 16, 65

Patch, Sam, 8, 19, 22, 45, 89, 142
Paulding, James Kirke, 177; *The new
  Mirror for Travellers*, 171
Pell, Stephen, 150
Pell, William, 70, 149, 150
Peru, N.Y., 15, 43
Philadelphia, Pa., 108
Picturesque: definitions, 7, 11, 50, 105,
  134, 146, 147, 154, 157, 159, 162,
  164, 165; descriptions, 15, 48, 100,
  106, 107, 109, 116, 132, 145, 160,
  175; travel, 27, 118, 132, 134, 139,
  144, 147, 151, 153, 154, 163–64,
  165, 169, 171, 177
Picturesque America, 111
Pierce, Franklin, 2, 10, 11, 153
Plattsburgh, N.Y., 15
Port Folio, 145
Portland, Maine, 29
Portsmouth, N.H., 11
Pratt, Henry Cheever, 7, 12, 21, 101

Quebec City, Quebec, 2, 9, 10

Reinagle, Henry, 145; *View of the Ruins
  of Ticonderoga Forts on Lake Champlain*,
  95 (ill.), 124
Revolutionary War, American (1775–
  81), 15, 16, 69, 96, 126, 132, 136,
  145
Rhine River, 7, 124
Richards, William Trost, 77
Ringe, Donald A., 124, 125, 126, 134
Rochester, N.Y., 18–19, 22, 45, 88 (ill.),
  90 (ill.), 108, 110–11

Saco River, 14, 27–28, 33, 76 (ill.), 104,
  157–58
Salem, Mass., 1–2, 3, 12, 21
Saratoga Springs, N.Y., 10, 16

Satire, 155, 161, 162, 166, 171, 172,
  175, 176, 180
Savannah, Ga., 108
Schuylkill River, 108
Shaw, Joshua: *Picturesque Views of Amer-
  ican Scenery*, 108, 132
Sheeler, Charles, 110
Sigourney, Lydia H., 103
Spafford, Horatio Gates, 19; *Pocket
  Guide for the Tourist and Traveller*, 163;
  satirized, 164
St. Clair, General Arthur, 65, 66, 147
St. Lawrence River, 18, 57, 61, 87 (ill.)
Sublime, 128, 175; definitions, 7, 11,
  63, 101, 119, 122, 128, 141, 177,
  179; descriptions, 8, 13, 15, 20, 61,
  110, 115, 116, 132, 156, 158, 159,
  160, 173, 175, 178; travel, 9, 27,
  135, 169
Switzerland: as symbol of freedom, 141
Syracuse, N.Y., 17, 18, 86 (ill.), 112,
  117, 139

Table Rock, 59, 61, 92–93 (ills.), 119,
  120, 122, 175, 178
Templeman, William, 134
Thousand Islands (of the St. Lawrence
  River), 18
Ti, N.Y., 65
Ticknor, William D., 25
Ticonderoga, Fort, N.Y., 15, 16, 65,
  95–98 (ills.), 124, 144
Ticonderoga From Mount Independence,
  125
The Token, 5
*The Traveller's Guide, or, a few weeks tour
  in the New-England States*, 9
Turner, Arlin, 1; *Hawthorne as Editor*,
  49
Twain, Mark, 128; *Innocents Abroad*,
  147

Utica, N.Y., 16, 17, 36, 38, 84 (ill.),
  113, 117, 118, 165

Vanderlyn, John: *Niagara Falls from Ta-
  ble Rock*, 93 (ill.), 119
Vandewater, Robert J., 18, 20, 165; *The
  Tourist*, 10, 86

Wadsworth, Daniel, 74

Wall, William Guy, 125; *Hudson River Portfolio*, 114, 132

Wallace, R. Stuart, 15

War of 1812 (1812–14), 143

Washington, George, 29, 132, 143

Washington, Mount, 3, 14, 22, 29, 32, 34, 74 (ill.), 78 (ill.), 102, 107, 141, 160

Weber, Alfred: *Die Entwicklung der Rahmenerzählungen Nathaniel Hawthornes*, 49, 62

West Point, N.Y., 66, 126, 132, 147

White Mountains, 3, 10, 12, 22, 28, 74–79 (ills.), 101, 140, 155, 159, 160; compared to the Swiss Alps, 141, 156; early tourism, 15; Notch, 14, 101, 103, 141, 159; Washington, Mount. *See* separate entry

Whitehall, N.Y., 65, 69

Willey family, 8, 13, 22, 102, 157

Willey House, 76 (ill.)

Willis, N. P., 103, 124, 146; *American Scenery*, 17, 105, 132

Winnipesaukee, Lake, 12

Wissahiccon Creek, 108